CALL SIGN EXTORTION 17

The Shoot-Down of SEAL Team Six

DON BROWN

Guilford, Connecticut

An imprint of Rowman & Littlefield

Distributed by NATIONAL BOOK NETWORK

British Library Cataloguing in Publication Information Available

Library of Congress Cataloging-in-Publication Data
Brown, Don, 1960-
  Call Sign Extortion 17 : the shoot-down of SEAL Team Six / Don Brown.
    pages cm
  ISBN 978-1-4930-0746-2
  1. Afghan War, 2001—Aerial operations, American. 2. United States. Navy. SEALs—History—21st century. 3. United States. Naval Special Warfare Development Group—History. 4. Chinook (Military transport helicopter) 5. Special operations (Military science)—United States. 6. Afghan War, 2001—Campaigns. I. Title. II. Title: Shoot-down of SEAL Team Six.
  DS371.412.B74 2015
  958.104'745—dc23

                                    2015002084

ISBN 978-1-4930-1732-4 (e-book)

♾™ The paper used in this publication meets the minimum requirements of American National Standard for Information Sciences—Permanence of Paper for Printed Library Materials, ANSI/NISO Z39.48-1992.

Contents

CONTENTS

CONTENTS

Prologue

BASE SHANK

LOGAR PROVINCE, AFGHANISTAN

AUGUST 6, 2011

Under the moonless sky in Logar Province, at just before two o'clock in the morning local time, thirty Americans, including seventeen members of the elite SEAL team that had killed Osama Bin Laden fourteen weeks earlier, were scrambled aboard a Vietnam-era US Army National Guard Chinook helicopter, code name Extortion 17. Sixty-six years earlier to the day, the United States had dropped an atomic bomb on Hiroshima.

The old Chinook was not the type of helicopter typically used by the SEALs. Special Forces units typically attack with specially equipped, highly armed Special Operations helicopters with highly sophisticated electronic and jamming systems, flown by Special Operations pilots trained to insert the SEALs with swiftness, speed, and surprise.

But the Chinook was not an assault helicopter. It did not have significant offensive capabilities, and it was not designed for high-speed assaults carried out by US Special Forces. The Chinook was a transport chopper and was not designed to fly into a hot combat zone. Its crew was a National Guard crew, trained to transport troops and equipment, but not trained or equipped for Special Operations in hot battle zones.

The Americans boarding the chopper ranged in age from the youngest, twenty-one-year-old Specialist Spencer C. Duncan of Olathe, Kansas, to the oldest of the group, forty-seven-year-old Chief Warrant Officer David Carter of Aurora, Colorado.

Two of the men, Lieutenant Commander Jonas Kelsall, the SEAL commander, and Chief Petty Officer Robert Reeves, had been best friends since their high school days in Shreveport, Louisiana, and even played on the same high school football team.

Sixteen of the men had wives back home in the United States, and thirty-two American children called these men "Daddy."

Three of the men, Navy Senior Chief Craig Vickers of Hawaii, Navy Chief (SEAL) Matt Mason of Kansas City, and Senior Chief Tommy Ratzlaff of Arkansas, had wives who were expecting their third child.

Vickers was on his last tour with the Navy and planned to retire and return home to his family in May 2012. Like Craig Vickers, forty-four-year-old Senior Chief Lou Langlais, one of the most highly decorated and experienced SEALs in the Navy, was also on his last combat deployment and planned to return to a stateside job as a trainer where he would reunite with his wife, Anya, and their two boys in Santa Monica.

Seven mysterious Afghan commandos, along with one Afghan interpreter, joined these remarkable Americans on the helicopter that night. The presence of the unknown Afghans, whose names were not on the flight manifest, breached all semblances of military and aviation protocol.

Within minutes of takeoff, every American on board Extortion 17 died a horrific, fiery death in a crash that would mark the deadliest single loss in the eleven-year-old Afghan war, and the single-largest loss in the history of US Special Forces.

Why did these men die?

Their children and wives deserve to know. Their parents and their country deserve an answer.

Powerful evidence now suggests there was a cover-up to prevent the truth from ever getting out.

What is being covered up?

Several signs suggest that the Taliban were tipped off as to the Chinook's flight path and were lying in wait with rocket-propelled grenades as it approached the landing zone. Invaluable forensic evidence has been inexcusably lost, negligently or intentionally destroyed by the military, or conveniently glossed over to obfuscate the truth as to why these men died.

Even if the Taliban had no inside information, which appears unlikely, the decision to order a platoon of US Navy SEALs and supporting troops onto a highly vulnerable and largely defenseless Vietnam-era National

Guard helicopter, a CH-47 Chinook piloted by a noble crew of National Guard aviators who were ill equipped and untrained in the Special Forces aviation techniques necessary to prosecute this mission, effectively sealed the death warrants for each and every American on board that night.

For the sake of the thirty-two children who lost their fathers, for the sixteen wives who lost their husbands, for the sake of sixty parents who lost their sons, and for the sake of a nation that deserves better from its leadership in protecting its treasured sons in times of war, hard questions need to be asked.

This is the story of the last flight of Extortion 17 and the cover-up that followed.

CHAPTER 1

Forward Operating Base "Shank"

LOGAR PROVINCE, EASTERN AFGHANISTAN

AUGUST 5, 2011

LATE EVENING HOURS

The crescent moon hung low over the horizon, dipping below the mountains off in the distance to the west.

It was 10:00 p.m. local time, and the night was not yet half gone. But soon, the moonless sky would yield to the faint blinking of the stars against the jet-black canopy of space, a placid contrast to the bloody jihad raging in the dark hills and valleys and riverbeds beyond the mountains.

Down below the starry firmament, in this forward-deployed military base occupied by Western forces in the ten-year-old "War on Terror," a buzz of activity arose from units of several US Special Forces, namely from US Army Rangers and the elite US Navy SEALs.

Here, in the midst of the Afghan night, they called this place "Base Shank," or officially, "Forward Operating Base Shank." And at first glance, with its wooden buildings and Quonset tents, concrete barriers and big green and sand-colored jeeps and dirt graders, FOB Shank could pass for 1950s-vintage from the Korean War—perhaps even the backstage of a Hollywood set constructed in the foothills of snow-capped mountains.

But technologically, and militarily, there was nothing Fifties-vintage about this place, nor was there anything about it that was Hollywood.

At this remote outpost 46 miles south of the Afghan capital at Kabul, and 100 miles west of the Pakistani border, the SEALs and the Rangers were deployed to the tip of the American military spear, poised to use their superior training and weaponry to take the fight straight to the Taliban in rugged and treacherous mountain peaks, in crags, and in rocks and valleys and remote riverbeds. Much of the SEAL unit was from the prestigious SEAL Team Six, the unit that ninety days earlier had killed the world's most notorious terrorist, Osama Bin Laden.

Their mission was to kill Taliban, and they were deadly effective at it.

On this night, as the SEALs and Rangers prepared their weapons of war, two US Army National Guard Chinook helicopters, call signs Extortion 16 and Extortion 17, prepared to transport two platoons of Army Rangers to the edge of the battle front, in this case in the Tangi River Valley in the mountainous Wardak Province a few miles to the west. Their job —to engage Taliban forces and hunt down a Taliban terrorist leader named Qari Tahir, whose code name was Lefty Grove.

Between ten and eleven o'clock, two platoons of Army Rangers, weapons loaded and in full combat gear, moved single-file toward the giant helicopters, their running lights blinking on the heliport, their twin engines shrieking loudly into the night.

As they boarded the choppers, the Rangers ducked their heads under twin rotary blades whirling in a wind-filled roar. Some probably covered their ears to block the noise and the wind. Within minutes, they had strapped themselves into their jump seats, and they were cleared for takeoff.

Like two giant locusts, with twin-engines spinning, the lumbering war birds lifted into the dark skies, dipped their noses, and set a course for the northwest.

Their destination—an area approximately 2 kilometers outside the battle zone in the Tangi River Valley in neighboring Wardak Province. The Tangi Valley cut across the border between Wardak and Logar Provinces and was an area where security had deteriorated over the past two years, bringing the insurgency closer to the capital, Kabul. It was a largely inaccessible area that had become a haven for insurgents.

In command of Extortion 17 was thirty-year-old CW2 Bryan J. Nichols, a member of the Kansas Air National Guard.

Bryan Nichols enlisted in the Army in 1996 as a ground soldier. He was deployed as an infantryman twice in Iraq, once in 2002 and again in 2003, and once in Kosovo in 2004, all of which occurred before he became an Army pilot.

Following his dream to become a US Army aviator, Bryan graduated from flight school in 2008; most of his flight training had taken place back in the United States.

But tonight marked a first for Bryan.

Base Shank, Afghanistan, marked his very first tour as a pilot in combat. For although he was experienced as a combat soldier, he had no experience as a combat pilot. Not yet, anyway. The dark, deadly skies of Afghanistan were about to change all that.

Bryan was on his second marriage when he deployed to Afghanistan, and left behind a ten-year-old son named Braydon. Braydon lived with his mother, Jessica Nichols, in Kansas City.

He had arrived in Afghanistan less than a week earlier, and as his chopper thundered to the northwest, full of elite US Army Rangers, perhaps his mind returned for a moment to Braydon. Bryan and Braydon were close, and though Bryan remarried, he and Braydon remained thick as thieves. When Bryan remarried and exchanged his vows with Mary in his service dress blue Army uniform, he had a miniature version of the uniform tailored for Braydon, who stood proudly beside his father during the ceremony. In the days since Bryan left Kansas, he and Braydon had frequently communicated by Skype and could not wait to see each other again.

In a few weeks, when he returned home, he planned to fulfill a promise to Braydon to take him to a Royals game. As his chopper sliced through the dark of the deadly night, perhaps his thoughts, for a flickering moment, turned to home, and to baseball, and to his boy.

Theirs was a reunion that would never take place.

—◆—

As Extortions 16 and 17 flew over the rugged, snow-capped Hindu-Kush mountain ranges, jagged peaks stretching from central Afghanistan to northern Pakistan, the American pilots charted their route to the initial drop-off point.

The battle for military control of these mountains, and the crags and valleys and riverbeds around them, had been wrapped in a long and ancient history of warfare. Darius the Great, the great king of Persia, once maintained an army here. Later, Alexander the Great explored these mountains.

But the exploits of Darius and the explorations of Alexander had come hundreds of years before the birth of a man named Muhammad, whose life and death would mark a geopolitical shift in the world. In the hundred years following Muhammad's death in AD 632, Islam would sweep by military conquest from the Arabian Peninsula to the west, all the way across the rim of North Africa and crossing Gibraltar into all of Spain. At the same time, the meteoric expansion of the Muslim empire stretched to the north and east, with Islamic warriors from Arabia capturing the cities of Damascus, Baghdad, and Kabul, and all the lands around them.

By the end of the Umayyad Caliphate in AD 750, the great Muslim empire had grown by military conquest into the largest empire in the history of the world. The land and mountains below these helicopters had been under Islamic control for twelve hundred years.

The ghosts of ten thousand fallen sons of a former superpower haunted the frozen snowcaps, crags, and cliffs of the harsh mountain terrain. Some had been shot. Others had been chopped apart or brutally decapitated. All spilled their blood for the lost cause of Soviet communism the last time a great power tried invading Afghanistan.

The Russians had defeated Napoleon, and the Soviets defeated the Nazis. But at the zenith of their strength as a nuclear superpower, with missiles and MIG jets and arsenals of sophisticated weaponry, the great Red Bear of the uttermost north could not defeat the Islamic mujahideen lurking behind the rocks of these unforgiving mountains. Afghanistan became the most humiliating defeat in the history of the Soviet Union.

Now, as two American helicopters closed in on their landing zone just two clicks (kilometers) from the battle zone, the sons of another superpower would try their hands at war in this harsh terrain that belonged to Islam. Perhaps if the ghosts of the Russians could speak, they would cry loudly into the night to warn the Rangers and the pilots of the danger lurking ahead. Perhaps that warning would have come out of respect for an old ally, a former ally that once joined Mother Russia in her fight against Nazism. Or perhaps their voices would have remained silent, content to hope that radical Islam would bring down their bitter-rival superpower, the Americans, just as their defeat in Afghanistan had jumpstarted the downward spiral of the Soviet Union.

Even if the Russian ghosts could have warned him with their loudest voices, Bryan Nichols was too focused on the task at hand to hear anything they would have said.

Using GPS instrumentation and night-vision goggles, Nichols slowed the Chinook over the landing zone and brought it down to a feathery landing just outside the Tangi River Valley, outside the "hot" combat area, in Afghanistan's Wardak Province.

Off to the side, his sister chopper, Extortion 16, also had set down. From the load area of both Chinooks, flight engineers and crews stepped out under the whirling rotary blades to open the cargo ramps. Rangers, wearing flak jackets and night-vision goggles, and carrying automatic rifles, began filing out in quick precision. The chopper had landed outside the fire zone, as Nichols and his crew had been trained to do, for the Chinooks were big and slow and unable to effectively defend themselves against any kind of sustained antiaircraft fire. Under the battle plan, the Rangers would depart the choppers and move by foot into the battle zone, to attack Taliban and capture or kill the target, Qari Tahir.

Having once been a ground soldier himself long before he became a pilot, Nichols could identify with the mission of the Rangers.

So far, so good.

In a few minutes, Nichols got an "all clear," most likely from his friend, Staff Sergeant Pat Hamburger, another National Guardsman who was from Nebraska, and served as the helicopter's flight engineer and gunner. The "all clear" meant that all the Rangers had cleared the cargo bay.

It was 11 p.m. local time.

"Thumbs ups" were exchanged, and the choppers' rotary blades, which had been spinning during the short drop-off of the Rangers, revved up. From the cockpit of Extortion 17, Nichols pulled up on the collective, the stick controlling vertical ascent, causing the big helicopter, sometimes described as an "airborne school bus," to lift off the ground. Using his cyclic to turn the chopper back to the southeast, Nichols set a course for

Base Shank and the Chinooks began their return journey through the air, over and around the mountains, back to the plains of Logar Province.

We will never know what was said by the five National Guardsmen on their return flight to Base Shank. Perhaps they discussed their families. Perhaps they discussed their mission. Perhaps they were buried in thought, silently contemplating their fate. Perhaps some had a premonition that they were about to die.

They knew they might be called back in a matter of hours to bring the Rangers back from the battle zone. Or, the Rangers might not be back for a day or more. Or the Rangers might never come back.

The only thing certain about war was the uncertainty.

They had no clue that shortly after returning to Base Shank, they would be called upon to fly another mission—this time with the super-elite SEAL Team Six.

They never knew that their next mission would be the last mission they would ever fly.

CHAPTER 2

Aboard Extortion 17

SOMEWHERE OVER THE HINDU KUSH MOUNTAINS HEADING SOUTHEAST

DESTINATION: BASE SHANK

AUGUST 5, 2011

SHORTLY AFTER 11 P.M. LOCAL TIME

As the old Chinook helicopter flew through the night along a course heading back to Base Shank, thirty-one-year-old Staff Sergeant Patrick "Pat" Hamburger, the chopper's flight engineer and gunner, sat strapped in his position at the back of the aircraft.

A well-liked soldier with closely cropped hair and an infectious smile, as flight engineer, Pat was the senior enlisted member of the crew, or the "crew chief," in military helicopter vernacular. This made him the most important crewmember behind the pilot and co-pilot.

Pat, a National Guardsman from Nebraska, was in charge of all logistical aspects of the helicopter's operations, including loading and offloading cargo, and loading and offloading passengers—and was in charge of loading and unloading the Ranger team that had just deployed. From that standpoint, the most important of his tasks for this mission was over once that last Ranger stepped out the back of the helicopter.

But loading and unloading cargo and personnel wasn't Hamburger's only duty aboard Extortion 17. He also served as the gunner, putting him in charge of firing any of the three M-240 lightweight machine guns aboard the aircraft.

The M-240's effectiveness was limited to close range, against enemy ground forces firing light weapons. For the 240s to work, the Chinook would need to be in a hover position, just above the ground, not much above treetop level, firing at enemy ground troops with rifles.

But against incoming rockets, antiaircraft fire, surface-to-air missiles, or rocket-propelled grenades, the machine guns were as effective as a pea-shooter in a gunfight at the OK Corral, a reality of which Pat Hamburger was all too aware.

Hamburger had practice-fired the weapons many times, but he had never fired the weapons in combat. Like his friend Bryan Nichols in the cockpit, this marked his first combat deployment to Afghanistan, his first foray into a war zone. Four of the five members of this Air National Guard flight crew were green from lack of experience.

The two young Air Guardsmen sitting with Hamburger in the cavernous cargo bay, twenty-four-year-old Corporal Alexander Bennett of Tacoma, Washington, and twenty-one-year-old Specialist Spencer C. Duncan of Olathe, Kansas, were also green when it came to combat.

Only the co-pilot, Chief Warrant Officer David Carter of Denver, who sat in the cockpit alongside Bryan Nichols to help guide him on this first combat mission, had any type of substantial flight experience.

Thankfully the Army had the good sense to draft an initial flight plan for this young crew to keep this bird away from known enemy antiaircraft positions. The initial flight plan would keep the Chinook away from the Tangi River Valley, where the Rangers were headed by foot and that had been the site of three attacks on American helicopters within the last ninety days. US military intelligence reported that in the last three months, the Taliban had deployed over one hundred fighters, armed with rocket-propelled grenades, solely for the purpose of shooting down a US helicopter.

Sending a Chinook over that valley, at least tonight, would be the equivalent of serving a sitting duck up at a point-blank target in front of a double-barrel twelve-gauge for target practice with lottery proceeds rewarded to the winner for the kill.

Thus, the initial flight plan, when deploying the Rangers, kept them from flying over that valley. In contrast to the later flight involving US Navy SEALs, the choppers would initially take the Rangers to a relatively safe zone, which had been pre-cleared of enemy insurgents. As will be seen, the second flight plan, involving members of SEAL Team Six, would prove to be irresponsibly dangerous, and indeed foolish given the level of training of the National Guard flight crew, the antiquated equipment, and poor rules of engagement that were guaranteed to get all the Americans killed. If the Taliban knew or even suspected that the Chinook was transporting Special Forces, their helicopter would become a significant target.

At 96 feet in length, the Chinook, an older Vietnam-era helicopter pawned off to the National Guard, had a maximum capacity of thirty-three in the cargo bay. But on the way back to Base Shank, under the dimmed cabin lights and the sonorous roar of the choppers' twin engines, and the *thwock-thwock-thwock* of the sixty-foot rotary blades slicing the night air, Hamburger and his young subordinates sat alone in the cavernous cargo bay, perhaps alone in their thoughts, perhaps wondering what would come next.

The guardsmen knew what they were getting into when they enlisted. America was at war. Her opponent in this "War on Terror" was a nebulous enemy, without conventional uniforms, without conventional tactics. The enemy was willing to kill, maim, and destroy without regard to any semblance of the civilized rules of war. The Geneva Conventions meant nothing to this enemy. These guardsmen knew this. None of them had been drafted. None had been forced to sign up.

Soldiers enlist in the Army for different reasons. Some enlist out of patriotic duty. Some enlist because they need jobs. Others join with a thirst for adventure.

The young guardsmen in the back of the chopper that night, Hamburger, Bennett, and Duncan, all knew that Afghanistan might one day call their names. From the relative safety of the Midwestern plains, or the foothills of the Rockies where their units trained, they all knew that from a faraway land, half a world away, American soldiers and sailors and marines were coming home in body bags.

Yet they were prepared to serve, voluntarily, every one of them.

Now they were here, in this war-torn place that had been a theoretical figment of their collective imaginations for years, knowing that some of the Rangers they had dropped off might never come home, knowing that for their own flight crew, survival was no guarantee, and knowing that their own deaths lurked around the corner.

Perhaps the flight back to Base Shank was like a cold, wet washrag to the face, reminding them that Afghanistan was no longer a vague notion, but a sobering reality where even the smallest mistake could be your last.

It has been said that a man thinks of family as death approaches.

At some point during the flight from the landing zone back to Base Shank, it's likely that thoughts of family flashed through Pat Hamburger's mind.

Pat's brother, Chris, was back in Nebraska. Pat had telephoned Chris on July 26th, only eleven days before. His family members had been nervous about Pat leaving the safety of the corn-plains of Nebraska for the deadly, war-torn mountains of Afghanistan. Pat loved to joke around, reassuring his brother with humor, and didn't even mention anything about his mission, only telling Chris that he had "stuff to do."

Anyone who knew Pat Hamburger knew of his loving kindness and tender heart as a father. As he flew in the back of the chopper through the dark passes of the Hindu Kush range, it is inconceivable to believe that he did not, at least for a moment, turn his thoughts to the two younger girls in his life. The tough National Guardsman had a marshmallow-of-a-heart for them both.

Thirteen-year-old Veronica, his girlfriend Candie's daughter, was not his daughter by birth. But Pat had for six years treated her as if she were his own. When he came home, she would hug him and squeeze him and kiss him as if he were her own daddy. And Pat was the principal father figure in Veronica's life. Then, two years earlier, in 2009, Candie had given birth to Pat's daughter Payton, and suddenly, Veronica had a baby stepsister. Oh how Veronica doted on her baby sister, and the thought of them together would bring a smile to Pat's face!

But it was Candie Reagan, the girl he'd met while he was working as a plumber at the Village Inn in Lincoln, who had changed Pat's life. Candie was "the girl behind the desk," and the initial attraction was instant, although a few months would pass before they solidified their relationship. Candie was an all-American girl, and she had made him a better man.

There can be little doubt that under the roar of those engines, Pat thought of Candie, for the last six years had been the sweetest of both their lives. Pat had shared his secret with his brother Chris. When he returned home to Nebraska, he would ask Candie to marry him. They would live together as husband and wife, and raise their daughters in a loving home.

Now, on his very first deployment overseas, Pat had everything to live for.

But first, he would have to find a way to survive the night.

CHAPTER 3

Base Shank

LOGAR PROVINCE, EASTERN AFGHANISTAN

2115 ZULU TIME; 1:45 A.M. LOCAL TIME

SATURDAY, AUGUST 6, 2011

The United States Military typically operates according to what is known as "Zulu time." This means that reports of military operations, worldwide, are given at whatever the current time is in Greenwich, England, at the moment the operation occurs. Therefore, the military, in the coordination and execution of its operations, is not a respecter of time zones. This practice can at first blush cause confusion to laypersons and civilians not familiar with military procedure, as there is a natural tendency to always think in local time. In addition, the practice of converting Zulu time to local time can often become more confusing in parts of the world where daylight savings time is sometimes in effect.

However, in order to best understand the events of the night of August 6, 2011, it is necessary to understand Zulu time and the relationship of Zulu or military time to the local times in the affected parts of the world.

Kabul, Afghanistan, the largest city in the area in question, is always four-and-a-half hours ahead of Zulu time. Therefore, noon Zulu time would be 1630 hours, or 4:30 in the afternoon local time in Afghanistan. Likewise, midnight Zulu time would translate to 0430 hours, or 4:30 in the morning local time in Afghanistan. On August 5, 2011, at 21:15 Zulu time it was already 1:45 the next morning at Base Shank in the Logar Province of Afghanistan. Extortions 16 and 17, the helicopters that earlier in the evening had dropped off two platoons of US Army Rangers in neighboring Wardak Province, had returned safely to base.

Bryan Nichols, Pat Hamburger, and the other Army National Guardsmen of Extortion 17 had gone to standby status, probably trying to grab some shut-eye, in the event they were called out on another mission.

Not far away from the Air National Guard members, members of the US military's most famous and elite fighting force, the internationally acclaimed SEAL Team Six, the group that ninety days earlier had killed the world's most notorious terrorist Osama Bin Laden, maintained a state of readiness, just in case.

SOC (SEAL) Aaron Vaughn, a six-foot-four-inch Tennessean with sandy-colored hair and radiant blue eyes, and a seasoned combat veteran, was among the members of the SEAL team's "Gold Squad" deployed at Base Shank that night.

A former SEAL instructor, Aaron was among the bravest and most decorated of America's warriors. But no matter how focused he became or dangerous his mission was, Aaron Vaughn's heart was never far from home.

As SEAL Team Six maintained its readiness in the dark hours of the Afghan morning, it was 5:15 p.m. back home in Virginia Beach, where Kimberly Vaughn was caring for the couples' two small children, Reagan and Chamberlain.

Kimberly Lineberger and Aaron Vaughn met in Guam in 2005, where Aaron was deployed as part of a rapid-action force to the Arabian Gulf region. He stood tall and handsome, a superhero, an American Navy SEAL.

Kimberly had been a Washington Redskins cheerleader on a mission to the South Pacific with the USO to entertain the troops about to deploy to the Middle East. Glamorous and beautiful, her instant chemistry with Aaron proved magnetic. Their story became the fairy-tale meeting of which romance novels are written—an NFL cheerleader and an elite American warrior. The initial attraction on a faraway island grew into an abiding and nourishing love, cemented across time and distance by a mutual commitment to their Christian faith.

Aaron and Kimberly were married in May of 2008, and shortly after that, Kimberly gave birth to their son Reagan. They made their home in Virginia Beach, and made plans to build their dream house. Three weeks before his final deployment to Afghanistan, Kimberly gave birth to their second child, a little girl named Chamberlain.

On the afternoon of August 5th, 2011, hours before the final flight of Extortion 17, as Kimberly drove along the interstates in Virginia Beach, with Reagan and Chamberlain strapped in their car seats, the cellphone rang. Aaron's voice came over the Bluetooth, and his family would hear him for the last time. For the final time, Aaron and Kimberly, separated worlds apart, on different continents across thousands of miles of ocean, would proclaim their love for one another.

At 2130 (9:30 p.m.) Zulu Time, or 0200 (2:00 a.m.) local time in Afghanistan, several hours after Aaron and Kimberly spoke by phone, all hell broke loose at Base Shank.

According to one version of the story, word came down that the two Army Ranger units were pinned down by the Taliban. These were the same units, apparently, that had been transported to the Tangi River Valley by the two Chinooks hours earlier the same evening.

We use the phrase "according to one version of the story," because the national and international press reported, in the days following the shoot-down, that the SEALs had been deployed to rescue the Rangers, who were supposedly "pinned down" by enemy Taliban forces. Later, the military seemed to back away from the "Rangers were being rescued" story, and reported that the SEALs were being deployed to capture the well-known terrorist Qari Tahir.

In what will later be described by a US Navy SEAL as one of the fastest and chaotic "spin ups" to a mission that he has ever seen, seventeen members of SEAL Team Six—the informal name given to the Navy's elite Special Forces Developmental Group (DEVGRU) based out of Virginia Beach—sprang into action. The SEALs gathered their weapons and rushed to the airstrip, where the two old Chinook helicopters, the same choppers that had transported the Rangers to the edge of the battle zone, were waiting, with engines running.

In recounting the chaotic minutes leading up to the launch, certain facts are clear, while other factors remain unclear. Perhaps the ambiguity surrounding this launch is a simple consequence of the fog of war. Perhaps the unanswered questions will linger for other reasons.

CHAPTER 4

SEALs Called to Action

Unfortunately, the only thing that was clear about the launch of Extortion 17 was the identity of the American servicemen being scrambled.

The SEAL team was at the core of this mission, which was at first portrayed as a "rescue" mission for the Army Rangers.

LIEUTENANT COMMANDER JONAS KELSALL, SEAL COMMANDER

The SEALs were under the command of thirty-three-year-old Lieutenant Commander Jonas Kelsall, of Shreveport, Louisiana. Commander Kelsall was the only naval officer on board the flight, and was the senior commissioned officer aboard the aircraft. Kelsall was one of the original members of SEAL Team Seven, which was formed in San Diego, before being transferred to SEAL Team Six in Virginia in 2008. A rising star in the special warfare community, he had already been awarded the Legion of Merit and two Bronze Stars for combat valor. He had been married to Victoria for three years, whom he met while a student at the University of Texas. The couple had no children.

MASTER CHIEF LOU LANGLAIS, SECOND-IN-COMMAND

Kelsall's next-in-command was forty-four-year-old Master Chief Lou Langlais, of Los Angeles. Langlais, a Canadian-born rock climber and twenty-five-year Navy veteran, was married with two young sons. This was his last deployment to Afghanistan. After this deployment, he planned to return to the United States as a SEAL team instructor, and then retire and spend time with his wife and boys. Master Chief Langlais was one of the Navy's most experienced SEALs and one of its most valuable members.

The team under Kelsall and Langlais was an experienced fighting unit full of combat veterans. Eleven of the seventeen SEAL team members were chief petty officers or above. To get an idea of the experience of these men, in the Navy it takes an average of about fourteen years to reach the rank of Chief. Next to Langlais, the highest-ranking of the chiefs was Senior Chief Petty Officer Thomas Ratzlaff.

SENIOR CHIEF PETTY OFFICER THOMAS RATZLAFF

Navy Senior Chief Petty Officer Thomas A. Ratzlaff, sometimes called "Tom," and more often referred by those closest to him simply as "Rat," was a thirty-four-year-old family man who had wanted to be a Navy SEAL ever since he was a young boy.

In the prime of his life, Tom Ratzlaff was living his dream, as a husband, as a father, and as a warrior. With a list of combat ribbons and medals across his chest that would make most warriors envious, Ratzlaff had already earned four Bronze Stars—with the Combat "V" device for valor—and had served in Kosovo, Afghanistan, and Iraq. Tom and his wife had two sons back home, and they were expecting their third child after Tom completed his tour in Afghanistan.

Time magazine reporter Eric Blehm wrote about Ratzlaff as both a family man and a man of faith in his article "The Navy SEALS' Dying Words," published on August 6, 2012, the one-year anniversary of Extortion 17:

> *Tom shared that whenever he boarded a helicopter for a mission, he said the Lord's Prayer silently, once he got seated, and then prayed for protection. "I don't ask for protection myself because that's in his hands. I ask him to look after my wife and kids. Then I ask him to protect all my buddies and forgive them of all their sins and me of my sins. Then I move straight into thinking about what I'm about to do—the target, the map study, making sure I know which way's north so I can call out things correctly on the target."*

CHIEF PETTY OFFICER ROBERT J. REEVES, USN

One of the experienced chiefs serving under Kelsall and Langlais was thirty-two-year-old Robert Reeves. Like Commander Kelsall, Chief Petty Officer Reeves was from Shreveport, Louisiana. Lieutenant Commander Kelsall and Chief Reeves had been best friends from childhood. They went to school together, and at Caddo Magnet High School in Shreveport, they were just "Jonas and Rob."

Jonas Kelsall had been described in high school as a "jokester" and a "prankster." With an athletic physique and mischievous grin, Jonas was a kid who always had girls hanging around his locker.

Rob, meanwhile, had been a star athlete in high school, excelling on the school's lacrosse and soccer teams, where Jonas, also an outstanding athlete, was his teammate. Rob had a kind side to him. Once Rob surprised his high school English teacher by giving her a book signed by her favorite author. As a young man, he was both driven and thoughtful.

From the time they were boys, Jonas and Rob were inseparable. The two best friends joined the Navy together, and made a pact to become SEALs together. When Jonas was picked up for the prestigious SEAL officer program, their paths diverged, but only for a short time. And while his best friend acclimated to the officer ranks, Rob Reeves forged his own heroic mark within the SEAL community, having been deployed to war zones more than a dozen times, and winning an impressive four Bronze Stars for combat.

Between the two of them, they came into this final mission as the pride of Caddo Magnet High School, with a Legion of Merit and six Bronze Stars for combat valor between them. Few modern high schools in America can boast such collective heroism as did Caddo Magnet.

Now they were both Navy SEALs, together on a mission, placed by fate in the very same elite fighting unit, at the very same moment in history on a continent thousands of miles from their childhood home. This was a coincidence that only fate could have dictated.

Jonas Kelsall had once said, "If I die on a mission, I'll die happy, because I'm doing something for my country."

Before the sun would rise, Jonas would die for his country, and he and Rob would die together. They would be close in life, and even closer in death.

—◆—

In addition to Kelsall, Langlais, Reeves, and Vaughn, there were thirteen other SEALS on the mission, bringing the number to seventeen members of SEAL Team Six who boarded the choppers for Wardak Province.

The seventeen SEALs were supported by five other US Navy members, including a cryptologist, a master-at-arms, two explosive ordnance experts, and an information systems specialist. Also scrambled were three US Air Force servicemen, working in support of the SEAL team, along with five members of the National Guard aircrew. Two of the three Air Force crewmen were Special Operations rescue operators, whose job would be to rescue and bring home any Americans downed in combat. The third was a Special Operations combat controller.

Thirty Americans scrambled into action aboard that old chopper in the dark, early hours of that fateful Afghan morning—that much is clear. But what happened after that, even at the very beginning of the flight, before the shoot-down, is murky at best. Questions have arisen that call into question the actions of the military and which to date the proper authorities have failed to credibly address.

QUESTION 1: WHY NOT BOARD TWO CHOPPERS?

Remember, two old helicopters were sitting on the tarmac. Both Extortion 16 and Extortion 17 had flown in the earlier mission that evening to deliver the Rangers to the edge of the battle zone. Both were operational. Both were going to fly in support of this mission. But rather than splitting the SEAL team into two groups and flying them to the battle site on two helicopters, all the SEALs were ordered onto one chopper, Extortion 17, making the whole team vulnerable in case of a single disaster. Extortion 16 will take off and fly with Extortion 17, but Extortion 16 will serve as an aerial decoy.

Four-star retired Navy admiral James "Ace" Lyons, the former commander of the United States Pacific Fleet, commented on this issue at a press conference on May 9, 2013, in Washington. Regarding the decision to cram the SEALs onto one helicopter, Admiral Lyons stated:

"Why and who decided to put twenty-five elite SEAL Team Six warriors in a single helicopter? That was my first question to myself when I heard about this tragedy. Sending them on a mission that was compromised? As you all know, we had to vet all our Special Operations plans, basically with all the Afghans. We might as well have turned them over to the Taliban."

Indeed, Admiral Lyons is correct in that the Afghans were informed in advance of this mission, and, in fact, every mission that the SEALs and Rangers have flown in Afghanistan. Obviously this raises a huge concern about mission integrity and avoiding compromising the safety of US forces, a topic discussed with greater detail later.

There still has been no satisfactory answer to the question of why all the SEALs were crammed onto one chopper when a second was available.

CHRONOLOGY FOR AUGUST 6, 2011: DAY OF SHOOT-DOWN

The official United States military investigation of the shoot down of Extortion was conducted in Afghanistan by a team headed by Army Brigadier General Jeffrey Colt, who had been an Army helicopter pilot. Brigadier General Colt had a team of officers and experts working at his disposal, with a goal of producing a report explaining the reasons for the shoot down.

More background on this report, referred to by the author as the "Colt report," will be presented in later chapters of this book, with a full background on the Colt Report beginning at Chapter Six, below.

For the time being, however, it is important to understand that the chronology of the shoot-down has been assembled from documentary evidence taken directly from the Colt Report.

At 0200 a.m. local time in Afghanistan, per "Enclosure H" of the Colt Report, the Tactical Operations Center directed Extortion 17 to move to the staging area at Base Shank to pick up twenty-five Special Operations personnel, including the US Navy SEALs. The SEALs are part of what is called an "Immediate Reaction Force." They are a contingency unit, designed to back up the US Army Rangers already on the ground, if the Rangers find themselves in need of help.

Seconds before Extortion 17 was directed to pick up the SEALs, a decision was made to increase the number of personnel in the Immediate Reaction Force from seventeen to twenty-five.

Five minutes later, at 0205 a.m., despite the fact that two helicopters were available for the mission, all twenty-five Special Operations American personnel were ordered onto a single helicopter, cramming the chopper to its maximum capacity, and endangering all souls aboard in the event of a shoot-down. The old chopper was about to be ordered to fly over an area heavily armed with Taliban, with RPGs and rockets capable of attacking allied helicopters, over a valley in which three Coalition helicopters had been attacked in the last ninety days.

Based upon the order to board a single chopper, the SEALs, under Lieutenant Commander Kelsall, rushed to the tarmac where both choppers awaited. Operational prudence and safety considerations dictated that the SEAL team be split, with Kelsall taking twelve team members on one chopper and Langlais taking the rest on the other. Remember that five of the thirty Americans were flight crew members. The other twenty-five were the SEAL team and its support crew.

But that's not the way it happened. Instead, every member of the American SEAL team, and every Navy and Air Force enlisted man, piled onto one of the choppers, Extortion 17. So all the risk was concentrated in one chopper at takeoff. But the strange decision to concentrate the entire SEAL team onto Extortion 17 was the first in a string of oddities that would plague the mission from start to finish.

By 0209 a.m., the SEAL team was on the chopper. Pilot Bryan Nichols reported that the Immediate Reaction Force was composed not of thirty-two, but of thirty-three members, nearly doubling the originally planned contingency of seventeen. Extortion 17 was now fully loaded, in fact almost overloaded, sitting on the tarmac at REDCON level 1, awaiting the order to take off.

Extortion 16, the other Chinook chopper that would fly this mission, and that earlier in the evening had infiltrated US Army Rangers into far less dangerous airspace alongside Extortion 17, was also ready for takeoff.

But Extortion 16, this time, is only manned by its aircrew. No SEALs are aboard. No Rangers are aboard. No ground forces are aboard. Aside from its aircrew, Extortion 16 is empty.

At 0222 a.m., local time, Extortion 17 lifted off for the last time, carrying the thirty Americans aboard to their eternal destiny.

From the time they lifted off, until they time they were shot down at 0239 a.m., seventeen minutes later, their flight was marred by inexplicable delays, losses in communication, and very odd movements by the helicopter.

At one point, a near panic set in at flight control, as controllers, planners, and officers fretted over why Extortion 17 appeared to be stalled in the air, seemingly hanging there as a sitting duck, as if making itself a target.

At one point, back at flight control, there was self-assured speculation that perhaps the chopper was hovering in the air, and some controllers speculated that perhaps the SEAL team was rappelling down to the ground.

But the SEALs were not rappelling to the ground. Instead, per reports coming out of flight control, the chopper was stalled in the air. What was going on inside that helicopter?

Yes, it was being piloted by a relatively inexperienced young National Guard pilot, CW2 Bryan Nichols. But his co-pilot, CW4 David Carter, was far more experienced.

Still, in this day of GPS navigation, there was no logical reason for Extortion 17's seeming difficulty finding the landing zone. Nor was there any reason for it to be stalled in the air.

All parties involved seem to agree that Extortion 17 was only 100 to 150 feet above the ground when it was shot down.

The Colt Report: August 7, 2011–September 13, 2011

The thirty-eight days or so immediately following the shoot-down, from August 7, 2011 to September 13, 2011, were crucial because of what the Army did and did not do and said and did not say during this period.

As soon as Extortion 17 was shot down, the commander of US Central Command, Marine general James Mattis, ordered Army brigadier general Jeffrey Colt to conduct an investigation of the shoot-down. That investigation, which involved twenty-three military investigators as part of the Air-Crash investigating team, analyzing evidence collected from the site, interviewing witnesses, and reviewing photographs, resulted in a 1,250-page report, originally classified as Top Secret. For reasons that are still unclear, it was largely declassified and later turned over to certain surviving family members of the SEAL team.

For ease of reference, the investigative report will be referred to herein simply as the "Colt Report."

The timing of the Colt Report's release in September 2011 was critical. That's because the initial report, which came in the form of an "Executive Summary" from Brigadier General Colt back to General Mattis, with numerous exhibits and recommendations, left out crucial information.

For starters, here are three relevant dates to keep in mind concerning the report itself, which raised grave suspicion of a cover-up.

The first date is August 7, 2011, the day after the crash. On this date, four-star US Marine general James Mattis, Commander of United States Central Command, sent a written directive to Brigadier General Jeffrey Colt to conduct a sweeping investigation as to the cause of the shoot-down of Extortion 17. Mattis gave Colt thirty days to complete his investigation.

The second date is September 9, 2011. By this time, Brigadier General Colt had completed the investigation ordered by General Mattis. Colt had some twenty-two military officers, mostly from the US Army, but a few from the Navy and Air Force, all subject-matter experts in various relevant fields, assist him in his investigation.

In addition to the twenty-two officers working directly on Colt's investigation team, a Joint Combat Assessment Team (JCAT) from Bagram Air Base in Afghanistan, using aviation crash experts, conducted a piece-by-piece, visual and forensics examination of the shot-down helicopter. They supplied Colt's investigation team with their own JCAT report, and their own conclusions about what happened.

Colt and his team had taken all this into consideration, had interviewed dozens of witnesses under oath, and by September 9, 2011, Colt was ready to report back to General Mattis.

So on September 9, 2011, Colt signed his Executive Summary to General Mattis, attaching more than one hundred exhibits and enclosures, with his (Colt's) written thoughts on the reason for the shoot-down.

Four days later, on September 13, 2011, General Colt issued his final report, hoping to close the chapter on any questions concerning the shoot-down of Extortion 17.

General Mattis's final report, perhaps not surprisingly, summarily concluded that no one was at fault, that the military made all the correct decisions, and that the shoot-down of Extortion 17 could not have been prevented.

Colt's summary and Mattis's report and conclusion will be contradicted by internal evidence on multiple fronts. It will be more than a year before all the report's glaring omissions come to light, in what can be explained only as an attempt by the military to sweep crucial and highly embarrassing information under the rug.

Aside from the report's failure to discuss the military's inexplicable inability to locate or otherwise account for the black box that was supposedly on board the helicopter, the reports ignore an even greater pink elephant in the room: On the night of the shoot-down, just minutes before Extortion 17 lifted off for the final time, the chopper was boarded by seven unidentified Afghans, in blatant violation of US military procedure and protocol. The Afghans' names were not on the flight manifest for Extortion 17.

In an era of disconcerting "Green-on-Blue" violence in which Afghan soldiers and security forces, purporting to be US allies, had been shooting Americans in the back for nearly a decade, one would think that the *final* report on the shoot-down of Extortion 17 would reveal and address such a big-time security breach.

But the report contained no explanation of how the Afghans violated US security procedures to get on the aircraft. There was no mention of their names. There was no assurance that their intentions were not sinister. In fact, not one single word was even mentioned about the incident by either Colt or Mattis.

On January 11, 2013, some fifteen months after the shoot-down, a brave and gutsy sergeant major in the US Army alerted Billy and Karen

Vaughn, parents of SOC Aaron Vaughn, that the Afghans were on the chopper, and that their security breach was a "very big deal."

The military's omission of this crucial breach raised all kinds of unanswered questions, and the military almost got away with covering it up.

Almost.

QUESTION NUMBER TWO: THE SEVEN UNIDENTIFIED AFGHANS

A second oddity, one of the biggest red flags of the entire mission, and one largely ignored by the press and even the US military itself, also occurred during the boarding process of Extortion 17.

This question, unless answered, will haunt the mission and will linger throughout the ages.

As the Navy SEAL team, which included Navy support personnel, rushed to the chopper along with the five-man Air National Guard crew, seven unidentified members of the Afghan military also boarded the chopper.

That fact is worth repeating, because it is crucial. Seven unidentified Afghans boarded that chopper. Their names are not known. They have not been identified, and we don't know what they were up to.

The identity of the Afghans is one of the great, looming questions unanswered by the military, as if it is of peripheral unimportance. But their identities are vitally important in fully understanding what happened.

Yet, the fact that unidentified Afghans infiltrated this chopper at the last second has been largely brushed over by the official military investigation and virtually ignored by the US press. The military investigation headed up by Brigadier General Colt in August of 2011, producing the 1,250-page report with testimony, photographs, real-time transcripts of air-traffic control, and a plethora of other information, barely even mentions the huge pink elephant—the mysterious Afghans, except in one testimonial exchange on page 118 of Exhibit 1.

But understand this. That testimonial exchange at page 118 of Exhibit 1, was a needle-in-a-haystack buried in a thousand-plus-page report. As previously stated, nothing is mentioned about the Afghans in either Brigadier General Colt's Executive Summary of September 9, 2011, or

General Mattis's final report of September 13, 2011, showing a finding of no-fault.

Yet, the questions remain constant, like an eerie, beating war-drum, on each page of the 1,250 pages: Who were these Afghans, and why were they on board a United States Army helicopter without proper permission or authority? Why does nobody account for them and why did nobody stop them from boarding?

Yet the Colt Report brushed over the existence of the seven unidentified Afghans, and made no substantial effort, at least no effort that is reported, to identify them, or to even acknowledge the existence of the severe security breach that allowed them to infiltrate Extortion 17 before it took off.

And as will be seen later, the cremation of the unknown Afghans, if that indeed happened, looms large in suggesting a cover-up, because cremating their bodies destroys DNA evidence, making it impossible to identify their remains.

In fact, their bodies were brought back to the United States and apparently cremated by the US military, thereby effectively destroying any chance to ever identify them. If this is truly the case, no one will ever know if they were terrorists. No one will ever know if they were Taliban collaborators.

The fact that Afghans boarded the US military transport helicopter was not in and of itself unusual, given the politically correct climate between the United States and Afghanistan in 2011. In fact, this Immediate Reaction Force of Navy SEALs had seven Afghan army personnel assigned to it. *But the oddity in this instance came when the seven Afghans who boarded were not the seven Afghans assigned to the team, but seven unidentified Afghans whose names were not on the flight manifest.*

There was a switch-out.

The unexplained presence of the seven unidentified Afghans was a violation of flight protocol, procedure, and security.

The official military investigation of the shoot-down of Extortion 17, conducted in the weeks following the shoot-down and overseen by Brigadier General Jeffrey Colt, did not even make a credible effort to identify these seven unidentified Afghans, nor did it even peripherally raise their non-identity as a security concern. Nothing was said at all about the Afghans in the initial report following the military's investigation. Their presence would be discovered, by happenchance, well over a year after the shoot-down.

It would seem reasonable to ask why. But only the military can answer that question, which they have failed to do to date. So these questions remain unanswered, looming like a mysterious fog over the graves of SEAL Team Six members of Extortion 17 at Arlington National Cemetery, and haunt the memory of this mission in perpetuity:

Who were these armed Afghans? And why were they allowed to board the helicopter in violation of US military protocol? And what did they do once the flight took off?

Before examining who these Afghans might have been, it is crucial to understand the backdrop of this mission—the international climate and instability in the ninety-seven days leading up to this fateful mission, beginning with the killing of Osama Bin Laden by members of SEAL Team Six on May 1, 2011.

CHAPTER 5

Ninety-Seven Days from Quintessential Glory to Unexplained Disaster

MAY 1, 2011–AUGUST 6, 2011

The announcement that the Japanese had bombed Pearl Harbor. The moment Germany surrendered. The Japanese surrender at Tokyo Bay. The assassinations of John Kennedy and Martin Luther King Jr. The moment Armstrong stepped on the moon. The explosion of the Space Shuttle *Challenger*. The fall of the Berlin Wall. The day the twin towers fell to the ground.

Moments like these are burned into the consciousness of a nation.

Most Americans, alive and alert enough to understand the issues threatening the nation at the time of these events, can recall exactly where they were and what they were doing when news came of these compelling moments in US history.

For many Americans, Sunday evening, May 1, 2011, would become one of those moments. They would always remember where they were and what they were doing when they heard the news—when President Barack Obama announced the death of the world's most hated terrorist, Osama Bin Laden.

The massive manhunt unleashed by President George W. Bush a decade earlier, seeking revenge against the man blamed for the most bloody, painful, and humiliating act of terror and mass murder ever perpetrated against the United States, was ended by an announcement from President Obama on national television from the White House that Sunday evening at 11:30 p.m. Washington time.

The announcement set off celebration and jubilation, and rightly so. On the afternoon of August 9, 1974, moments after President Nixon had resigned and was in flight back to San Clemente, President Gerald Ford said that "our long national nightmare is over." Though President Obama did not reference Ford's words in his address to the nation, there was a collective feeling that another long national nightmare had ended on May 1, 2011, one that had begun a decade earlier with horrific images of Manhattan's tallest buildings collapsing from a blaze of fire to a mountain of destroyed concrete and rubble, had finally come to an end.

All presidents are remembered by their greatest achievements, and many by their most profound failures, whether they fully deserve those achievements or whether they are fully responsible for those failures. Herbert Hoover is blamed for the Great Depression; Lyndon Johnson for the Vietnam War. John Kennedy is remembered for his bold vision of putting a man on the moon. Jimmy Carter gets credit for Camp David. Ronald Reagan is credited for the collapse of the Soviet Union and the fall of the Berlin Wall.

For President Obama, politically beleaguered on many fronts, the death of Bin Laden is likely to go down in history as his crowning achievement, the one moment the nation was wholly unified by a grand decision he had made.

Yes, there would be some who would argue that President George W. Bush set the military apparatus in place for Bin Laden's final demise, and that it was SEAL Team Six, and not Obama, who actually killed Bin Laden.

All that is technically true. But it was Obama who gave the order to send the SEALs into Pakistan to kill Bin Laden, and the heroic mission occurred on his watch. And for that, he deserves credit.

But as history would have it, a mere ninety-seven days would separate the most glorious achievement in all of Seal Team Six's history from its deadliest disaster. That disaster would not be the fault of the SEALs, but rather, would rest squarely on the shoulders of those above them in the chain of command who ordered them into battle in tenuous and questionable circumstances, on an old helicopter built before most of them were born, in a hot fire-zone in the skies that would completely neutralize their ability to do what they do better than anyone in the world—fight on the ground and in the sea.

For the families of thirty Americans, mostly US Navy SEALs, the glory of May Day, 2011, would within three months and one week fade into unimaginable pain, heartbreak, and personal loss. The loss and pain these families, and indeed the nation would soon suffer, in part because of a series of curious and foolish actions by certain members of the Obama Administration who would insist on reckless public blabbing, in violation of a vow of silence, and also because of certain inexplicable actions by the US military, who would execute a battle plan wholly lacking in common sense.

The Planning of Neptune Spear

On May 1, 2011, US Navy SEALs, attached to DEVGRU Red Squad, formerly known and still colloquially known as Seal Team Six, executed Operation Neptune Spear, slipping into Pakistan aboard Special Ops helicopters and killing Osama Bin Laden. Prior to execution of the mission, an internal debate had gone on inside the White House.

Among those in on the pre-mission planning were President Obama, Vice President Joe Biden, Secretary of Defense Robert Gates, CIA director Leon Panetta, members of the National Security Council, and then–Vice Admiral William McRaven, the three-star Navy SEAL who led the US Joint Special Operations Command. (Admiral McRaven, perhaps somewhat ironically, would later receive his fourth star on August 9, 2011, the same day that the bodies of the SEAL Team Six members who died on board Extortion 17 were brought back from Afghanistan and honored at Dover Air Force Base.)

Active planning for Neptune Spear had begun in March 2011, with the operational details in the planning phase masterminded by Vice Admiral McRaven, who briefed President Obama regularly.

The National Command Authority knew by this time that Bin Laden was holed up in Abbottabad, Pakistan, a highland town north of Islamabad. By all accounts, an internal debate ensued within the Administration on what to do about it. The execution of the plan would involve sending the SEAL team from Afghanistan across the border into neighboring

Pakistan, sending US forces into a foreign country, a country that on paper was a US ally, without first notifying the host government.

Various options were discussed, including striking the Bin Laden compound with drones. Vice President Biden was opposed to the mission altogether, concerned that it was too risky. But President Obama favored the option presented by Admiral McRaven that would send the SEAL team directly into Bin Laden's compound.

Obama wanted to make sure that they killed their man, and that they got the body. He overrode the vice president, and the order to execute Neptune Spear quickly moved down the chain of command to the SEAL team, waiting in eastern Afghanistan for presidential orders.

The next point is important. At the White House on the night of the raid, a group including the president, the vice president, and other senior Administration officials and military officers privy to the Top Secret plans accepted Secretary of Defense Robert Gates's suggestion not to reveal the identity of the unit that would kill Bin Laden. There was collective agreement that revealing the specific unit that ultimately killed Bin Laden would endanger the unit's members, and possibly their families as well.

When President Obama announced to a national television audience that Bin Laden was dead, he was criticized in some corners for appearing to take too much personal credit for the operation. That sort of criticism happens in the rough-and-tumble world of politics.

All that aside, to his credit, President Obama was careful not to publicly announce the name of the unit that killed Bin Laden, honoring the commitment made in the White House Situation Room not to provide specific information on the unit carrying out the mission.

President Obama, in his initial comments, announces only that "a small team of Americans" had killed Bin Laden. The president made no other comments that could be used to identify the team. A "small team of Americans" could have been CIA, or Army Rangers, or Navy SEALs, or US Marines, or Delta Force, or regular military. The specific identity of the unit would be anybody's guess.

Immediately after the shoot-down, other senior White House and military officials also declined to provide specific information on unit identity or numbers. Former national security advisor (now CIA director)

John Brennan, his former deputy Denis McDonough, and senior military spokesmen at the Pentagon all, when asked, specifically declined to divulge unit identity or unit numbers.

Despite the failure of US authorities to divulge the identities of the assassins, the Taliban did not take long to vow revenge.

On May 2, 2011, the day after Neptune Spear, a Taliban commander in Afghanistan, identified as "Qudos" and claiming to operate in the northern province of Baghlan, vowed that the Taliban would avenge Bin Laden's death. The commander said his fighters planned to launch an operation called "Operation Badrto to avenge the killing of Osama" and claimed many other similar operations would be launched to avenge Bin Laden.

MAY 3, 2011: THE VICE PRESIDENT'S BREACH OF PROMISE

On May 3, 2011, two days after Neptune Spear, and following a slew of Taliban retaliation vows, Vice President Biden, visibly giddy over the Administration's crowning achievement, appeared at Washington's Ritz-Carlton Hotel to mark the fiftieth anniversary of the Atlantic Council. For reasons that still cannot be explained, Biden violated the sacred Situation Room agreement not to identify the units involved, and twice mentioned the SEALs as the Special Forces unit responsible.

Biden began by recognizing James Stavridis, a highly decorated four-star admiral who had served as Commander of US European Command, Supreme Allied Commander Europe, and Commander of US Southern Command. The vice president addressed Admiral Stavridis with these comments: "Let me briefly acknowledge tonight's distinguished honorees. Admiral James Stavridis is the real deal. He can tell you more about and understands the incredible, the phenomenal, the just almost unbelievable capacity of his Navy SEALs and what they did last Sunday."

Those remarks, if that's all the vice president had said, were enough to immediately send a shockwave throughout the Administration and the SEAL community. But Biden was not finished with his remarks about the SEALs.

Later in his speech, he returned to the topic of the SEALs again. "Folks, I'd be remiss also if I didn't say an extra word about the incredible events, extraordinary events of this past Sunday. As vice president of the United States, as an American, I was in absolute awe of the capacity and dedication of the entire team, both the intelligence community, the CIA, the SEALs. It just was extraordinary."

Biden's inexplicable breach of trust would stun the SEAL community and cause SEAL families to fear for their safety. The SEALs, who pride themselves on operating in secrecy and shun the glory that the world thrusts on them, had been "outed" by the vice commander-in-chief.

Indeed, the concern and dismay over Biden's remarks spread swiftly. On May 4, 2011, the day after the vice president announced that Navy SEALs had taken out Bin Laden, and four days after Operation Neptune Spear, Aaron Vaughn, who would later be killed in Extortion 17, telephoned his parents and informed them that SEAL Team Six now had a "target" on its backs.

Vaughn instructed Billy and Karen Vaughn to remove all their presence from social media, for fear that they were now in danger. Aaron Vaughn reported that this fear was a pervasive concern throughout the unit. According to Karen Vaughn, Aaron said, " 'Mom, you need to wipe your social media clean . . . your life is in danger, our lives are in danger, so clean it up right now.' "

On May 6, 2011, three days after the Biden speech, the Taliban again vowed public revenge against the unit that killed Bin Laden. For the first time, Al Qaeda also vowed revenge.

MAY 11, 2011: TALIBAN POSITIONS FORCES TO SHOOT DOWN US HELICOPTER IN TANGI RIVER VALLEY

It appeared that the Taliban was serious about carrying out retaliation, and was determined to do, specifically, by shooting down a US military helicopter carrying US Special Forces. On May 11, 2011, US military intelligence received information that more than one hundred Taliban fighters were being moved into the Tangi River Valley (where Extortion 17 was shot down) for the express purpose of "shooting down an American Helicopter."

At this juncture it was known that the war against the Taliban in eastern Afghanistan was being largely and effectively prosecuted by US

Special Forces. President Obama had made a tactical decision to step up Special Forces Operations in 2009. It was also known that those US Special Forces fighting the war were primarily either US Navy SEALs or US Army Rangers.

On May 12, 2011, Defense Secretary Gates, speaking at Camp Lejeune, North Carolina, expressed concern over Administration leaks identifying Navy SEALs as the Special Forces unit that killed Bin Laden. Gates indicated that he was dismayed that an agreement made in the Situation Room that officials would not talk about any operation details of the Bin Laden raid "lasted only fifteen hours." In corroborating the veracity of Aaron Vaughn's call to his parents, Secretary Gates confirmed that Navy SEALs involved in the operation were concerned about the safety of their families.

Gates was about to step down and be replaced by Leon Panetta. In a response to a question from a Marine Corps medical logistics officer at a meeting with Marines at Camp Lejeune on May 12, 2011, Gates expressed frustration that the agreement to maintain secrecy for the protection of the SEALs had fallen apart. When asked in this open meeting with the press present, the Marine, obviously concerned about the safety of the SEALs' families, asked: "What measures are being taken to protect the identities and the lives of the SEAL team members, as well as the lives of military forces deployed that might have to face extreme retaliation from terrorist organizations that want to have those identities known?"

Here's how Secretary Gates responded: "Frankly, a week ago Sunday, in the Situation Room, we all agreed that we would not release any operational details from the effort to take out Bin Laden. That all fell apart on Monday—the next day." He went on to say that "there is an awareness that the threat of retaliation is increased because . . . of the action against Bin Laden."

Secretary Gates also talked about meeting with members of the SEAL team, who expressed concern about the safety of their families as a result of Biden's betrayal of confidence. On May 12, 2011, he was quoted by ABC News as saying, "when I met with the team last Thursday, they expressed a concern about that, and particularly with respect to their families . . . I can't get into the details in this forum, but we are looking at what measures can be taken to pump up the security."

Clearly, Gates was not happy about the vice president's inexplicable blabbing and breach of trust, and was frank in his comments to that effect. Unfortunately, Biden was not the only senior Administration official to violate the no-details agreement reached in the Situation Room.

PANETTA'S GAFFE

On June 24, 2011, while he was still CIA director, and four days before he would succeed Robert Gates as secretary of defense, Leon Panetta went even further than Vice President Biden, and specifically disclosed both Secret and Top Secret information concerning the SEAL team's operation against the Bin Laden compound to filmmakers working on the movie *Zero Dark Thirty*, which would chronicle the attack by the SEALs on the Bin Laden compound.

Panetta revealed details to the scriptwriter Mark Boal, who had been invited to CIA headquarters for a briefing that Panetta was giving on the details of Operation Neptune Spear. How coincidental that the Hollywood writer of the movie that would chronicle the event, thus placing the Obama Administration in a positive light, would happen to have been invited to a briefing given by the CIA director on Top Secret operational details of the event.

Information concerning Panetta's breach was discovered through Freedom of Information Act requests served by the Washington-based watchdog group Judicial Watch, the same group that would later uncover previously unreleased details from the White House about those responsible for the "it's a video" meme that would be trumpeted by the Administration in the wake of the Benghazi terror attacks against the US consulate.

On June 15, 2013, the Pentagon inspector general reported that Panetta also discussed classified information designated as Top Secret and Secret during his presentation at an awards ceremony honoring the SEAL team, according to a draft of the inspector general's report published by the Project on Government Oversight.

With the inspector general confirming the improper release of classified information by Mr. Panetta, leaving no doubt that it actually happened, Mr. Panetta had little choice but to respond. His stated excuse was that he did not know that Mr. Boal (or anyone else lacking the proper security clearance) was in the room.

Even if Panetta was telling the truth, that he "did not know" that Boal was in the room, that sort of error would still be an inexcusable act of sloppiness in protecting national security. For Panetta to reveal Top Secret information to an audience without knowing who was listening showed an incredible sloppiness in protecting state secrets designed to save American lives, and was an incredible lapse in professionalism. It was a mistake that the CIA director, of all people, should never have made. For the CIA to be so sloppy as to give someone like Boal access to Top Secret information, and then to hide behind the claim that he somehow slipped into a briefing without proper clearance, looms as an even scarier event than Mr. Biden's loose lips.

Regardless, by the time Biden, Panetta, and others were finished with their talking, at the end of June 2011, SEAL Team Six had an Administration-enhanced target on its back, because the vice president of the United States and the director of the CIA (soon to become secretary of defense when Secretary Gates stepped down) could not keep their lips closed.

In the summer of 2011, the Taliban, following up on promises for retaliation, and following the babbling sessions by Biden and Panetta, opened up hunting season on US helicopters flying over the Tangi River Valley in Afghanistan.

On June 4, 2011, just three weeks after US intelligence discovered that the Taliban was moving one hundred insurgents into the valley, and thirty-one days after the vice president's gaffe, the Taliban opened fire on a United States UH-60L Black Hawk helicopter. The chopper survived, but barely, as "rounds burned out within 1 rotor disk of the aircraft." In other words, the Black Hawk escaped by virtue of a near miss.

Two days later, on June 6, 2011, the Taliban unloaded against a Chinook CH-47D, firing fourteen rocket-propelled grenades, along with small arms fire, from five different points of origin on the ground. Fortunately, the Chinook in this case, unlike Extortion 17, was not at point-blank range, and the pilot was able to maneuver it to safety.

Yet again, on July 20, 2011, only seventeen days prior to the Extortion 17 shoot-down, a Special Ops MH-47 chopper was fired at from Taliban ground forces over the Tangi River Valley. The Special Ops chopper was hit by small arms fire, but survived the attack and completed its mission.

THE TALIBAN RESPONSE

So in the midst of babbling by Biden and Panetta, in the summer of 2011, the Taliban launched three attacks against helicopters flying over the Tangi Valley. Fortunately, they were 0 for 3 at this point, but it was very clear that the Taliban was determined to shoot down an American helicopter, both from their threats and their actions.

The military was aware of heavy antiaircraft fire on the ground in the Tangi River Valley, and was aware of the vulnerability of the CH-47 to ground fire only days before, but still dispatched the SEAL team on a CH-47, without pre-suppression fire.

On August 5, 2011, a crescent moon hung over Afghanistan. The moon set at 2200 hours (10:00 p.m.), leaving the skies over Pakistan dark in the hours after midnight.

On the ground, the men of SEAL Team Six, their backs now targeted by the sloppy negligence of their own vice president and secretary of defense, sat and waited for duty to call.

Because of a sloppy inability or unwillingness to maintain public secrecy by two of the highest-ranking officials in the Obama Administration, the SEALs would go into this, their last mission, knowing that they had been singled out and effectively painted as targets by Washington politicians eager to take political credit for their unit's heroic performance in Operation Neptune Spear.

CHAPTER 6

Background on the Colt Report

The official military investigation of the shoot-down produced the Colt Report. The report collected information gathered during a quickly assembled investigation conducted over a period of approximately thirty days, from August 7, 2011, the day after the shoot-down, to September 7, 2011, the day Brigadier General Colt submitted the report to General James "Mad Dog" Mattis, then commander of CENTCOM (US Central Command).

Colt, a one-star US Army general who had been a helicopter pilot, ran the investigation and delivered his report to four-star general James Mattis, because it was General Mattis who ordered Colt to conduct the investigation to begin with.

To better understand the chain-of-command structure under which this investigation was ordered, it is important to know that CENTCOM is one of nine different "Unified Combatant Commands." All these Unified Combatant Commands are commanded by a four-star officer, either a flag officer (Navy) or a general officer (Army, Air Force, Marine Corps).

The commanders of these Unified Commands report directly to the secretary of defense, who reports to the president. These commanders have actual warfighting capabilities as opposed to some other four-star officers, such as the officers on the Joint Chiefs of Staff, who serve as military advisors to the president but are not in the chain of command for issuing orders for military operations.

Six of the nine unified commands are geographically centered, giving the flag/general officer warfighting command in a certain part of the world. These include African Command (AFRICOM), Central

Command (CENTCOM), European Command (EUCOM), Northern Command (NORTHCOM), US Pacific Command (PACCOM) and Southern Command (SOUTHCOM).

This means that if conflict breaks out in any given part of the world, the four-star officer in charge of that Unified Command issues operational orders to US military forces in that region. For example, in recent discussions of the 2012 terrorist attack on the US consulate in Libya, focus centered on Army general Carter Ham, who was the general commanding AFRICOM, because Libya is located in Africa, and the commander of AFRICOM is the general with actual warfighting authority in the chain of command in Africa. Likewise, CENTCOM, headquartered at MacDill Air Base in Florida, also has a geographic responsibility for theater and wartime operations that includes the Middle East, Central Asia, Iraq, and Afghanistan. Because Extortion 17 was operating in Afghanistan, it fell under CENTCOM's area of responsibility, which is why General Mattis gave the investigation assignment to Brigadier General Colt, who in turn reported back to Mattis.

The 1,250-page report included eighty-nine multi-paged exhibits, ten enclosures, and covered the sworn testimony of numerous witnesses, including the aircrews of Apache gunships and an AC-130 that were in the air when Extortion 17 was shot down.

THE MYSTERIOUS RELEASE OF THE COLT REPORT

How did the Colt Report get released to the public to begin with?

The report was immediately classified as Secret, and how it would end up being largely declassified and released to certain SEAL family members in October of 2011 is not clear. But shortly after the report's release to a limited number of family members, high-ranking Pentagon brass discussed a plan to try to get it back, but ultimately did not pursue that strategy, perhaps for legal reasons, or perhaps because trying to get the report back might have proved disastrous for public relations reasons.

Most likely, its declassification was the work of senior enlisted men and mid-grade officers in the military who wanted to get the truth out about the mission. Indeed, a number of senior enlisted Special Forces members and mid-grade officers have provided crucial off-the-record information about this mission, showing a dogged determination to get the truth out to the American people. Their willingness to talk may have been a product of the apparent tension between the lower-level soldiers and the Pentagon's upper brass and Administration officials over the foolish rules of engagement set forth by the Obama Administration, which many with personal knowledge of this mission believe were responsible for the deaths of the Extortion 17 crew.

There is no way to be certain about why the report was declassified. But one thing *is* certain: Certain evidence revealed in the Colt Report leads to concerns about the military's official position, and contains numerous contradictions and omissions that point to a cover-up of the truth about the SEALs.

Only a few copies of the report are in the hands of the public. A handful are in the possession of Extortion 17 family members, although, based upon the author's discussion with several family members, because of the extreme pain of coming face-to-face with the circumstances of their loved ones' deaths, it appears that very few have actually read the 1,250-page report, at least not in its totality.

One copy is in the hands of the *Washington Times*, which has run several stories on the shoot-down, some based on the report.

One copy of the report is in the hands of the author.

The following chapters examine the report with a view toward forensic, testimonial, and other evidence, approaching the shoot-down as a prosecutor would conduct an initial investigation to determine exactly what happened, based on a total overview of all the evidence available, and to determine who is responsible for the shoot-down of the SEAL team.

CHAPTER 7

The Colt Report: A General Overview

The internal evidence in the Colt Report on the shoot-down of Extortion 17 reveals numerous inconsistencies and contradictions that suggest a cover-up to prevent the American public from knowing the truth.

The military, and civilian Pentagon officials, claimed that the death of these men was "just one of those things," or words to that effect, and "could not have been prevented."

But the evidence will show that nothing could be further from the truth.

COLT REPORT UNDERMINES MILITARY'S PREVIOUS POSITION
The Colt Report's limited release, in October of 2011, effectively undercut public positions taken by the military a month earlier, in September of 2011.

A similar approach was taken one year later in the immediate aftermath of the Benghazi terror attacks. Initial reports released by the Executive Branch noted that the US consulate was attacked when an angry mob gathered around it was incited by a video. In the weeks and months to follow, additional evidence surfaced leading to the conclusion that the "it was a video that incited a demonstration" narrative was inaccurate. Much in the same way, the military and the government would make initial claims about the shoot-down, which later proved to be false in the face of clear evidence leaked by the Colt Report. For example, the military claimed that the rocket-propelled grenade that brought down Extortion 17 was fired from a building 220 meters away, but evidence in the Colt Report proved that claim to be inaccurate.

Just three days after the shoot-down on August 9, 2011, the military stated that none of the bodies of the SEALs and Afghans on Extortion 17 could be identified because they were so badly burned. But once the Colt Report leaked out, along with the results of independently released autopsies, that claim was proven to be false.

Not only would contradictions within the Colt report debunking the military's self-serving claims about the shoot-down prove to be significant, but conspicuous and inexplicable omissions from the report would prove to be just as if not more significant.

SPIN AFTER THE SHOOT-DOWN

Essentially, much like the inaccurate "it was a video" meme played over and over again after Benghazi, the military tried desperately to spin a "we did nothing wrong" narrative to absolve itself of the death of thirty Americans.

But from the foolish rules of engagement that provided these men of Extortion 17 with no pre-suppression fire, to the selection of a defenseless, Vietnam-era helicopter with a National Guard flight crew that flew the SEAL team into a "hot zone" where the Taliban had vowed to shoot down an American helicopter, to the incredibly irresponsible decision by the vice president and CIA director to publicly "out" the identity of the SEAL team that killed Bin Laden, both the military and the Obama Administration did virtually everything wrong in the ordering, planning, and execution of this mission.

If Operation Neptune Spear, the mission that killed Bin Laden, was perfectly and sublimely executed, then Operation Lefty Grove, the name of the operation underway when this chopper was shot down, was the epitome of negligent callousness, a textbook example of how to get men killed.

The contradictions and omissions in the Colt Report, and evidence from outside sources, including the autopsies of SEALs that revealed bullets in their bodies, and British press reports citing the Afghan government's claims that the Taliban knew the exact flight path of Extortion 17, all served to undermine the government's claim that they did nothing wrong.

Allowing seven unidentified Afghans to board that aircraft, without authority, and allowing that aircraft to take off and fly into a hot zone to face hostile fire was a major security breach by both the military and civilians at the Pentagon.

Keep these dates in mind:

Extortion 17 was shot down on August 6, 2011. The bodies of all thirty Americans plus the bodies of eight Afghans (seven unidentified Afghan commandos plus an interpreter) were flown back to Dover Air Force Base three days later, on August 9, 2011, where grieving and distraught families were met by President Obama.

That same day, August 9, 2011, the military publicly took the position that "Given the nature of the attack, there were 'no identifiable remains' of the 30 troops." Those senior military officers publicly reporting that there were "no identifiable remains" had no way of knowing that less than three months later, the Colt Report would be released to families and would contradict the strange "no identifiable remains" claim.

These and other public claims made by the military, including conclusions made by Brigadier General Colt himself, would later be contradicted by internal evidence shown in the report, which was somehow released, to the probable surprise of senior military officials.

Why would the military release clearly false information that there were "no identifiable remains"? Again, no one knows except the Pentagon. But given that some family members had been told by US military officers that the bodies had been cremated, the "no identifiable remains" line could have been placed out there to either (a) justify cremation of the bodies, or (b) justify cremation of some of the bodies, or (c) create the impression that bodies had been cremated, whether they had or had not been cremated.

Why would the military want to create such an impression?

If the bodies had been cremated, or if the public thought the bodies had been cremated, there would be no way to determine who the Afghans were who boarded Extortion 17. And if there was no way to determine who the Afghans were, then there was no way to say, one way or the other, whether they were Taliban sympathizers who played a role in bringing that chopper down.

A senior Navy JAG officer, Captain Al Rudy, long since retired, once said, "The mark of a good lawyer isn't his ability to give all the answers, but rather, to ask all the right questions."

The following chapters scrutinize the evidence from the Colt Report and other sources, including autopsies, witnesses, credible press reports, and the House National Security Subcommittee's February 2014 hearing on Extortion 17, exposing numerous contradictions and omissions that undermine the official story.

Perhaps most important, as Captain Rudy once suggested all those years ago, this book will ask a lot of questions, questions the Colt investigation and the National Security Subcommittee of the House Oversight Committee should have asked, but failed to ask, questions that the families have demanded, and even a number of questions that the families haven't demanded because they don't yet know enough about the evidence to ask them.

The preponderance of evidence points to the conclusion reported by the British press—that the Taliban was tipped off and knew where Extortion 17 was flying, and lay in wait, ready to ambush the chopper as it approached the landing zone.

The evidence will also show that if pre-suppression fire had been allowed by the American rules of engagement and had been employed, the thirty Americans on board Extortion 17 would still be alive today.

CHAPTER 8

The Colt Report 101:
Points to Keep in Mind in
Examining Evidence

With two exceptions, the Colt Report never used real names. This was for security purposes and for the protection of the military personnel involved. If, for example, a Lieutenant John Doe from Pamlico was named in the report, that would potentially put a target on the back of the fictitious officer, making the officer or his/her family vulnerable to Al Qaeda or the Taliban. We can't have that. (Excuse the irony here.) Therefore, the only proper names that appeared in the Colt Report were the names of Brigadier General Colt, the one-star general conducting the investigation, and General James Mattis, the four-star general who ordered the report.

Everyone else identified in the Colt Report was identified by military acronyms. Those acronyms denote what job or mission the person speaking carried out. For example, on the night of the shoot-down, two US Army helicopter gunships accompanied Extortion 17 into the landing zone. The pilots and flight officers from those Apaches were interviewed, under oath, about what they saw and what they knew in connection with the shoot-down of the Chinook. However, the testimony of those witnesses (pilots and flight officers) did not include their actual names or ranks.

The interpretation process isn't that complicated; it's sort of like reading the key of a map. Just as a map might have a star denoting the capital city of a state, there is an acronym for the pilots of the Apache helicopters who were interviewed (PB65BS). There's another acronym for the co-pilots (PB65FS) and still other acronyms for additional military personnel testifying.

At first blush, some of the acronyms might look a bit strange for those not versed in military matters, and some are translated into layman's terms to eliminate ambiguity as to who is speaking in the record.

In many ways the Colt Report was extremely detailed, providing candid testimony from US military officers and enlisted members about the downing of the chopper, and showing detailed photographs and diagrams.

In many other ways, however, the Colt Report was incredibly lacking, not even addressing areas critical to an accurate determination of what happened to Extortion 17, such as the blatant failure to pursue the identity of the Afghans who boarded that chopper without authority. The reason for this failure will be covered later in the book, and it has to do with General Mattis's charging order to Brigadier General Colt, which, frankly, tied Colt's hands in many ways.

But for now, the Colt Report can be best understood, broadly, as both a wealth of crucial, detailed information about the crash and, at the same time, a big, black gaping hole, as if someone took a shovel and deliberately dug out crucial data and information absolutely essential to a determination of the truth, tossing that data into a secret abyss.

These inexcusable gaping black holes in the report—including the failure to interview any Afghans familiar with the mission, the failure to even have a meaningful discussion about the identity of the seven unidentified Afghans who broke all protocol and entered the chopper moments before takeoff, and the failure to report on any forensics testing of small arms carried by those Afghans or by any of the SEALs—simply raise more questions and raise suspicion that the military was hiding something that if released, could prove highly embarrassing.

This leads to another question: How did the Colt Report get out of the hands of the military to begin with?

What really happened remains unclear. By stark contrast to the wealth of information provided in the Colt Report, as of early 2014, virtually no inside information had yet been released by the government on the Benghazi terror attack. In a conversation between an Extortion 17 parent and Mr. Charles Woods, the father of former Navy SEAL Tyrone Woods, who along with former SEAL Glen Doherty was murdered in Benghazi attempting to defend Ambassador Chris Stevens against a mob that greatly outnumbered them, Mr. Woods is reported to have said that the Benghazi families have, in contrast, received virtually no information from the government on what occurred.

But in the case of Extortion 17, the Colt Report, originally classified as Secret, was declassified and given to various family members of the fallen SEAL team upon their requests by certain Navy officials.

Once the report had been released, some high-level officer apparently asked to get it back from several family members, but did not receive the families' cooperation. As of early February of 2014, the report had been provided to the *Washington Times*, and to this author. However, before publication of this book, it still had not been widely disseminated nor analyzed.

CHAPTER 9

The Pink Elephant Escapes

The biggest pink elephant in the room was the identity of the seven unidentified Afghans who rushed aboard the chopper prior to its shoot-down.

FLIGHT MANIFEST TESTIMONY

A portion of the Colt Report transcript included testimony about the flight manifest, the official list of all personnel aboard the aircraft. Military regulations require the list to be accurate.

In an interview conducted on August 15, 2011, nine days after the fatal crash, officers testifying under oath offered the Colt Report's only glimpse into the key questions surrounding the seven unidentified Afghans in Exhibit 1, at page 118. Remember, as a roadmap has keys, so does the Colt Report.

IO-DEP was the deputy investigating officer, the principal officer assisting General Colt in the investigation of the shoot-down. General Colt was the investigating officer. The deputy investigating officer was the guy doing a lot of the "heavy lifting," so to speak, by asking a large number of questions on the record.

JSOTF J3 was the joint/combined operations officer for the Joint Services Theater of Operations. This title was often shortened to "J3," or the "operations officer."

JSOTF CDR was the commander for the Joint Services Theater of Operations. This officer was ranked above the JSOTF J3. Put another way, this officer was the J3 or the operations officer's boss. This officer is also not specifically named in the report.

Note how the operations officer (J3) brings up the topic of the unidentified Afghans, and note how quickly his boss, the JSOTF commander, cuts him off and changes the subject:

IO-DEP: *Was there a manifest for that aircraft back at the—*
   JSOTF J3 (Operations Officer): *Yes, sir. And I'm sure you know by now the manifest was accurate with the exception of the [Afghan] personnel that were on. So the [Afghan] personnel, they were the incorrect—all seven names were incorrect. And I cannot talk to the back story of why, but—*
   JSOTF CDR: *But the bottom line is: We knew the total number that were on the aircraft. We knew the total number that we were trying to account for on the ground.*

In the interest of full disclosure, the word "Afghan" had been redacted from the initial written report as shown above when originally released by the Navy to the families, perhaps to reduce the types of questions about be asked in this book and by others wanting answers. The word has been reinserted for our purposes here, to make the testimony easier to follow. But junior- and senior-level US Navy and Army officials as well as others have repeatedly admitted to Extortion 17 family members that seven unidentified Afghans boarded the aircraft.

Now in analyzing the portion of the testimony on the unidentified Afghans, note how the J3, the operations officer, basically said that the manifest was accurate except for the seven Afghans. The names were incorrect because seven other Afghans had been assigned for the mission, but were mysteriously switched out at the last second.

Note too, how the JSOTF commander abruptly cut off the operations officer midsentence when the operations officer started talking about possible reasons for the switch-out.

Again, the operations officer said, "So the [Afghan] personnel, they were the incorrect—all seven names were incorrect. And I cannot talk to the back story of why, but—"

The commander then cuts him off midstream, interjecting his own "but" midsentence, and goes on to give his "bottom line" analysis.

JSOTF CDR: *But the bottom line is: We knew the total number that were on the aircraft. We knew the total number that we were trying to account for on the ground.*

The commander clearly wanted no part of an extended conversation on the record about the Afghans, and immediately changed the subject.

But the cat was now out of the bag, and the needle was now in the haystack. It would take a while before that needle—the fleeting reference to the Afghan infiltrators—was found, but later, with the help of a senior sergeant major in the US Army who cared about the truth and who apparently didn't care much about political correctness, it would be found.

Consider just how important the issue of passenger manifest accuracy is to the military. The requirement for accuracy is clear, as set forth in the Defense Department Transportation Regulation of October 15, 2012.

Consider first the mandated requirement set forth in Paragraph J, entitled PREPARATION AND USE OF DD FORM 2131, PASSENGER MANIFEST. The Defense Department's instructions are clear, and set forth as follows:

J. PREPARATION AND USE OF DD FORM 2131, PASSENGER MANIFEST
   1. Use the DD Form 2131, Passenger Manifest, Figure V-21, to list the names of the deploying personnel. Units may use a typed list in place of the DD Form 2131 if the form is not available.

However, the typed list must include all the information required on the DD Form 2131. The troop commander signs the anti-hijacking statement (shown below) on the passenger manifest, regardless of the form used.

First off, we see from the above that the names of the deploying personnel must be listed.

Looking down to Section J (2)(a), the requirement is even more specific. The troop commander is required to "Prepare Form 2131 as follows:" At paragraph "g," the manifest must be completed as follows:

g. Block 7: PASSENGER INFORMATION

(1) Block 7a: NAME. Last, First, Middle name of passenger.

(2) Block 7b: RANK. Military/DOD civilian passenger grade (e.g., O-3, E-4, W-2, GS-11).

(3) Block 7c: SSN. Enter Social Security Number of passenger.

(4) Block 7d: STATUS. Enter status of each passenger (e.g., Active, Civilian, Guard/Reserve).

(5) Block 7e: ULN. Enter ULN.

(6) Block 7f: LINE NO. Enter Line Number. Defense Transportation Regulation – Part III 15 October 2012 Mobility III-V-11.

(7) Block 7g: SVC. Enter Service.

(8) Block 7h: CHECKED BAGGAGE. Enter number of pieces of checked baggage and total weight.

(9) Block 7i: CARRY-ON WEIGHT. Enter weight of carry-on baggage.

(10) Block 7j: PAX WEIGHT. Enter actual weight of passenger.

(11) Block 7k: EMERGENCY CONTACT INFORMATION. Enter Name (Last, First, Middle).

(12) Block 7l: EMERGENCY CONTACT INFORMATION. Enter telephone number (Include area code).

The Department of Defense very clearly requires not only the names of every member boarding a US military aircraft, but much more information, including twelve specific subcategories here alone.

In addition, there is also a requirement that the commander sign an "anti-hijacking statement," as set forth in section J (1), requiring the commander to certify as follows:

The troop commander signs the anti-hijacking statement (shown below) on the passenger manifest, regardless of the form used.

"I certify that no unauthorized weapons/ammunition/explosive devices, or other prohibited items are in the possession of those personnel for whom I am the designated manifesting representative or troop commander, and that their authorized weapons have been cleared."

Note that the anti-hijacking statement requires a certification that no unauthorized weapons or explosives have been brought on the aircraft. Note also the certification that *"their authorized weapons have been cleared."*

Clearly, the manifest process and the manifest procedure is in place, to ensure flight security, and to ensure that no unauthorized persons or weapons enter the aircraft. The ultimate goal is to keep the aircraft and the American military personnel onboard secure.

Why, then, did the task force commander change the subject when his subordinate was asked about the manifest, and when asked about the unidentified Afghans?

Why is there no concerted effort in the Colt investigation to figure out who they were? Why shut this down and ignore it?

Was the Army not concerned that the unidentified Afghans could have been Taliban infiltrators? Wasn't the Army concerned about whether the unidentified Afghans brought unauthorized weapons aboard? The manifest requirement from the Department of Defense mandates a certification that "authorized weapons have been cleared."

Yet the Colt Report blew this off as if it was a nonissue. Why?

BILLY VAUGHN AND THE DISCOVERY OF THE MANIFEST DISCREPANCY

Although the issue of the seven unidentified Afghans has never been substantively reported by the press, perhaps because they have not yet realized its importance, it was first discovered outside the confines of the military by Billy Vaughn, father of deceased Navy SEAL Aaron Vaughn.

Mr. Vaughn discovered the issue in a review of the 1,250-page Colt Report when he read the very same passage at Page 118 of Exhibit 1 that is cited here. In other words, Mr. Vaughn discovered the "needle in the haystack." But because so very little was said about the unidentified Afghans on the flight manifest in the transcript, he initially assumed that the presence of the Afghans on board must not have been significant.

Mr. Vaughn first raised this issue with military officials on January 11, 2013, fifteen months after the shoot-down, when he and his wife Karen were visited in their home by then-Admiral William "Billy" McRaven, and the admiral's senior enlisted advisor, a senior sergeant major in the Army.

Both at the time of the Bin Laden raid and the Extortion 17 shoot-down, Admiral McRaven was the commander of Joint Special Operations Command, a post he held until August 8, 2011. Only two days after the Extortion 17 incident, he was promoted to commander of US Special Operations Command, with that Command being headquartered at MacDill Air Force Base in Tampa, Florida.

In his position as commander of Joint Special Operations Command, McRaven ultimately oversaw and commanded the logistical operations of Operation Neptune Spear, and although he did not fly with that mission, he was often referred to as the "mastermind" of the mission that got Bin Laden.

Both Operation Neptune Spear, the SEALs' greatest triumph, and Extortion 17, the SEALs' greatest tragedy, occurred on McRaven's watch.

As a result of his leadership both as commander of Joint Special Operations Command, and then as commander of Special Operations Command, and due to the fact that he was also a Navy SEAL, Admiral McRaven often had communications with family members of the fallen Navy SEALs of Extortion 17.

On or about Friday, January 11, 2013, Admiral McRaven traveled to the Florida home of Billy and Karen Vaughn, parents of deceased SEAL Aaron Vaughn.

During the meeting, Billy Vaughn mentioned that he had read in the transcript of the investigation that seven unidentified Afghans had boarded Extortion 17, and Mr. Vaughn casually made the comment that, "This must not be a big deal."

But the admiral's aide, the sergeant major, spoke up and corrected Mr. Vaughn's assumption. "Mr. Vaughn, it's a very big deal. [Speaking of the unidentified Afghans infiltrating the aircraft.] Because it was passed over. It's a very big deal. That should never happen." The sergeant major then added, "In fact, after the crash, we had to notify the men we thought were on the chopper. We had to notify them and tell them their sons were okay."

The sergeant major, whose name is being withheld here for his own protection, was taking it upon himself to alert the Vaughns about a major issue that had been overlooked. His words were heard by both Billy and Karen Vaughn, and it is important to note, by Admiral McRaven, who was sitting in the Vaughns' living room beside the sergeant major. According to the Vaughns, McRaven sat silently and did not say a word.

The timing of this revelation was significant. The Vaughns were alerted to this breach as being "a very big deal" on January 11, 2013, some seventeen months after the shoot-down. Up until this point, the military had been successful in keeping people's attentions off the security break, in part because it was buried in a very brief exchange, at page 118, in which the subject was quickly changed.

That's how close the military came to burying this information altogether.

So why were they hiding the mysterious Afghans—if they were even mysterious? Why weren't they admitting their error and trying to find out who the Afghans were? And why did the Joint Task Force commander so abruptly cut off his subordinate (the J3 operations officer) when the subject of the unidentified Afghans on board Extortion 17 came up?

It isn't hard to figure out that they had something to hide, and that whatever they were hiding about those unidentified Afghans was probably very embarrassing to the military.

But it is just as interesting to consider the great lengths that General Mattis (four-star general in command of CENTCOM) went to in order to ensure that the Colt investigation stayed away from the topic of the seven missing Afghans.

Put another way, the cover-up about the seven Afghans begins much earlier, with the initial instructions given by General Mattis to Brigadier General Colt.

CHAPTER 10

CENTCOM Handcuffs
Colt's Investigation

Billy and Karen Vaughn were informed about the issue of the seven unidentified Afghans being of concern for the first time at the meeting with Admiral McRaven and his enlisted aide on January 11, 2013. This revelation came some sixteen months after Brigadier General Colt finished his investigation.

Some may believe it odd that Colt's report failed to attempt to identify the seven Afghans who boarded Extortion 17. Such concern is well placed. But looking further into Colt's marching orders, it seems evident that the restraints placed on him by General Mattis were designed to whitewash the investigation from the beginning.

The order from Mattis to Colt was an odd mix which, on the one hand, appeared to give General Colt all the authority he needed to conduct an investigation to get to the facts of what happened, but on the other, tied Colt's hands and ensured that the final findings would amount to a whitewash designed to suppress the truth about what happened to Extortion 17.

Why is this? Because Mattis's order included contradictory parameters and placed legal shackles on Colt's hands that prevented him (Colt) from even asking all the questions he needed to ask to get to the truth.

The order commissioning Colt to conduct the official military investigation of the crash of Extortion 17 was handed down by written directive from Mattis on August 7, 2011, the day following the crash.

Mattis's order entitled "Memorandum of Appointment" was attached to the Colt Report as "Exhibit A." Brigadier General Colt was given one month, up to and including September 7, 2011, to complete the investigation.

SWEEPING POWERS BUT CONTRADICTORY ORDERS

In the three-page directive, Mattis instructed Colt to "conduct your investigation in whatever matter you believe necessary and proper." At first blush, nothing was constrained, at least not in the report. General Mattis provided that "you [BGEN Colt] may request any additional individuals or subject matter experts be appointed to accompany you or assist you in your investigation."

So Colt, at least it appears at first glance, was given the broad, sweeping power to ask anybody anything about the details of this tragedy. General Mattis told him, specifically, "You may order any witness to provide a statement, if you believe that they have relevant information that would not incriminate themselves." And Mattis went on to write, "you may consider any evidence that you determine to be relevant and material to the incident."

Mattis further ordered Colt to provide (a) an executive summary with both classified and unclassified versions, (b) an index of all exhibits, (c) a chronology of the investigation, and (d) a list of persons interviewed and those from whom no statement was taken.

Mattis directed that "if it is impracticable to obtain a written and/or sworn statement from a particular witness, you will swear to the accuracy of any transcription or summary of such witness testimony in whatever form it appears within your report of investigation."

So at face value, Mattis's instructions seem like an order to look under every rock, behind every corner, to illuminate every shadow, and to leave no stones uncovered to get at the truth about Extortion 17.

Did Colt not consider the possibility that Extortion 17 had been infiltrated by seven Taliban sympathizers, something that might be relevant to the investigation? Perhaps not, because his 1,250-page report treated the Afghans' identity as a nonissue.

One thing is for sure. It is absolutely impossible to believe that Colt did not at least consider the possibility of Taliban sympathizers infiltrating that aircraft prior to takeoff, given the serious breach of protocol and the very serious history of "Green-on-Blue" violence in Afghanistan.

Perhaps, based on Mattis's instructions complete with Article 31 self-incrimination restrictions, Colt considered the topic of the seven mysterious Afghans to be a kettle of worms that he knew better than to stick his shackled hands into.

Mattis gave Colt an out if he felt that relevant evidence might incriminate someone. Rather than issuing an order to Colt to investigate the shoot-down and get to the truth of what happened no matter what, Mattis issued a half-baked order designed in part to protect the legal rights of US service members who might give incriminating statements during the course of the investigation.

For example, consider the following statement signed off by Mattis to Colt in the order to start investigations: "You may order any witness to provide a statement, if you believe that they have relevant information that would not incriminate themselves."

Putting that in layman's terms, General Mattis was really saying, "If you think any of our guys messed up in any way, don't ask them any questions and especially if they could get court-martialed for messing up."

Could this explain why the seven missing Afghans' identity is not inquired about? Was there a possibility that someone could be prosecuted for dereliction of duty in allowing those infiltrators on the helicopter?

Of course this looks to be the case. Somebody messed up, big-time, on the American side by letting those Afghans board that aircraft.

Colt had an out, because his superior, General Mattis, essentially ordered him not to include relevant information, at least not in the form of any statements that might lead to self-incrimination. If he had been given statements by anyone who knew, or should have known, that the seven Afghan infiltrators were not friendly to American forces, there was a possibility that those statements could have led to criminal prosecution under the Uniform Code of Military Justice, colloquially referred to as the "UCMJ."

It is hard to envision any scenario under which those seven unidentified Afghans slipped onto that American helicopter just before the shoot-down without someone being at fault, and potentially subject to prosecution for dereliction of duty under the UCMJ.

Suppose, for example, an American military member failed to double-check the manifest. Such an admission would be a criminal offense under the UCMJ. Suppose someone was in charge of making sure the right Afghans, the ones whose names were actually on the manifest, boarded the helicopter, but failed to do so. Again, such an admission could be a criminal offense under the UCMJ and subject the one committing the offense to court-martial for a crime known as dereliction of duty.

⁓

Dereliction of duty under US military law is not the functional equivalent of a misdemeanor speeding ticket. Quite the contrary. It is a very serious offense, especially in times of war. *In fact, during times of war, the UCMJ provides, at Article 92, that dereliction of duty is punishable by the death penalty.*

It cannot be disputed that somebody dropped the ball by allowing the Afghan infiltration into that chopper. Even if those unidentified Afghans were as sweet and as kind as the seven sisters of the poor, there is absolutely no doubt that certain persons within the US chain of command failed to ensure the security of that aircraft. There can be little doubt that under Article 92, someone could be prosecuted if the right questions were asked.

An officer of Colt's experience and professionalism should have been able to see the relevance of identifying those Afghans in seeking the full explanation of what went wrong.

But when we look at his marching orders from CENTCOM and General Mattis, it is clear that Colt was actually prohibited from ordering witness statements that might lead to a criminal offense. At paragraph 7, he is told by General Mattis, "no military or civilian witness can be ordered to provide information that may incriminate him or herself."

In that same paragraph, General Mattis goes even further in shackling Brigadier General Colt's investigative parameters. Mattis tells Colt,

"If in the course of your investigation, you suspect any specific person may have committed a crime, you will promptly consult with your legal advisor, and then inform me. You should not attempt to elicit any information from any suspect without first discussing the matter with your legal advisor and then provide the requisite advice and warnings required by Art. 31, UCMJ or other applicable US law or regulation."

In other words, Mattis is saying, "Hey BGEN Colt. If you suspect somebody screwed up, you don't say a word to anybody until you talk to me first."

Talk about a chilling effect on the investigation! General Mattis's caveat is just that. Just as significant to these instructions is what was left unsaid: "Tell me if someone violated the UCMJ."

Here is what was unsaid between the lines of these instructions. "Look. We all see the pink elephant in the room. The pink elephant is those seven unidentified Afghans. We all know that somebody screwed up here when those Afghans, who weren't in the flight manifest, entered that chopper. It was a big-time mistake and a big-time breach of procedure. Heads could roll for having allowed this. We have to conduct an investigation. We have no choice. But it could become highly embarrassing to the military and highly embarrassing to the administration if the public's attention is riveted on this issue."

By the way, "warnings required by Art. 31, UCMJ," are the military's equivalent of what are typically referred to as "Miranda warnings." Anyone over fifty years old who ever saw the TV show *Dragnet* is intimately familiar with Miranda warnings.

Likewise, those Miranda warnings are codified in the UCMJ, whereby a military member suspected of a crime under the UCMJ is told he has the right to remain silent, that anything he says can be used against him, that he has a right to speak with an attorney, and have an attorney present during questioning.

So Mattis in his order went overboard, again and again, to discourage Colt from investigating anything, or asking any questions that might lead to a criminal offense under the UCMJ.

In General Colt's defense, his hands were strapped from the beginning. There was no way Colt could get into the question of the identities

CENTCOM HANDCUFFS COLT'S INVESTIGATION

of the Afghans without asking questions such as, "Who had a duty to check the manifest?" or "Who had had a duty to make sure they matched the manifest?" or "Who had the duty to make sure the right crew was on board?" or "Who had a duty to vet the Afghans who boarded Extortion 17 to make sure they were not dangerous?"

Each and every one of these questions leads to the possibility of a dereliction-of-duty charge, which is potentially a criminal offense—which, based on General Mattis's order, meant that Colt could not go there, not of his own accord, no matter how relevant the issue, or how pink the elephant.

So what started as a written mandate for a factual investigation into the cause of the shoot-down morphed into a mandate filled with cautionary legal restraints, forcing Colt to proceed with one hand behind his back.

The unsaid implication is clear. "Don't ask those questions, period." This is classic "don't ask, don't tell" put into action, in this case to protect exposing a major breach that might never have gotten out if not for a sliver of commentary by the J3 officer at page 118 of Exhibit 1.

All this points to a bigger strategic and policy consideration: Which was more important? Protecting a potential military defendant's Article 31 Rights, or getting to the truth about why thirty Americans, including members of the military's most elite fighting force, were unnecessarily dead?

Mattis's instruction to Colt made it appear that Mattis was just as concerned about protecting personnel from making potentially incriminating statements as he was with finding the truth.

Mattis did not have to clamp Colt's hands with all the Article 31 warning language.

To understand why Mattis had another option, one must examine the basic fundamentals of how a prosecution works within the military.

US MILITARY LAW 101

To understand why General Mattis did not have to muddle the waters with these Article 31 warnings, it is first important to understand the purpose of the military justice system.

On one hand, the military justice system mirrors and is identical to, although generally much more efficient than, its civilian counterpart. For example, a military murder charge might have exactly the same elements as a civilian murder charge. The military rules of evidence substantially mirror the federal rules of evidence, and thus, military judges often make the same type of evidentiary rulings as civilian federal judges.

But on the other hand, the military justice system is substantially different from its civilian counterpart in this regard: *The military mission is more important to the military than the criminal justice system operating within the military.* That's because the principal purpose of the military is to win wars.

General Norman Schwarzkopf, who gained fame as ground commander in Operation Desert Storm, once said that "The job of the military is to go to war and win, not to be instruments of social experimentation." The former Navy SEAL and author, John Carl Roat, has been quoted as saying, "war is about killing people and breaking things." A variation of Roat's quote was later rendered by General Colin Powell, who said, during the First Persian Gulf War, that "an army is for killing people and breaking things."

The great Third Army commander, Lieutenant General George S. Patton Jr. said that, "An army is a team. It lives, eats, sleeps, fights as a team. This individuality stuff is a bunch of bullshit." One of the greatest of all Marines, Lieutenant General Chester Puller said, "Paper-work will ruin any military force."

The point in citing these great military men is to underscore the point that the dominant purpose of any American military force is first and foremost to win in battle, not to protect the legal and constitutional rights of its troops. Not that the legal and constitutional rights of military members aren't important—they are vitally important. But they take a position of secondary importance to battlefield victory and to winning wars.

The purpose of the military justice system is first and foremost to support the war-fighting purpose of the military, by maintaining good order and discipline. Sometimes, but not always, that involves prosecuting military members who have violated the UCMJ.

But there are priorities. Protecting a service member's rights under Article 31 of the UCMJ does not rise to the same level of importance as preserving the warfighting and the war-winning capability of the US military, nor should it.

To promote good order and discipline to assist American forces in winning at war, the *Manual for Courts-Martial* exemplifies three types of courts-martial that military commanders may use in this goal. And remember, because this too is unique, it is the military commander, and not some lawyer or some prosecutor in the JAG Corps that decides to bring charges. These three courts-martial are:

A summary court-martial is for the most minor of offenses, applies to enlisted members only, and caps its punishment at thirty days confinement. It's often used by commanders for typical squabbles, fights, and other minor disciplinary problems.

A special court-martial is used for most misdemeanor-level criminal charges, either unique military charges such as unauthorized absence, or traditional criminal charges that you would find in civilian courts, such as assault, battery, and petit larceny. Punishment at a special court-martial is capped at one year's confinement.

A general court-martial is the highest and most serious level of court-martial under the UCMJ.

Remember again, the purpose of the US military is to win wars, not to serve as a laboratory for social experimentation or a safe haven for the full implementation of one's constitutional rights. Certain constitutional rights that one enjoys outside the military are checked and left at the door once an individual enters active duty. For example, the First Amendment guarantees freedom of speech. But if you decide to openly criticize your commanding officer in the military, you could wind up prosecuted.

Here's the point to understand. While the military justice system in some ways is almost identical to its civilian counterpart—it uses an evidence code virtually identical to the federal rules of evidence, for example, and certain crimes such as murder, rape, and larceny for the most part have the exact same elements of the same crime in civilian courts—it is also in many ways very different from civilian courts and has crimes that are unique to the military.

In many cases the military justice system criminalizes conduct that would not be criminal outside that system. For instance, being late for work or being absent from work can be criminalized. Negligence, a civil tort in the civilian world, is criminalized in the military.

The crime of dereliction of duty is unique to the military. Dereliction of duty basically takes the civil tort of negligence and turns it into a criminal act. If you make an innocent mistake in civilian life, you might get sued for negligence, but you don't potentially go to the brig.

If you make a mistake in the military, even if you did not mean to or simply forgot—say if you fail to check a flight manifest to keep intruders off an aircraft—not only could you possibly go to jail, but in times of war, in theory, you could potentially be executed.

That's a big difference.

Other crimes unique to the military with no civilian counterparts include unauthorized absence, desertion, missing movement, and conduct unbecoming an officer. Understand that all these crimes that are uniquely military are designed to support the mission and effectiveness of the military, which first and foremost, is to win wars, and not to serve as a laboratory for social experimentation.

———

Against this backdrop, here's another aspect of the military justice system that makes it unique and different from the civilian system. In the civilian system, criminal charges are initiated by prosecutors. Usually, it is the district attorney at the state level or the US attorney at the federal level who initiates the process by which charges are filed—whether by seeking a grand jury indictment or presenting affidavits to a magistrate. The prosecutor has the discretion to charge or not to charge.

In the military, neither the JAG officer serving as the prosecutor nor any other prosecutor has the discretion to bring criminal charges against a military defendant. *Instead, it is the military commander and only the military commander who has authority to bring charges or not to bring charges.* The decision to charge anyone with a crime—say with the crime of dereliction of duty for failure to ensure that seven Afghans illegally boarded an American aircraft—is left up to the commander.

For a general court-martial, the military commander with the discretion to bring charges or not is a flag or a general officer, meaning a general or admiral, just like General Mattis. A general officer who brings charges is known as a "convening authority" in the military.

A convening authority, that is the military commander in the chain of command, asks this question and makes a decision: "Which is more important? Is it more important to the mission of the military to get to the facts, so that we can take corrective action and save lives in the future? Even if that means possibly forgoing criminal prosecutions because the method of gathering evidence might preclude it?

"Or is it more important for me to protect the rights of a defendant so that defendant is protected at a potential court-martial, even if protecting the civil rights of a defendant means I might not get to the bottom-line of what happened, even if not getting to the bottom-line might cost the lives of more of my men in the future, because I might not have the evidence that I need to take corrective action?"

General Mattis ultimately had to, at some level, make this value judgment in setting forth his marching orders to Brigadier General Colt to convene the investigation of Extortion 17. Though he probably would not admit it, Mattis had to decide whether to focus on protecting the rights of a potential criminal defendant in the event of a court-martial or getting to the bottom of why Americans died that day in Afghanistan.

That value judgment, at some level, went into the crafting of General Mattis's order to Colt, and all the "Article 31" warning instructions that shackled Colt's hands.

If Mattis were determined to get to the bottom line at all costs, he did not have to include "Article 31" instructions in his letter to Colt. But for whatever reason, he made a decision to do so.

The results of that unfortunate decision are obvious throughout the 1,250-page Colt Report.

The question "who were the Afghans on that chopper?" was never asked.

The question "who was responsible for checking the flight manifest and making sure unauthorized intruders didn't enter the aircraft?" was never asked.

The question "who was responsible for vetting the Afghans who entered that aircraft?" was never asked, not by Brigadier General Colt, or by a single expert working under his command.

An even more pressing question is this: Why wouldn't General Mattis want to know the names of those Afghans? Why wouldn't the Army want to know if they were Taliban sympathizers? Why wouldn't they want to know if, perhaps, those Afghans had any role in bringing down Extortion 17?

Could it be because the information, if revealed, might be embarrassing to the Army or to the mission? Could it be because revealing their identities might lead to questioning the wisdom of sharing sensitive military information with Afghan forces? Even if it means not prosecuting someone at a court-martial, surely getting to the absolute truth and absolute facts in a case like this would be far more important to national security and to protecting and safeguarding future missions. From a standpoint of good order and discipline, there are other ways of dealing with dereliction of duty short of military prosecution.

Moreover, getting to the actual facts of what happened and why might shed some additional insight on the wisdom, or lack thereof, of forcing US Special Operations forces to operate with Afghan forces, or any other foreign military forces for that matter, who have shown violent tendencies toward allied forces.

No one put a gun to Mattis's head and forced him to give a written directive to Colt instructing him to Mirandize anyone who may have committed an offense, or to avoid even asking questions that might lead to prosecution. This instruction placed a huge chilling effect on the investigation.

Had Mattis left all the instructions about Article 31 out of his order to Colt, and had he not ordered Colt to avoid asking questions that might incriminate someone, then Colt would have had the freedom, at least legally, to ask whatever questions he wanted to ask to find out why Extortion 17 was infiltrated by unauthorized and unidentified Afghans.

⸺◆⸺

Suppose some junior-level officer or enlisted man said, "I'm the one who screwed up. I forgot to double-check the manifest to make sure the right Afghanis were on board."

Or suppose a senior enlisted man said, "I'm sorry, I forgot these guys that got on the chopper, and it turns out that two were Taliban sympathizers."

If that junior-level officer made that admission, and Article 31 rights had not been read, here's what that means. It means that the military might not be able to prosecute those guys in a court-martial. It would probably mean that the statements given could not be used in a court-martial, because the military's version of the Miranda warnings had not been read.

But consider the upside. Sure, you may or may not be able to prosecute. But at least you might know exactly what went wrong, and if you know exactly what went wrong, maybe you can take painful efforts to prevent the same mistake from happening again in the future.

General Mattis wanted sworn testimony, and he got it. But he got no sworn testimony about the Afghans, other than the J3's slipup, or perhaps his intentional slip-in, that they weren't accounted for on the manifest. It appears that Mattis did not want, for whatever reason, the full truth, including the "good, the bad, and the ugly" of what really happened. At least he didn't want the full truth on the record. All the precautionary language on Article 31 ensured that this would not happen.

In General Mattis's final conclusion that followed the Colt report, he did not mention the seven unidentified Afghans, nor did he address the odd loss of the helicopter's "black box," nor did he address the odd question of why the military apparently cremated all bodies, thus destroying DNA evidence and making it forever impossible to positively identify the missing Afghans, nor did he touch on the issue of why several autopsies of US service members who died on Extortion 17 revealed that bullets had been found in their bodies.

Isn't it odd that Mattis's memorandum, approving Colt's report, like Colt's report itself, again, conveniently ignores the pink elephant in the room, namely the seven unidentified Afghans?

The general's conclusion simply whitewashes the findings in a neat, tidy, conclusive memorandum, not pointing the finger anywhere, and not raising the issue of the seven unidentified Afghans, and certainly not attempting to determine, one way or the other, whether they were friendly to the Taliban or friendly to America.

CHAPTER 11

The Seven Missing Afghans Discovered by Happenchance

JANUARY 2013

The apparent decision to try to de-emphasize and stay away from a discussion about the Afghans on the aircraft almost worked.

Almost.

It isn't clear whether the brief revelation by the J3 was intentional, to try and get the truth out, or accidental. All we know is that he was shut down by his boss, the Joint Special Operations Task Force commander, who kept him from saying another word about it.

This much we know. Mid-grade officers, who are not so influenced by political considerations, and senior enlisted men, who have seen it all, and often do not give a rat's derrière about political bull, are the heart and soul of the US military.

These are the men and women who make the US military engine run. They generally care about truth, duty, honor, and country. They aren't interested in B.S. rules of engagement or official cover-ups, and they especially aren't interested in protecting a cover-up if a cover-up is intended to minimize responsibility for loss of life. They know that they, or their buddies, could be next on the short-end of some politician's decision to use the military in a foolish way.

So given this, it would not be surprising if the J3 officer intentionally allowed just enough of a slip about these Afghans to get the truth out. That's speculation, based on the author's knowledge of the heart of the military. But if he did, God bless him.

But the truth always finds a way of percolating to the surface. They could not hide the pink elephant forever.

How did this J3 officer finally see the light of day? Remember that Extortion 17 was shot down August 6, 2011. It was not until January 11, 2013, seventeen months later, that a senior enlisted soldier in the Army, the sergeant major who accompanied Admiral McRaven into the Vaughns' home, alerted families that failure to account for the seven missing Afghans was "a very big deal."

Here's the way this came down the pike.

Billy Vaughn, the father of slain SEAL Aaron Vaughn, was one of the few family members who actually received and read the Colt Report.

Seventeen months had now passed since his son's death, but Mr. Vaughn recalled a small sliver of testimony that stuck out in his mind concerning Afghans on board his son's helicopter before it crashed. That testimony was the testimony of the J3 officer.

Again, here's that sliver of testimony, from Exhibit 1, page 118, that Mr. Vaughn remembered:

> **IO-DEP:** *Was there a manifest for that aircraft back at the—*
> **JSOTF J3 (Operations Officer):** *Yes, sir. And I'm sure you know by now the manifest was accurate with the exception of the [Afghan] personnel that were on. So the [Afghan] personnel, they were the incorrect—all seven names were incorrect. And I cannot talk to the back story of why, but—*
> **JSOTF CDR:** *But the bottom line is: We knew the total number that were on the aircraft. We knew the total number that we were trying to account for on the ground.*

Mr. Vaughn had kept that exchange of testimony in the back of his mind, but had not paid much attention to it, because the testimony was so short, and unlike the issue of the missing black box and other matters, the military had said nothing about it.

Because nothing had been said about it by the military, *because it was not included in the final Executive Summary of the Colt Report*, and because so very little had been said about the issue (of the seven Afghans infiltrating the chopper), Mr. Vaughn assumed that the issue must not have been important.

But as Admiral McRaven and his senior enlisted advisor sat across from him in his home in Florida on that January day in 2013, the sliver of testimony floating around in the back of Mr. Vaughn's mind popped to the forefront.

Eyeing the two highly decorated military men sitting across from him, Mr. Vaughn, as related in his book (co-authored by Monica Morrill and Cari Blake) entitled *Betrayed: The Shocking True Story of Extortion 17 as Told by a Navy SEAL's Father,* asked the question, almost as an after-thought, about those seven Afghans getting on that chopper right before they took off.

"I guess it wasn't a big deal, right? Because that was all that was said about it and it was then just passed over," Mr. Vaughn asked the men, referring to the J3 officer's testimony.

A moment passed. Admiral McRaven sat still and said absolutely nothing. But then, when it became obvious that McRaven was not going to answer, the sergeant major spoke up.

"It was a very big deal, Mr. Vaughn," the sergeant major said. "That should never have happened. In fact, all of the Afghan families who had previously been notified of their loved ones' death had to be re-notified that they were, in fact, alive. What actually happened was, at the last minute, the commander wanted to swap out those listed for the seven Afghanis who were actually on the chopper."

Again, even after the sergeant major spoke up, Admiral McRaven still did not address the subject.

Bear in mind that at the time of this conversation, the Colt investigation had been out for sixteen months, and the Executive Summary had been issued, wrapped in a tidy conclusion that the military had done nothing wrong, and conveniently omitting any reference to this "very big deal."

Bear in mind also the earlier observation that mid-level officers and senior enlisted generally aren't interested in B.S. rules of engagement or official cover-ups, and they especially aren't interested in protecting a cover-up if a cover-up is intended to minimize responsibility for loss of life. The whitewash was on, and the pink elephant, thanks now to the sergeant major who had the guts to speak up, had barged onto the scene.

After the men left, Mr. Vaughn became more bothered about all this, his stomach more twisted than ever.

Cover-ups lead to more questions, and the first question in Mr. Vaughn's mind was "what commander authorized the swap-out?" Was the sergeant major talking about an American commander? Or was he talking about an Afghan commander who may have authorized the swap-out?

With the question nagging him and sticking in his gut, Mr. Vaughn picked up the phone and called an Army lieutenant colonel at Special Operations Command who had been involved in the investigation.

Mr. Vaughn posed the question to the colonel.

"Can you tell me who that commander was [who authorized the swap-out of the Afghans]?"

The lieutenant colonel hesitated momentarily then spoke with a quiet, but clearly perplexed tone, "Mr. Vaughn, we [the crash investigative team] weren't told about that [the last-minute swap, which left the manifest incorrect]."

Mr. Vaughn also recounts this conversation in his book *Betrayed: The Shocking True Story of Extortion 17 as Told by a Navy SEAL's Father.*

In other words, as a follow-up to the J3's testimony, then the sergeant major's revelation, we now have a lieutenant colonel, a member of the team investigating the crash, saying that members of the investigating team were not even informed about this unauthorized infiltration by the Afghans.

Why was information concerning the infiltration by these unauthorized Afghans withheld from the investigating team? Who is trying to hide what?

The issue of the seven unidentified Afghans was whitewashed in at least four instances: It was ignored in the 1,250-page Colt Report, the Executive Summary of that report, and in General Mattis's memorandum approving the report, and information was even kept from members of Colt's investigating team.

The issue also was not addressed in a ninety-minute congressional subcommittee hearing held on February 27, 2014, discussed in more detail later, a fifth lost opportunity. All this raises more questions pointing to a cover-up. Why, for example, would General Mattis not give Brigadier General Colt the full authority, not restricted by self-incrimination issues of potential military defendants, to get to the bottom of what happened?

And going back to the testimony at Exhibit 1, page 118 of the Colt Report, why, during that testimony, did the commander cut off his subordinate, to prevent any discussion on the record about the seven unidentified Afghans? Is the commander trying to hide something by cutting off the topic and changing the subject?

What was the operations officer about to say that necessitated the cut-off by his commander?

Was he going to say, "But their presence was unauthorized"? Or "but . . . their presence was a breach of safety protocol"? Or "but . . . our men have concerns that seven unidentified Afghans may have compromised the safety of this mission"?

What were they trying to hide?

There is no way to know, because the brusque interruption by the Task Force commander kept the operations' comments off the record, and successfully changed the subject.

The Joint Special Operations Task Force commander who cut off his subordinate's thoughts on the unidentified Afghans was the same person who ordered the SEAL team into that chopper to begin with. This was revealed at page 99 of Exhibit 1, when Brigadier General Colt asked who ordered the ill-fated mission. Here's that exchange:

BG Colt: *At 2130 Zulu, the IRF was directed to infill by whom?*

JSOTF J3: *Sir, Task Force Commander was the guy that controlled the immediate reaction force. We actually have—discussing it before; there've been reports about the ground force commander, asking for the immediate reaction force to handle, to interdict those orders. Actually, it was from Task Force. They recommended to call over to the ground force commander and said, "Hey, we have got the immediate reaction force that we can employ against this thing, and that's where it came from."*

There is no way to know if the Task Force commander allowed the seven mysterious Afghans on board, because the Afghans have their own commander.

After the Joint Special Operations Task Force commander cut off his subordinate's testimony midstream, the subject of the investigation changed to testimony about how the bodies were extracted from the crash site. Nothing else was mentioned about the unidentified Afghans, of any substance, in the entire 1,250-page report—not even a peep. Nor is there any suggestion in the Colt Report's recommendation or in General Mattis's final conclusions that the military did anything wrong in the deaths of thirty Americans.

Why not?

Why no attempt to at least identify these guys? Why conduct days of investigation on flight approach, rescue operations, ground movement of enemy forces, and gloss over the identity of seven unidentified intruders on the aircraft?

It's as if the unidentified Afghan infiltrators were the big pink elephant in the room that no one wants to talk about.

Why is this question significant?

The answer has to do with the concept of "Green-on-Blue" violence.

CHAPTER 12

"Green-on-Blue" Violence:
"Friendly" Afghans Killing Americans

The phrase "Green on Blue" refers to the dangerously widespread practice of Afghan forces masquerading as American allies, yet then shooting Coalition elements in the back and subversively cooperating with the Taliban. The Colt Report's failure to even address the potential security concerns the Afghan "Mystery Seven" might have presented was nothing less than shocking.

Why won't the military deal with the question of their identity? Why ignore this inexcusable breach of security in the Colt Report as if it's a nonissue?

The failure to address the identity of the "Mystery Seven," and the apparent cremation of their bodies so as to destroy DNA evidence, was one of the linchpin failures in this investigation that points to a cover-up. This failure is so important that it's crucial to pause and consider the problem of Green-on-Blue attacks.

THE BACKGROUND ON GREEN-ON-BLUE VIOLENCE
Ever since the United States inserted forces into Afghanistan in 2001, there has been an effort to work with the government of President Hamid Karzai, beginning in 2001 when the United States toppled the Taliban-controlled Afghan government at the beginning of Operation Enduring Freedom.

Karzai was not Taliban, and had been installed as interim president of Afghanistan at a conference in Bonn, Germany, in December of 2001, with said conference operating under the approval of the United Nations. Karzai was chosen first as head of the Afghan Interim Authority, and later was elected president of the country. Karzai, when he became president, appointed anti-Taliban leaders into high positions in his government.

The United States, and other NATO forces, for political and other reasons, now sought to have an ally on the ground in the "host" country in which it was prosecuting the "War on Terror."

That host government on the ground was now the government of Hamid Karzai. This alliance would lead to a military alliance, at least on paper, in the "War on Terror," in which Afghan Army and other military forces would be pitted alongside US forces to go after and kill Taliban.

That type of arrangement might have looked good on paper. But there was a practical problem with it. In many cases, pro-Karzai Afghans in the Afghan Army who were ordered to fight alongside the Americans, for religious and political reasons, felt a stronger alliance with their stated enemies, namely Afghan Taliban, than with their politically mandated military allies, namely the Americans. Put another way, many Afghan Army members in Karzai's army felt a much stronger allegiance to fellow Muslim Afghan Taliban members than to the members of the US military who had orders to kill Muslim Afghan Taliban members. For religious reasons, and for nationalistic reasons, the Afghan Army–Taliban tie was often much stronger than the Afghan Army–NATO tie.

The results of this strong and often natural alliance between regular Afghan military and police forces and their Afghan Taliban brethren often proved deadly and disastrous for American forces in Afghanistan. Numerous reports surfaced of Afghan Army and police forces shooting and murdering Coalition forces, which were composed primarily of American forces. Thus, the phrase "Green-on-Blue" attack was born.

It should be noted that the phrase "Green-on-Blue" has nothing to do with the color of uniforms or anything else other than the standardized military symbols used to designate different forces on maps. In the military's system, the color blue is used for friendly forces, red for hostile forces, green for neutral forces, and yellow for unknown forces. Thus, Blue-on-Blue shootings are incidents in which members of the same force fire on one another. Green-on-Blue, technically, would refer to neutral forces firing on friendly forces. The phrase in this context means Afghan forces firing on ISAF Coalition (primarily NATO) forces.

2011: A Bloody Year for Green-on-Blue Violence

In 2011 alone, leading up to the shoot-down of Extortion 17 on August 6, 2011, there had already been at least twelve reports of such Green-on-Blue attacks, or murders, or attempted murders of Coalition forces by Afghan forces who were supposed to be US allies. This is according to statistics compiled by the *Long War Journal*, in an article by Bill Roggio and Lisa Lundquist, first published August 23, 2012, and updated October 26, 2013, which documented the following Green-on-Blue attacks in 2011, leading up to the Extortion 17 flight.

Attack 1: January 15, 2011:
An Afghan soldier argued with a Marine in the Sangin district in Helmand, threatened him, and later returned and aimed his weapon at the Marine. When the Afghan soldier failed to put his rifle down, the Marine shot him.

Attack 2: January 18, 2011:
An Afghan soldier shot two Italian soldiers at a combat outpost in the Bala Murghab district of Badghis province, killing one and wounding the other before escaping.

Attack 3: February 18, 2011:
An Afghan soldier opened fire on German soldiers at a base in Baghlan province, killing three German soldiers and wounding six others. The attacker was killed in return fire.

Attack 4: March 19, 2011:
An Afghan hired by Tundra Security Group to provide security at Forward Operating Base Frontenac in the Argandab Valley in Kandahar Province shot six US soldiers as they were cleaning their weapons, killing two and wounding four more. The attacker was shot and killed in return fire by three other US soldiers.

Attack 5: April 4, 2011:

An Afghan Border Police officer guarding a meeting between a Border Police commander and US military trainers in Maimana, the capital of Faryab Province, shot and killed two US soldiers, then fled. ISAF reported on April 7 that the attacker was killed when he displayed hostile intent after being tracked down in Maimana; two other insurgents were arrested during the raid.

Attack 6: April 4, 2011:

An Afghan soldier opened fire on ISAF vehicles in Kandahar Province; no casualties were reported.

Attack 7: April 16, 2011:

A newly recruited Afghan soldier who was a Taliban suicide bomber detonated at Forward Operating Base Gamberi in Laghman Province near the border with Nangarhar Province, killing five NATO troops and four Afghan soldiers. Eight other Afghans were wounded, including four interpreters.

Attack 8: April 27, 2011:

A veteran Afghan air force pilot opened fire inside a NATO military base in Kabul, killing eight NATO troops and a contractor. According to the Washington Post, *the shooter, a two-decade veteran of the Afghan air force named Ahmad Gul, jumped out a window after the attack, injuring his leg.*

Attack 9: May 13, 2011:

Two NATO soldiers who were mentoring an Afghan National Civil Order brigade were shot and killed inside a police compound in Helmand Province by a man wearing an Afghan police uniform. The gunman was wounded by return fire and taken to a hospital.

Attack 10: May 30, 2011:

An Afghan soldier killed an ISAF soldier in southern Afghanistan. According to an Australian Department of Defense press release, an Australian soldier from the Mentoring Task Force was shot while manning a guard tower at patrol base MASHAL in the Chorah Valley in Uruzgan province by another guard, a soldier from the Afghan army, who fled.

Attack 11: July 16, 2011:
An Afghan soldier killed an ISAF soldier in southern Afghanistan. According to The Telegraph, *a NATO soldier was shot by an Afghan soldier not far from Lashkar Gah in Helmand Province during a joint patrol. The attacker ran away after the shooting.*
Attack 12: Aug. 4, 2011:
An Afghan soldier killed an ISAF soldier in eastern Afghanistan. According to the Turkish Weekly, *someone wearing an Afghan police uniform killed an ISAF soldier in Paktika Province.*

So based on these reports, as set forth in the *Long War Journal,* a total of twenty-six NATO/Allied were murdered in Green-on-Blue attacks in 2011 alone, leading up to the flight of Extortion 17. This was a problem that the military was well aware of. Yet, the fact that seven unidentified Afghans infiltrated the flight was mentioned only peripherally in the report, substantially brushed over, and no time or resources were spent on trying to identify who these men were.

Two *New York Times* Articles on Taliban Infiltration
New York Times reporter Ray Rivera published two articles examining the problem of Taliban infiltration into supposedly friendly Afghan forces. The first article, entitled "Taliban Fan Fears of Infiltration in Afghan Forces" and published on April 20, 2011, began by recounting a November 29, 2010, incident on the Pakistan border in which an Afghan border policeman, who was "well thought of by his superiors suddenly opened fire on American soldiers, killing six." The article went on to cite another incident in April of 2011 in which insurgents, dressed in Afghan uniforms, attacked "three heavily secured government locations." Even though the Rivera article reported intelligence officials as saying there was "no evidence the infiltration is widespread," it concludes that "concern over sleeper agents still run high among NATO and Afghan officials."

On June 27, 2011, and *only forty days before the Extortion 17 shootdown,* Rivera wrote a second article on the subject of Taliban infiltration into the Afghan military. This article, entitled "Afghans Build Security, and Hope to Avoid Infiltrators," featured the story of a Taliban insurgent named Akmal, who very easily infiltrated the Afghan army, and later took part in two suicide bombings. At the time of the article, Akmal was facing the death penalty.

Rivera reported that, "In the past two and a half years, 47 NATO soldiers have been killed by Afghan soldiers or police officers. Many of those deaths were the result of arguments that turned violent. But infiltrators are suspected in some of the cases, including one in which an Afghan soldier detonated a vest at an Afghan military base and another when a police officer killed the police chief at the Kandahar police headquarters."

Green-on-Blue violence was nothing new to the US military, and they were clearly aware of the issue of Taliban infiltration of the Afghan military. Indeed the mainstream press was picking up on it, as evidenced by both of Mr. Rivera's articles.

One Extortion 17 parent relayed the words of his late son, a member of SEAL Team Six. "It's hard to get the Afghans to fight. Sometimes they won't move. Sometimes they want to stay in the chopper." The father related his son's concerns that the SEALs were "far more worried about getting shot in the back by the Afghans we have to take on these missions than by the Taliban we're fighting against."

Indeed, the overwhelming evidence of Taliban infiltration into the regular Afghan military—the same military that NATO forces were forced to work with as "allies"—was so disconcerting that General John Allen, former commander of US forces in Afghanistan and former commander of the combined International Security Assistance Force (ISAF), estimated that 25 percent of all Green-on-Blue attacks were carried out by Taliban infiltrators. General Allen's conclusions were reported by Mike Mount of CNN on August 23, 2012. Allen, who was the top NATO commander at the time, indicated that the 25 percent infiltration was significantly higher than an earlier 10 percent infiltration estimate put out by the Pentagon.

In an interview from the Pentagon, Allen was quoted as saying, "So if it's just pure Taliban infiltration, that is one number. If you add to that impersonation the potential that someone is pulling the trigger because the Taliban have coerced the family members, that's a different number," he said.

CHAPTER 13

An Ambassador's Blunt Warnings

In a September 17, 2012 speech to the Carnegie Endowment for International Peace, recently retired US ambassador to Afghanistan Ryan Crocker estimated infiltration to be higher than 25 percent, the estimate given by US military commanders.

In an article on the well-respected military.com website, dated September 18, 2012, and entitled *Crocker: Taliban Infiltration Worse than Estimated,* reporter Richard Sisk quoted part of former US Ambassador Ryan Crocker's remarks to the Carnegie Endowment for International Peace on the previous day, September 17, 2012.

> *We've talked about security and security forces simply to say the threats as we have seen are very much there, whether it be that coordinated attack on Camp Bastion that destroyed a number of aircraft—only 15 or so gunmen, but they clearly knew what they were doing—the high profile attacks, which haven't worked that well, by and large, as headline grabbers, after the attack on the embassy last year and again in April, and the very troubling green-on-blue attacks.*
>
> *You know, I'm not there. But I would put the percentage of attackers who have some affiliation with the Taliban rather higher than the percentages I have seen [referring to the 25 percent estimate from military sources]. I think they're finding that a relatively easy [thing] to do—and our own vetting in the US military is not that great, let's face it. We've got a lot of prison barracks at military facilities for people who never should have gotten in the first place and didn't get out of boot camp housed in Afghanistan. I think the Taliban have found*

a niche. Obviously not the whole story; I don't discount the personal grudge, the cultural insensitivity and the rest of it. But I think we underestimate at our peril a resilient enemy finding a new—a new mechanism with effect.

Ambassador Crocker was no rookie to the US Foreign Service. He had served as US ambassador to Afghanistan from July 25, 2011 through July 13, 2012. Prior to that, he had served as ambassador to Lebanon, Kuwait, Syria, Pakistan, and Iraq.

Note several salient points from Ambassador Crocker's speech.

First, Crocker thought the problem of Taliban infiltration might be even worse than General Allen thought it was. And of course General Allen thought it was worse than the official Pentagon estimates, in part because Allen was taking into account "Taliban influence" even if the Green-on-Blue attackers might not always technically have been Taliban members.

Second, the ambassador refers to the Green-on-Blue attacks as being "very troubling." If these attacks were "very troubling" to the former US ambassador to Afghanistan, then why didn't the official military investigation, in the 1,250-page report, make any effort to account for the names or the identities of the seven unidentified Afghans, if for no other reason than to rule out possible Taliban infiltration of that mission? Was there no concern that they could have been hostile to the American forces, given the clear history of Green-on-Blue violence?

Third, when Ambassador Crocker estimated that Taliban infiltration might be higher than the military has first estimated, he went on to say, "—and our own vetting in the US military is not that great, let's face it." So Crocker was openly questioning the military's ability to effectively vet Afghan forces to root out Taliban membership and Taliban influence.

That dangerous problem was manifestly evident on August 6, 2011, as twenty-six NATO forces had already been murdered in Green–on-Blue attacks in 2011 alone. Why not even make an attempt to identify the seven unidentified Afghans? Or at the very least, why not address the possibility that the seven unidentified Afghans could have been Taliban infiltrators or sympathizers? Or why not at least try and eliminate the possibility that Extortion 17 had been infiltrated from the beginning by seven Taliban infiltrators or sympathizers?

The military's silence on the question is telling.

The failure to even address this question marks either inexcusable negligence or a sleight-of-hand cover-up.

CHAPTER 14

A Forced Suicide Mission

It is important to understand a bit about the "platform" for Extortion 17's mission. In military-speak, a "platform" usually is the type of ship, plane, or vehicle that is being used to advance a military mission.

For example, there could be multiple platforms for launching a Tomahawk cruise missile: a B-52 bomber, a US naval cruiser, or a submarine, just to name a few.

Likewise a helicopter is a type of platform used to advance a military mission. As platforms, helicopters are often designed primarily for particular types of missions.

The CH-47D Chinook helicopters, code-named Extortion 16 and Extortion 17, were old helicopters, whose primary mission was and remains troop and cargo transport. The Chinooks were designed to carry troops to the edge of a battle zone. That's exactly what Extortions 16 and 17 had done earlier in the evening on August 5, 2011.

But the Chinooks were vulnerable if ordered into a hot zone with substantial antiaircraft fire, especially if they had to fly into those zones unprotected.

Unfortunately, both the Colt Report and General Mattis's conclusions failed to address this issue, and in fact, General Mattis's conclusion was misleading in several respects on the issue of mission planning and execution.

The selection of this particular aircrew, to fly this particular mission, in this particular area, despite the "we did nothing wrong" claim set forth by the military, amounted to nothing less than sending American forces on a suicide mission. The National Guard aviators were not adequately trained nor experienced enough to fly this mission, which should have required Special Forces aviators from the 160th Special Operations Airborne Regiment out of Fort Campbell, Kentucky, the unit the SEALs usually fly with.

In other words, even if we assume that there was no Taliban infiltration aboard the aircraft, the mission planning was still very foolish. They sent pilots trained for one thing, in an aircraft designed for one thing, on a mission demanding pilots trained in another area, and on a mission requiring another type of aircraft—that is if the military commanders wanted their men to have the best chance of surviving.

But the military tried whitewashing this foolish mission planning, as shown by the Colt Report's Executive Summary (September 7, 2011) and General Mattis's approval of that summary (September 13, 2011), which included many misleading statements claiming that the selection of the flight crew and the aircraft were appropriate.

On September 13, 2011, General Mattis signed the Memorandum for the Record approving the factual conclusions of the report, finding no fault with the Army pilots and concluding that Extortion 17 had not been "shot down " as "the result of a baited ambush." This Memorandum for the Record, was attached to and made part of the 1,250-page Colt Report as Exhibit B.

One example of a misleading finding appeared at Paragraph 3 of that Memorandum:

> 3. I specifically agree with the conclusions that the Army aviators were fully qualified to perform all required tasks, that the aircraft was fully mission capable, and that loading the Immediate Reaction Force (SEAL Team and SOC operators) onto one aircraft was tactically sound. The aircrew, having flown into the valley only hours before to insert the initial force, was the most familiar aircrew available to effectively carry out this mission. I believe that the shoot down was not the result of a baited ambush by the enemy; instead the enemy was in a heightened state of alert due to 3 1/2 hours of ongoing coalition force operations in the area prior to the CH-47's arrival.

On the surface, this claim might be just accurate enough to deflect questions at a superficial level. But under the surface, paragraph 3 was manifestly misleading.

Pilot Bryan Nichols and co-pilot Dave Carter certainly were trained to fly the Chinook, and Carter was in fact a very experienced Army pilot. There is no evidence that either aviator did anything wrong during the course of this mission.

But here's what was misleading. Nichols and Carter were National Guard pilots. They were not Special Forces aviators, had not been trained as Special Forces aviators, and were not flying in a Special Forces aircraft. Moreover, although it's technically true that they had already flown a mission earlier in the evening, it is not true that the mission they flew took them into the same, dangerous, Taliban-infested airspace that their final, fateful flight did.

In the earlier mission, the aviators had dropped the US Army Rangers two to three clicks (kilometers) outside the edge of the battle zone. On the final mission, they were ordered to fly a different course, this time over the Tangi River Valley into an airspace in which there had been three attacks on US helicopters, even Special Forces helicopters, within the previous ninety days.

Why didn't the general's report make this distinction between the dangerous airspace over the Tangi River Valley where the Seal team was shot down, and the original landing zone from the earlier mission, which did not have any known Taliban forces?

Instead, it implied that the earlier mission that inserted the Rangers outside the hot zone was just as dangerous as the subsequent mission that flew the SEALs over the hot zone, which simply was not true.

To better understand how these conclusions were misleading, it is important to understand some basic concepts about US Special Forces.

Each branch of the military has a Special Forces component. For example, the US Army has the Rangers and the Green Berets. The Marines boast their Combat RECON and Scout Sniper units. The Air Force has its para-rescue teams, Combat Rescue and Combat Control. The Navy has its EOD (Explosive Ordnance) Teams. The vaunted Navy SEALs have become the most famous Special Forces unit of all.

On board Extortion 17 that fateful night, every American who was not a part of the five-member National Guard flight crew was a Special Forces operator. The SEAL team was the best known, but even the three Air Force men who died were also Special Forces.

In each branch of the service, Special Forces members are chosen from a highly competitive field. They are trained to carry out missions with speed, stealth, and deadly precision that give them a role that is often distinct from the regular members of the US military. Quite often Special Forces units carry out the most dangerous missions in the military, and the most potentially deadly missions.

The National Guard pilots who flew that helicopter were not Special Forces aviators. That does not mean that they were any less important or less patriotic. Nor does it mean that they were not brave or willing to carry out their mission or give their lives for their country. They were all these things. This simply means that their military roles were typically very different from the Special Forces aviation units.

It should be noted that Special Forces, such as the SEALs, typically train with and fly on helicopters that are part of Special Forces Aviation. The best-known command for Special Forces Aviation is the 160th Special Operations Aviation Regiment (SOAR). The 160th SOAR is often referred to as the "Night Stalkers." Based out of Fort Campbell, Kentucky, the Night Stalkers are part of the US Special Operations Command, meaning they transport Special Forces from all branches, including the Navy SEALs. Their pilots are specially trained, for example, to fly in quickly, low, to avoid enemy radar, to attack at high rates of speed, to insert ground troops quickly, and to get out quickly. The stated role of the Night Stalkers is to "provide aviation support to special operations forces." Night Stalkers typically do not operate aircraft as antiquated as the CH-47 Chinook, but rather, operate the more advanced MH-47G Chinook, the MH-60 Black Hawk, and the MH/AH-6M Little Bird.

US Special Forces will typically be inserted into hot battle zones by helicopter. But Special Forces, including the SEAL units, typically operate with helicopters that are faster, and are "souped up" with more armament, heavier weaponry, electronic-warfare gadgetry, and jamming mechanisms.

As an example, in Operation Neptune Spear, the raid that killed Osama Bin Laden on May 1, 2011, the SEAL team was paired with the Army's Night Stalker pilots, who flew the SEAL team into Pakistan on a modified version of two MH-60 Black Hawks.

The Night Stalkers are trained to fly into hot zones, at low altitudes, at fast rates of speed to avoid detection, with sophisticated weaponry and electronic jamming mechanisms on their aircraft. Put another way, the Night Stalkers are specifically trained for the type of highly dangerous mission that the SEALs were attempting to execute, and they fly souped-up, sophisticated aircraft capable of carrying out those missions.

The National Guard aircrew simply was not trained in the same way, nor were they flying Special Operations helicopters designed for these types of missions.

CHAPTER 15

Extortion 17 Pilots: Underequipped and Untrained for Special Ops

Army Chief Warrant Officer 4th Class David Carter was forty-seven years old at the time of the Extortion 17 mission. Described as a pillar of his community of Centennial, Colorado, and as a man of great faith, he was a full-time National Guardsman. The father of two daughters, had he lived, David and his wife Laura would have celebrated their twenty-fifth wedding anniversary in December 2011.

A rock of stability who was trusted by all who knew him, David was the type of man that most people, under ordinary circumstances, would want in the cockpit. Indeed, he had logged over seven hundred hours flying, and enthusiastically served as a flight instructor for younger pilots.

So on the surface, General Mattis's conclusions about the experience of the Chinook's aviators beared a superficial semblance of truth, at least with regard to Carter.

However, these were not ordinary circumstances, and as experienced as he was as a general forces military pilot, Carter was not trained as a Special Operations aviator. Also, Carter was not the lead pilot in command of the aircraft.

That job fell onto the shoulders of Carter's younger counterpart of seventeen years, thirty-year-old Bryan Nichols.

Nichols was a brave American who, as a combat soldier, had been deployed to three different combat zones before he became a pilot in 2008, twice to Iraq and once to Kosovo.

He had enlisted in the Army in 1996, so at the time of his death, on August 6, 2011, he had fifteen years of service under his belt. Nichols was a credit to his country and a credit to the Army, and later to the National Guard. He was also a fabulous father, and was the ultimate hero, and rightly so, to his ten-year-old son, Braydon.

But when one looks at how Bryan Nichols's fifteen-year history in the military was allocated, we discover that twelve of those fifteen years had been primarily as a foot soldier, and only three of those years (from 2008 to 2011) had been served as a pilot.

And when one considers the fact that like David Carter, Bryan was not a Special Forces pilot, and on top of that, *he was the lead pilot in command of the aircraft*, General Mattis's conclusion about the aviators' so-called "experience" becomes even harder to swallow.

David Carter was an experienced pilot, but was not experienced as a Special Forces pilot. Bryan Nichols, the lead pilot, was an experienced infantryman, but was not overly experienced as a pilot, and in fact, had never before flown into any type of wartime environment before this deployment.

Once again, there is no apparent evidence that either Carter or Nichols did anything wrong on this mission. They simply followed orders that led to their deaths.

But why were they ordered to fly this mission? Why weren't Special Forces aviators ordered to fly the mission in Special Forces helicopters?

Putting an experienced National Guard pilot on a mission that should have required a Special Operations pilot was manifestly unfair, not only to the National Guard pilot, but also to every man, including the Navy SEAL team, that the National Guard pilot was flying with.

Would it have made a difference?

Perhaps.

Most likely, a Special Ops flight crew would have flown at a different flight trajectory and would have approached the target more quickly, flying with weapons and equipment that gave them a superior ability to fight back.

Pat Hamburger is reported to have told family members that he would be flying with Special Forces, but that National Guard helicopters would drop Special Forces off several clicks (kilometers) from the battle lines, as happened with the Ranger unit earlier in the evening.

In other words, it did not appear, at least from Hamburger's comments, that National Guard aviators were going to be required to fly directly into ultra-dangerous aviation hot zones, like the airspace over the Tangi Valley that normally would be assigned to Special Forces aviators. Indeed, despite the insinuation in the Colt Report that the National Guard helicopters flew the same type of mission with the Rangers as they did with the SEALs, this is not accurate. The National Guard helicopters earlier in the evening did not fly the Rangers directly into the teeth of Taliban RPGs as later happened with the SEALs. The Rangers, earlier on, were flown over far less dangerous airspace, and not straight down the gut of the Tangi Valley, where Taliban insurgents were known to be waiting to shoot down an American helicopter. Put another way, there was a reason that the highly trained Night Stalkers were chosen for the Bin Laden raid over a National Guard crew with a Vietnam-era helicopter.

Again, this in no way degrades the bravery or the professionalism of the National Guard crew or its pilots. They were forced into a mission for which they, through no fault of their own, were neither fully trained for nor equipped to prosecute.

NATIONAL GUARD PILOTS A BAD CHOICE FOR MISSION

The inadequate training and inadequate capabilities of National Guard pilots to fly Special Forces missions was set forth clearly in sworn testimony in the Colt Report.

At Exhibit 49, General Colt and his assistants interviewed the commander of the 10th Combat Aviation Brigade (CAB) in Afghanistan concerning the readiness of the National Guard pilots (as opposed to Special Forces Aviation) to fly night missions in combat. Extortion 17 and other National Guard air units were assigned to the 10th CAB.

Part of the problem was that the National Guard pilots were ill equipped to fly combat missions at night.

The parties involved in the testimony at page 60 of Exhibit 49 include: (1) the SME-NGB, which stands for Special Missions Expert—National Guard Bureau. This officer was assigned to General Colt's staff for his expertise in National Guard matters; (2) 10th CAB, which stands for Commander of the 10th Combat Aviation Brigade This officer was a full-bird colonel in the US Army Aviation Corps, typically a helicopter pilot; and (3) the BDE, who is the brigade serial commander for the CH-47s. That means that this officer was the regular Army officer (not National Guard) who was in charge of all the CH-47s who were in the air for this particular mission, which included Extortions 16 and 17.

SME-NGB (Special Missions Expert–National Guard Bureau): *Sir, just one last question: The reserve component guys, are they coming in fully RL1 qualified, day/night NVG? Are there any training issues when they get here, or—and, I guess, equipment shortages. Are [that are] equipment shortages that are significant?*

10th CAB (Commander 10th Combat Aviation Brigade): *Let me ask ESP to go ahead and talk about the training readiness.*

BDE (CH-47 Serial Commander): *This is kind of a prickly subject for us. But for the most part, they bring crews in who are day/night NVG RL1 on paper. However, if you look at the numbers they have as far as experience level, goggles, the killer for us—I don't want to use that term lightly. But the worse part here is the fact they have very limited NVG experience.*

Notice the CH-47 Serial Commander here expresses very frank concern about the National Guard pilots' ability to fly night missions.

On one hand, the National Guard pilots were technically qualified on paper, which gave General Mattis cover for his questionable conclusion that, "the Army aviators flying this mission were fully qualified to perform all required tasks."

On the other hand, despite technically qualifying on paper, the National Guard pilots were not up to speed with sufficient night flying experience to make regular Army aviators confident in their abilities to fly dangerous nighttime combat missions. The serial commander's testimony is disconcerting. "But the worse part here is the fact they have very limited NVG experience."

Again, questions arise. Why send pilots with "very limited NVG" experience into the cockpit, in a dangerous hot zone, on night missions, when crucial consequences of life-or-death are at hand?

The foolishness of choosing this particular flight crew for this very dangerous mission was further evidenced in this same document, Exhibit 49 of the Colt Report, in an exchange between the deputy investigating officer and the brigade commander. Note that the deputy investigating officer, denoted as "IO-DEP" below, formed his question by acknowledging that the experience level of the pilot of Extortion 17 was not only "low," but was in fact "very low" [author's emphasis].

> **IO-DEP:** *The skill set or experience level of the pilot and co-pilot. Do you know that handy?*
>
> **10th CAB:** *Yes, sir.*
>
> **IO-DEP:** *I just want your opinion, if you think that's* consistent—basically, the PC is very low experience; *however, it looks like there's potentially some risk mitigation by a very, very experienced co-pilot on this particular mission. I want to determine if this is getting at the core of what you are discussing—*
>
> **10th CAB:** *Yes.*
>
> **IO-DEP:** *—about on paper versus—or in qualifications or currency versus proficiency.*
>
> **10th CAB:** *This particular aircraft, the pilot in command was three years out of flight school, 672 hours of total time, 99 hours of combat time, 588 CH-47 Delta time. 156 hours of goggle time, and only 46 hours of TC time.* He was, essentially, a brand new PZ appointment within the last 30 days or so.

In considering the very frank testimony concerning Bryan Nichols's low experience level as a pilot, with the deputy investigating officer describing him as Pilot in Command (PC) with "very low experience," and saying that there is "potentially some risk mitigation" by having an experienced co-pilot, and with the Combat Air Brigade commander testifying that Bryan was, "essentially, a brand new PZ appointment within the last 30 days or so," the foolishness for selecting this particular crew for this particular mission is magnified.

Now this constant refrain about the inexperience of the lead pilot, sprinkled throughout the testimony from various witnesses, was curiously and inexplicably minimized by General Colt in his final Executive Summary to General Mattis, of September 9, 2011.

Recall that in his charging order of August 7, 2011, Mattis charged Colt with providing for him an "Executive Summary of the evidence" concerning the shoot-down of Extortion 17.

Colt did comply with that order, and signed his Executive Summary back to General Mattis, on September 9, 2011. This five-page report was attached to the Colt Report as Enclosure C.

There was also another document, signed by Colt on September 9, 2011, entitled *Investigation Findings and Recommendations*. That document was attached to the Colt Report as Enclosure B, and is discussed later in the book.

In Enclosure C, the Executive Summary, Colt appears to inexplicably whitewash the concerns expressed by various witnesses about the inexperience of the lead pilot.

Clearly, Colt was trying to suggest that David Carter, the co-pilot, might have been piloting the aircraft at the time of the shoot-down. While admitting that the evidence is "not conclusive," which is an understatement, the suggestion is perplexing.

Not only was the evidence "not conclusive" that David Carter "may have been piloting the aircraft," the evidence was nonexistent. In fact, there is not one shred of evidence in the Colt Report even remotely suggesting that the more experienced co-pilot was at the controls of the aircraft. Not a single witness even suggested that anyone other than the pilot in command, Bryan Nichols, was piloting that aircraft. In fact, multiple witnesses, as shown above, expressed concerns about Nichols's experience level.

Remember the question posed by General Colt's own deputy investigating officer, who described the PC with "very low experience," and noting that having an experienced co-pilot might help. And remember the Combat Air Brigade commander's testimony that Bryan was, essentially, "a brand new PZ appointment within the last 30 days or so."

Why would Colt suggest such a thing in his Executive Summary (that the more experienced co-pilot "may have been" piloting the aircraft) when there is absolutely no evidence of that?

Colt's unfounded comments here appear designed to whitewash and or mitigate the serious mistake in judgment of assigning such a young pilot command of a very dangerous and deadly mission with thirty American lives at stake.

Recall that in the ninety days prior to August 6, the three American helicopters had already been attacked in the Valley. All escaped, but barely. American helicopters at low altitudes had become red-hot targets in the region. The Taliban had become obsessed with shooting down American helicopters since the killing of Bin Laden because the Taliban knew Special Forces were likely to be aboard those choppers.

The military threw an inadequately trained young pilot in an old, defenseless helicopter into a hopeless situation.

INEXPERIENCED PILOTS THROWN INTO A HOT ZONE

Keep in mind that Extortion 17's first flight that night, to drop off the US Army Rangers, did not follow a route consistent with its second flight, over the more dangerous Tangi Valley.

This marks another misleading statement by General Mattis in his conclusion, when he states, again, at paragraph 3, "the air crew, having flown into the valley only hours before to insert the initial force, was the most familiar aircrew available to effectively carry out this mission."

One would think, by General Mattis's statement, that the National Guard crew flew the very same route on the second mission as they did the first. But this was simply not the case. Why make that type of misleading statement?

How green were these Air National Guard Units?

Recall that there were two Chinook choppers involved in the mission that night, both Air National Guard choppers. Their code names were Extortion 16 and Extortion 17.

The Choppers carried men from two Air Guard regiments back home. These units were the 7th Battalion (General Support), 158th Aviation Regiment Air National Guard Unit, headquartered out of Fort Hood, with a number of its members from the Kansas City area, and the 2nd Battalion, 135th Aviation Regiment, out of Colorado. Bryan Nichols, Spencer Duncan, and Alex Bennett came from the 7th/158th, while David Carter came from the Colorado-based 2nd/135th.

After the shoot-down, General Colt, as part of his investigation, interviewed members of both units. Their testimony does not match with Mattis's assertion in the Colt Report that "the Army aviators flying this mission were fully qualified to perform all required tasks, that the aircraft was mission capable."

On August 18, 2011, as part of his official investigation, Colt and his team took testimony from the crew of the other National Guard CH47-D Chinook helicopter flying alongside Extortion 17 that night, Extortion 16. This testimony appeared in its entirety in Exhibit 46 of the Colt Report, and reflects the startling lack of experience of the National Guard crews. The testimony below begins at page 2 of Exhibit 46.

BG Colt: *Okay. Can you tell us how many Team missions you have done up to this point approximately.*

FLT AMC (Flight Air Missions Commander): *Yes, sir. That was my first one that night.*

PC (Pilot in Command): *A handful, sir. I would have to go back to get—*

BG Colt: *How long have you been on a mission doing this particular—*

PC (Pilot in Command): *About four to six weeks.*

BG Colt: *Four to six weeks?*

PC: *Yes, sir.*

BG Colt: *Okay. Doing about two missions ever [sic] three days or so?*

PC: *For a while, it was every third day.*

RAMP (Remote Access Missions Planner): *Roughly, the same amount, sir.*

FLT AMC: *I think I've been doing it for about two weeks. And I've done about four to eight missions, something like that.*

Right Door: *It was my second mission.*

These units were not very experienced. One air missions commander was on his very first mission. A pilot had been flying every third day for four to six weeks. Another air missions commander responded that he'd "been doing it for about two weeks." For the right door gunner, August 6, 2011 was only his "second mission."

At page 49 of the interview, the National Guard subject matter expert, who is questioning the witnesses, asks the surviving pilot point-blank if he expected to be flying direct support of Special Forces missions prior to his arrival in Afghanistan. The pilot's response is eye-opening.

SME-NGB: *Were you—did you have in mind that you would be direct support to special operations type support?*

PC: *Not until we got here, sir.*

Thus, the National Guard pilots were not even expecting to fly in support of Special Operations until they had arrived in Afghanistan. Clearly, and despite General Mattis's conclusions, these pilots were not qualified to fly this type of mission. These pilots were thrown into the lion's den, and not only were they not adequately trained for it, but they weren't expecting it.

CHAPTER 16

The Deadly Record of
CH-47D in Afghanistan

One of the many things the report did not cover was the very deadly record of the CH-47D Chinook in Afghanistan. Recall that Extortion 17 was a CH-47D Chinook. Nearly half the shoot-downs suffered by American choppers in the Afghan war prior to the Extortion 17 incident involved the CH-47D.

One such shoot-down, oddly not disclosed in the Executive Summary of the Colt Report, occurred just *twelve days before the Extortion 17 shoot-down.*

NATIONAL GUARD CHINOOK
CRASH LANDING

TWELVE DAYS BEFORE EXTORTION 17

It was unfair to put these general aviation National Guard aircrews into the midst of a Special Forces operation. In fact, just twelve days before the Extortion 17 shoot-down on July 25, 2011, a Chinook from the 7th Battalion (General Support), 158th Aviation Regiment, the National Guard regiment that supplied three out of five aircrew members of Extortion 17, was involved in a hard landing so severe that one of its crew members nearly died.

This incident was reported in the *Kansas City Star* on March 22, 2012, in an article by Lee Hill Kavanaugh entitled "After a Grim Year in Afghanistan, Chinook Unit Is Home at Last." After recapping the

Extortion 17 shoot-down, the article reveals a near-death incident with a Chinook in the month prior to the shoot-down:

The month before, a Chinook had a hard landing, injuring Ezekiel Crozier and Kirk Kuykendall. The men were told at one point Crozier probably wouldn't live. But both men were waiting in this crowd, too, to welcome home their buddies.

A guardsman named Staff Sergeant Ezekiel "Zeke" Crozier of Gardner, Kansas, a native of Spring Hill, Kansas, nearly died in the incident, which Congressman Yoder referred to in the congressional record as a "violent crash."

Sergeant Crozier received a severe traumatic brain injury and miraculously dodged death, spending the next two and a half years rehabilitating in the United States. Incredibly, this brave young American, in a story that is shamefully repeated over and over again in America, was wrongly denied medical coverage by heartless bureaucrats from the Veterans Administration, despite receiving the Purple Heart for being injured in combat.

The National Guard Chinook that Staff Sergeant Crozier was in did not just suffer from a "hard landing" as was later spun. Staff sergeants in the US Army do not receive the Purple Heart for injuries suffered in a "hard landing." The Purple Heart is awarded for injuries in battle, in times of combat. In fact Staff Sergeant Crozier's Purple Heart was awarded because his National Guard Chinook was actually *shot down* by Taliban RPGs.

Although no deaths occurred from this July attack, this shoot-down was reported in at least two sources at the time, yet was conveniently omitted from the Colt Report.

The military press covered the July 25th shoot-down of the other Chinook from the same squadron, so it is not as if the military commanders were unaware of the earlier incident when they sent Extortion 17 into harm's way. Consider, for example, the article in Defense-Update.com, written by Tamir Eshel on July 26, 2011, entitled "Chinook Downed by

Taliban RPG Fire in Eastern Afghanistan." The exact wording of the opening of that article was as follows:

> *A CH-47 Chinook helicopter [was] downed by Taliban RPG fire in Eastern Afghanistan on Monday. The helicopter was hit by an RPG fired by Taliban, as it was descending, approaching to land at 'Camp Joyce' Forward Operating Base (FOB) in Eastern Afghanistan. According to the* Stars and Stripes, *The [sic] helicopter was carrying about 20 US and Afghan troops, two suffered minor injuries from shrapnel. The helicopter was hit shortly after midnight, when the rocket hit the rear of the helicopter on its descent into Nangalam Base in the Pech River Valley of Kunar province.*

The report of the July 25th shoot-down also appeared in other publications, including the respected *Long War Journal*, which published an article by reporter Bill Roggio on July 26, 2011, the day after the shoot-down.

> *The US military confirmed that the Taliban shot down a helicopter in the contested province of Kunar in eastern Afghanistan.*
>
> *The International Security Assistance Force Chinook helicopter was shot down by the Taliban yesterday and "crashed about 100 yards outside" of a military base in Kunar, a spokesman for Regional Command East told* The New York Times. *The attack took place just outside of the Nangalam Base in the Pech River Valley, according to* Stars & Stripes. *Nangalam is an Afghan Army base that used to be known as Camp Blessing.*
>
> *ISAF reported the crash of the Chinook yesterday, but did not indicate it crashed due to enemy fire. No US military deaths were reported; two soldiers were lightly wounded in the attack.*
>
> *The Taliban ambushed a rescue force that moved to the crash site, ISAF reported yesterday. "As coalition rescue forces approached the crash site, they came under enemy fire," ISAF stated in a press release on the incident. "Coalition forces returned fire, with small arms, while working to secure the site of the crash. All passengers*

and crew members have been secured and safely transported to a nearby base."

In a statement released on their website, Voice of Jihad, the Taliban claimed credit for the shoot down, and said two of their fighters were killed during the operation. The Taliban fighters "shot off rocket propelled grenades from a close distance to bring down the enemy helicopter last night at approximately 1:00 am local time," the statement on Voice of Jihad said.

On the day of the shoot-down, the principal newspaper for the US Armed Forces, *Stars and Stripes*, reported the incident as follows:

FORWARD OPERATING BASE JOYCE, Afghanistan—Minor casualties were reported after a rocket-propelled grenade downed a Chinook helicopter carrying US and Afghanistan soldiers as it attempted to land at a coalition forces base in eastern Afghanistan early Monday.

The crash happened shortly after midnight when the rocket hit the rear of the helicopter on its descent into Nangalam Base in the Pech River Valley of Kunar province.

At least two soldiers suffered non–life-threatening shrapnel wounds. Some 20 people were on board, including soldiers and crew.

A rescue team that responded to the crash came under small-arms fire, drawing return fire from US and Afghan soldiers. No further coalition casualties were reported.

Then, on August 4, 2011, less than forty-eight hours before the Extortion 17 mission, the *Stars and Stripes* published yet another article about the July 25th shoot-down, which was eerily prophetic and bone-chilling considering what was about to happen to Extortion 17. In fact, the approach, the time of day, and the danger from the ground in the July 25th attack were all similar to what Extortion 17 was about to face.

To understand the similarities in their missions and degrees of danger, it is first important to understand the mission of the National Guard Chinook on July 25, 2011.

It should be noted that many of the injuries to US forces referenced in these articles were minor, although Crozier's were not minor at all.

The point, however, is not so much about the severity of the injuries in these missions leading up to Extortion 17, but rather to show that (a) the military was on notice that the antiquated CH-47D was a dangerous platform in which to fly these special forces missions, and it should have used modified Special Forces aviation helicopters like the MH-47, and (b) the Colt Report did not reveal these pre-Extortion 17 mission shoot-downs, making it tougher for the reader to realize that the military knew, or should have known, of the unnecessary fatal danger it placed upon Extortion 17 by ordering the SEALs to board the old Chinook, unless someone bothered to do the research on similar missions with the CH-47D.

In the Vietnam era, American forces would spill blood to take a hill, then abandon a hill, and then spill blood to take the hill all over again. US forces were employing a similar tactic in July of 2011 in Kunar Province on the Pakistani border, approximately 80 miles northeast of Kabul.

The Kunar Province, in the northeastern corner of the country, had been a US stronghold against the Taliban since the beginning of the war. But by February 15, 2011, six months before the Extortion 17 shoot-down, US forces had begun the process of withdrawing from the once-strategic Pech Valley in Kunar Province that was central to the American campaign against the Taliban.

The *New York Times* reported on the pullback in an article published on February 24, 2011, by C. J. Chivers, Alissa J. Rubin, and Wesley Morgan, entitled "US Pulling Back in Afghan Valley It Called Vital to War." The *Times* article revealed the military's intent to fully withdraw from the region within a period of two months to turn the area over to the Afghan military and police forces to fight the Taliban on their own.

US forces did substantially withdraw from the province, leaving the region under Afghan control. The problem arose, however, when Afghan military and security forces proved so inept and hapless in fighting against the Taliban that the United States was forced, at least temporarily, to re-enforce the area.

The mission flown by the National Guard Chinook on July 25, 2011, was part of the effort to temporarily re-insert American forces into the area after the Afghans had made such a mess of it.

The article published in *Stars and Stripes* two days prior to the Extortion 17 shoot-down vividly describes that Chinook's approach into the Taliban-infested Kunar Province.

FORWARD OPERATING BASE JOYCE, Afghanistan—Minor casualties were reported after a rocket-propelled grenade downed a Chinook helicopter carrying US and Afghanistan soldiers as it attempted to land at a coalition forces base in eastern Afghanistan early Monday.

The crash happened shortly after midnight when the rocket hit the rear of the helicopter on its descent into Nangalam Base in the Pech River Valley of Kunar province.

At least two soldiers suffered non-life-threatening shrapnel wounds. Some 20 people were on board, including soldiers and crew.

A rescue team that responded to the crash came under small-arms fire, drawing return fire from US and Afghan soldiers. No further coalition casualties were reported.

There was no immediate word on who was responsible for the attack.

The Pech River Valley and several adjoining valleys, including the Korengal and Shuryak, are considered Taliban strongholds, and attacks on coalition forces remain a regular occurrence as the Afghanistan war approaches the 10-year mark.

A battalion of the Afghanistan National Army is stationed at Nangalam Base, formerly known as Forward Operating Base Blessing. The US military handed over control of the base to Afghan forces earlier this year.

All three of these articles, and others like them, are significant, because they prove that another Chinook from the same National Guard unit was shot down just twelve days prior to Extortion 17, flying a mission that was not nearly as dangerous as the deadly mission the Extortion 17 Chinook was ordered to undertake.

Moreover, the July 25th shoot-down, it turned out, was flown in circumstances similar to the Extortion 17 shoot-down—into a Taliban-infested region, on a high, slow, loping approach to landing in the dark, after midnight, by a National Guard flight crew not trained for special air operations.

Despite knowing about this shoot-down, which fortunately did not result in any loss of life, but which occurred only twelve days prior to August 6, 2011, someone ordered the SEAL team on board the Chinook for a highly dangerous mission to the Tangi Valley.

As will be shown below in more detail, the Colt Report revealed three separate Taliban attacks on helicopters in the Tangi Valley area in the ninety days prior to August 6, 2011. The Colt Report claimed that the last known helicopter attack was purported to be against a Special Forces MH-47, seventeen days before August 6, 2011. Nothing was mentioned in the Colt Report about the shoot-down of the National Guard Chinook on July 25, 2011, in eastern Afghanistan, the shoot-down that nearly killed Staff Sergeant Zeke Crozier.

Why was the report of the July 25th shoot-down involving the same type of chopper piloted by a National Guard crew from the same unit left out of the Colt Report? Could it be because revealing the information in the Colt Report might have made the decision to send the SEALs on an even more dangerous mission aboard Extortion 17 indefensible?

In an ironic twist of fate, it may be that the near-death experience suffered by Staff Sergeant Crozier may have eventually saved his life. After the July 25th shoot-down, Sergeant Crozier was sent back home to begin his long and arduous journey toward rehabilitation. Were it not for his near-death experience that day, he might very well have been aboard Extortion 17 in the fateful dark hours of the morning of August 6, 2011.

Again, the question here has nothing to do with the bravery or professionalism of our Chinook crews. Given the designed limitations of those crews and those aircraft, why were they forced to fly what in effect were suicide missions?

CH-47D CHINOOK: DOCUMENTED DEATH TRAP

A review of the section of the Colt Report that discussed the use of the CH-47D Chinook shows that General Mattis whitewashed the real danger and ignored real data showing that these choppers had been the principal deathtraps among all Coalition aircraft in Afghanistan.

As of February of 2014, more CH-47D Chinooks had been shot down in Afghanistan than any other Coalition aircraft, not to mention that the total shoot-down numbers for the CH-47D Chinooks accounted for almost half of all aircraft shot down! Colt and Mattis did not reveal any of these shoot-down statistics in the Colt Report.

On September 9, 2011, as a follow-up to the 1,250-page Colt Report, Brigadier General Colt prepared a memorandum for General Mattis, with the subject line, "SUBJECT: Investigation Findings and Recommendations (Crash of CH-47D Aircraft in Wardak Province, Afghanistan on 06 August 2011). That memorandum, attached to the Colt Report as Enclosure B, was used, at least in part, as a basis for General Mattis's final findings of no-fault by the military.

Even though Mattis hid certain bits of evidence, such as the infiltration of the Afghans on board the chopper, certain factors were obvious and needed to be addressed.

One of these factors was the "threat assessment," and thus, the wisdom of sending a highly trained SEAL team on board a defenseless Air National Guard chopper into a hot zone where there had been multiple recent attempts to shoot down Coalition helicopters, with a hundred Taliban operatives in the area vowing to shoot down Coalition choppers, and with rules of engagement that prohibited pre-assault fire.

At page 6 of Colt's memorandum, the general authors a section entitled "Threat Assessment."

As that "Threat Assessment" is reprinted here, with the dates of most recent attacks bolded, bear in mind that an Army Air National Guard aircrew, with a lead pilot who had never flown in combat before and who had been a pilot only three years, was being asked to fly a highly trained US Navy SEAL team into a high-risk zone. Again, this language is directly from the Colt Report [author's emphasis]:

The Tangi Valley was assessed as a moderate to high threat to coalition forces based on reported enemy activities, historical surface-to-air fire reports by coalition forces aircraft, and the lack of coalition forces presence in the valley. On 5 August 2011, 10th Combat Aviation Brigade (10th CAB) intelligence analysts assessed the threat in the valley as high risk *due to: historical enemy activities including RPG and small arms fire, an assessed early warning network, the lack of coalition force presence in the valley, the significance of the target (Qari Tahir) and the corresponding actions the Tangi Valley Taliban would likely take to prevent his capture.*

Taliban insurgents operating in the Tangi Valley maintain an early warning network in order to detect coalition forces' ground and air movements within the valley. Forty-five days prior to the EXTORTION 17 shoot-down, coalition forces aircraft reported three surface-to-air incidents within the Tangi Valley. On 06 June 2011, two CH-47D Chinook helicopters aborted a mission *to insert a strike force into Tangi Valley after they were engaged with multiple RPGs (rocket propelled grenades) from several locations in the valley, the helicopters returned to Forward Base (name redacted) without further incident.* Later that evening, an MH-47F Army Special Operations Aviation (ARSOA) Chinook helicopter was engaged with RPGs *from multiple locations while inserting the same strike force for the same mission; no damage to the aircraft was reported.* Seventeen days prior to the shoot-down of EXTORTION 17, another MH-47G was engaged by small arms fire *and two RPGs and reported small caliber bullet damage to the aircraft. These surface-to-air fire events indicated insurgent capability and intent to engage coalition forces operating in the Tangi Valley.*

Note that these three incidents were shoot-down *attempts*. Nothing was mentioned about the shoot-down of the Chinook on July 25th, 2011.

Each omission from the Colt Report raises yet another question. Why was the nighttime shoot-down of the Chinook CH-47D on July

25th not mentioned in the risk assessment? Because it technically wasn't over the Tangi Valley but was 100 miles away? If that's the case, the reasoning for omitting this shoot-down is poor. The July 25th shoot-down was further evidence of how vulnerable these big, slow, poorly defended CH-47Ds were to RPG attack from the ground.

The Colt Report also failed to acknowledge that the Chinook CH-47D had been by far the most vulnerable aircraft in the American fleet during the Afghan war, a popular shoot-down target for the Taliban.

While the Colt Report did note that three helicopters had been shot at by Taliban forces in the forty-five days prior to the Extortion 17 mission, and it also reported that the Task Force commander assessed the risk in using the CH-47 and this flight crew as being a "high risk," the report still does not go far enough in revealing the real danger, of using the CH-47 Chinook on missions such as the one demanded of the SEALs and the flight crew of Extortion 17.

Statistically, in Afghanistan, the CH-47 Chinook was by far the most dangerous chopper to fly in, and there's not even a close second. This was especially true when it was misused as it was in the Extortion 17 mission, when someone came up with the idea of using the CH-47 with a National Guard crew as a platform for delivering US Navy SEALs on a dangerous and covert mission.

As of February 2014, Coalition forces—primarily from the United States—had seen a total of twenty-seven helicopters shot down during the Afghan war.

Of those nearly half, a total of thirteen, were CH-47D Chinooks. Bear in mind that Coalition forces had used at least twenty-three different types of helicopters in the war effort.

In fact, three and a half times as many CH-47 Chinooks have been shot down than the next largest total, the UH-60 Black Hawk, of which five have been shot down. Other shoot-down losses in the ten-year span include 3 OH-58 Kiowas, 2 HH-60 Pave Hawks, 1 AH-1W Supercobra, 1 CH-53 Sea Stallion, 1 Mil Mi-24, and 1 Westland Sea King. None of these statistics appear in the Colt Report.

And here is yet another statistic that was also notably absent concerning the MH-47 Special Forces chopper, the type of Special Operations

Aviation chopper that the SEALs use for training purposes. As of February 2014, not one single MH-47 had been shot down in Afghanistan.

A retired US Army Ranger who was at the Extortion 17 crash site in Afghanistan but who for his own personal safety asked that his name not be used, made this comment about Special Forces being forced to fly in the CH-47: "We were scared to death every time we had to go out in those choppers. Everyone knows they're not safe. They can't avert attack like the MH-47Gs. We knew our lives were in danger every time we stepped into one . . . The MH-47 flies low and fast, like a roller coaster ride, due to its quick, agile abilities in air. The conventional CH-47Ds fly really high and slow with no evasive maneuvers. They're a huge target up there, like a train coming in for landing. They do 6–8 push-ups before landing, while the MH-47 burns straight in."

The words of this Ranger are poignant in describing the CH-47's flight path into the landing zone. "CH-47Ds fly really high and slow with no evasive maneuvers. They're a huge target up there, like a train coming in for landing."

Given this, is it any wonder that the CH-47 accounted for virtually half of all the Taliban shoot-downs since the beginning of the Afghan war?

Why weren't the SEALs allowed to carry out this mission in the chopper they were trained in? And why were no MH-47s pre-deployed at Forward Operating Base Shank? Had the order been given to use an MH-47, instead of a CH-47, based upon the statistics alone, there's a good chance that those SEALs and the Extortion 17 flight crew would have lived.

Here is the unfortunate historical timeline of CH-47 shoot-downs in Afghanistan, most of which was left out of the Colt Report, and unfortunately, which did not deter the very foolish decision to order the SEAL team aboard the CH-47D Chinook in the early morning hours of August 6, 2011:

September 11, 2012 (same day of Al Qaeda attack on US embassy in Libya): A NATO official said that three members of the Afghan National Security Forces have been killed after a CH-47 Chinook helicopter was hit by munitions fired into Bagram Airfield. An investigation was under way to establish the details of what happened.

August 6, 2011: A NATO CH-47 Chinook (Extortion 17) helicopter being flown by the 7th Battalion, 158th Aviation Regiment and 2nd Battalion, 135th Aviation Regiment was shot down by the Taliban using an RPG with thirty American and eight Afghan casualties (seven unidentified commandos and one interpreter), as well as a dog.

Documented Shoot-Downs Prior to Extortion 17

July 25, 2011: A CH-47F Chinook was shot down by an RPG near Camp Nangalam in Kunar Province. Two Coalition service members were injured.

October 12, 2010: A US Army CH-47 Chinook helicopter had just landed and had been off-loading when an RPG was fired into the cargo bay. An Afghan interpreter was killed and seven ISAF service members and an Afghan Border Police officer were injured.

August 5, 2010: A Canadian CH-47D Chinook was shot down in Kandahar Province, Afghanistan. It made a hard landing and burned out on the ground, wounding eight soldiers.

August 20, 2009: A British CH-47 Chinook (S/N ZA709) was shot down in the Sangin area of Helmand Province. The crew survived.

January 17, 2009: A US CH-47 made a hard landing in Kunar Province after being hit by small arms fire and an RPG. CH-47 was struck in the left main fuel tank by an RPG causing left side to become engulfed in flames and #1 engine failed due to fuel starvation. Upon landing, A/C rolled onto its right side and was destroyed in post-crash fire.

May 30, 2007: A US CH-47 Chinook was shot down, in the upper Sangin Valley, killing five American, one British, and one Canadian soldier.

December 4, 2005: A CH-47 Chinook helicopter 91-00269 was struck by small arms fire. There were two injuries and the aircraft was consumed in the post-landing fire.

September 25, 2005: Five US soldiers were killed when a CH-47 Chinook helicopter crashed in Zabul Province while returning from an operation. Though initially reported as an accident, the crash was later confirmed to have been caused by hostile fire.

June 28, 2005: A US CH-47 Chinook helicopter was shot down in Kunar Province by Taliban commander Qari Ismail, killing all sixteen US Special Operations servicemen on board. The US military says it was shot down by a rocket-propelled grenade.

March 4, 2002: Two CH-47 Chinook helicopters were hit by RPGs and gunfire during Operation Anaconda. Two were killed in the first helicopter, which was dropping off a SEAL team. The second Chinook came in later that day to try to rescue the crew of the first CH-47, and subsequently was shot down, killing four.

Of the thirteen CH-47 shoot-downs documented above, all by the Taliban, eleven occurred prior to Extortion 17. While the three incidents in the Tangi Valley were cited in the Colt Report, not a single one of these eleven pre-August 6th shoot-downs were cited, including the July 25th shoot-down of the National Guard Chinook in Kunar Province that nearly killed Staff Sergeant Crozier.

The Colt Report did not come even close to painting the full picture of the CH-47's dangerous record in combat situations. But it's no wonder that the Task Force commander deemed the use of the CH-47D and this aircrew to be a "high risk."

Note also some of the very pointed language from the one-star general (Brigadier General Colt) to his four-star boss (General Mattis), in which Colt uses phrases such as "the threat in the valley as high risk," and warns of three shoot-down attempts of American helicopters in the last ninety days, and "intent to engage coalition forces operating in the Tangi Valley" (Colt Report, Enclosure B—Investigation Findings and Recommendations—Threat Assessment Section).

But Brigadier General Colt was not finished with his assessment. At page 7 of the same document, Colt begins another assessment under a subcategory entitled "Risk and GPF Aviation Support."

GPF in this case stands for "General Purpose Forces" Aviation. In other words, aviation that is not designated as "Special Forces," would fall under "General Purpose Forces." The Chinook and the National Guard aircrew fall under this category. Once again, the threat was clearly high. Here are Colt's warnings to Mattis [author's emphasis]:

> *The TF (meaning "Task Force") Commander was responsible for the initial risk assessment for the CH-47Ds (Extortion 17 was a CH-47D) and AH-64Ds in direct support of [redacted—but referring to Special Forces].* He assessed all missions with a high risk based on the compressed planning timeline required to support their high pace of operations.
>
> *His TF (Task Force) helicopters had conducted missions in support of [redacted—but referring to Special Forces] over the previous 10 months,* all of which were assessed as high risk for CH-47D aircrews.

Now we see a specific warning of *high risk* not only because of the dangerous area in which the CH-47 would be flying, but also because of the very high tempo of the operations. Put another way, general forces aviators simply are not trained to operate at the same quick tempo of air operations, nor with the same speed and daring approach.

But General Colt's revelation gets even more pointed. Again, in the same document, in the next section entitled "Risk Assessment, Risk Management," Colt reveals the much greater risk that this mission was to the ill-fated Chinook helicopter than it was to the Apache attack helicopters. Consider this warning [author's emphasis]:

> *The CH-47D Air Mission Commander completed an Electronic Risk Assessment Worksheet (ERAW) and determined the mission to be high*

*risk based on low illumination condition and one crew chief's rela-
tively low experience level.*

So how does the mission commander's assessment (high risk based
on low illumination levels and on crew chief's relatively low experience
level) square with General Mattis's conclusion that "I specifically agree
that the Army aviators flying this mission were fully qualified to perform
all required tasks, that the aircraft was mission capable"?

It doesn't square well at all with the mission commander's deep concerns about using this old helicopter, and using this Air National Guard
crew with US Navy SEALs on such a high-risk mission.

RISK ASSESSMENT:

Chinooks versus Apaches

In the same paragraph as the warnings about the Chinook, Colt reports
that the Apache (AH-64D) helicopters were better equipped for this
dangerous mission because of superior aircrew experience and superior
equipment. Here is the risk assessment for the Apaches presented to
General Mattis:

> *The AH-64D Air Mission Commander also completed an indepen-
> dent risk assessment for his element and determined their risk to be
> moderate because of crew experience, and because the AH-64D air-
> crews used the Modern Target Acquisition and Detection system,
> which mitigated the low illumination.*

Now note the contrast in risk levels given to the different helicopters
on the mission. For the old Chinook, which was shot out of the air and
on which thirty Americans died, the pre-planning risk assessment was
"high risk." For the more modern Apaches, with more experienced crews
and superior equipment on the aircraft, the risk assessment was deemed
to be only "moderate."

Think about this. A "high risk" assessment from the very beginning,
based upon an inferior aircraft and a flight crew not trained for this type

of mission, meant that the SEAL team, and indeed, the entire comple-
ment of Americans, including the flight crew, were in danger the moment
they embarked on their mission.

That's worth repeating. With the high risk assessment assigned to
this mission from the beginning, based upon inferior aviation equipment
and a crew not adequately trained for this type of mission, the SEAL
team and flight crew were probably doomed to die before Extortion 17
ever lifted off the ground.

Someone higher in the chain of command was playing Russian rou-
lette with a US Navy SEAL team and the entire flight crew. Even if
the unidentified Afghans were not Taliban sympathizers, the calculus for
this mission meant probable death for every American serviceman aboard
Extortion 17 from the beginning.

General Mattis may have chosen to whitewash the story, to author
a conclusion chock-full of revisionist history, making it appear that the
mission planning was sound, that the aircraft was adequate, and that
the flight crew was adequately trained for this highly risky and dangerous mission. However, his local commanders on the ground and Special
Forces operators, that is the men whose necks were actually on the line,
begged to differ.

CHAPTER 17

Task Force Commander Concerns:
Conventional Aviation with Special Forces

As part of his investigation, General Colt heard some blunt and compelling testimony about the perils of using general aviation pilots and antiquated aircraft on Special Forces missions.

These excerpts of testimony began at page 41, Exhibit 48 of the Colt Report, in which Colt and his team were interviewing the Task Force commander, a Special Operations officer who oversaw deployment of the SEAL team from Base Shank.

In this exchange, the serviceman being primarily interviewed was the Special Forces Ground Force commander, whose name was not identified for security reasons, but who was most likely a US Navy SEAL or an Army Ranger. The Task Force commander is noted below as "TF-CDR."

In this exchange, the acronym SME-GFA stands for "Subject Matter Expert—Ground Forces Army Advisor." So this officer, again whose name is not identified for security purposes, was an Army officer, assigned to Colt's team as an expert, asking questions of the Special Forces Task Force commander about the SEAL's comfort level in working with general, as opposed to special aviation crews.

The acronym "ARSOA" below is crucial, because it refers to Army Special Operations, or the Night Stalkers that Special Forces such as the SEALs are accustomed to operating with.

> **SME-GFA:** *What's your comfort level of flying with these guys? Is there any friction points, or issues that come to mind besides just the*

normal three-hour timeline, and trying to get out the door quickly and they can't do it still?

TF CDR: *I would say, you know, we train in everything always with ARSOA. So comfort level is low because they don't fly like ARSOA—They don't plan like ARSOA. They don't land like ARSOA. They will either, you know, kind of, do a runway landing. Or if it's a different crew that trains different areas, they will do the pinnacle landing. So we are starting to understand different crews landed differently and needed different set ups for exfils and pick-ups.*

TF SEA: *It was a popular topic of discussion.*

TF CDR: *It's tough. I mean, and I gave them guidance to make it work. And they were making it work. But it limited our effectiveness. It made our options and our tactical flexibility [sic]. Our agility was clearly limited by our air platform infill—where we could go. How quickly we could get there. So when I talk about it, I briefed the boss and he knew it that, Hey, [sic] we're missing the enemy sometimes because we just can't get there. We can't adapt fast enough.*

The Task Force commander goes on, at page 45 of Exhibit 48, to explain that the Special Forces comfort level in flying with conventional helicopters was "very low." Consider this equally blunt testimony, in which he said that the SEAL's comfort level in flying with conventional helos was "low":

TF CDR: *But the bottom line is their comfort level is low. If we don't train with conventional helos, we learn to plan with conventional helos here. They brief us in on the process. It's very different than any SOF process that we've been in. Because it's not a SOF process. It's conventional planning to a SOF mission.*

Again, one must ask how this very blunt testimony squared with General Mattis's hunky-dory conclusion that the general aviation Army National Guard aviators were fully qualified to conduct the mission.

The testimony speaks for itself. There was evidence that the Chinook was at high risk because of its lack of equipment and crew experience level, and because of the frequency of attacks against choppers over the Tangi Valley, and there was very clear evidence that US Special Forces operators were only comfortable operating with Army Special Operations aircraft.

As a matter of fact, Extortion 17 was executing one of those slow "runway landings," as described by the Task Force commander, when it was blown out of the sky—coming in slowly, with no pre-assault fire, like a sitting duck floating upon a pond.

One SEAL officer at DEVGRU (SEAL Team Six), Commander Howard, made this comment to family members: "If the MH-47 had been hit in the same spot, the results would have been the same. The question is . . . would it have been hit?"

The question remains unanswered, and thirty-two children who lost their fathers deserve this answer: Why was CENTCOM (General Mattis) trying to whitewash the very clear defects in the poor mission planning that led to their deaths, and why did they not acknowledge the very clear warnings of Special Forces in the field?

But the facts raise more questions. Why subject the SEAL team to a high-risk aviation situation that was probably going to fail from the beginning? Why not paint a full and accurate picture in the Colt Report of the risky history involving the CH-47? Why include only three reports of helicopter attacks over the Tangi Valley, none of which actually brought choppers down, but leave out documented reports where the CH-47s were actually shot down by Taliban RPGs?

And why, when this was clearly not the case, would General Mattis conclude that "I specifically agree with the conclusions that the Army aviators were fully qualified to perform all required tasks, that the aircraft was fully mission capable, and that loading the Immediate Reaction Force [SEAL team and SOC operators] onto one aircraft was tactically sound"?

Only the general or others higher in the chain of command can answer this question.

Whoever insisted on this mission combination signed the death warrants for the SEALs, the Air Force SOC operators, and the National Guard flight crew.

CHAPTER 18

Pre-Flight Intelligence:
Taliban Targeting US Helicopters

Colt Report testimony revealed that the Taliban was specifically target-ing US helicopters in the Tangi Valley, and that in the ninety days prior to the Extortion 17 flight, and since the death of Osama Bin Laden, the Taliban had moved an additional one hundred fighters to the Tangi Val-ley, specifically for the purpose of shooting down Coalition helicopters.

Whether this increased determination to shoot down a US chopper was in retaliation for the death of Osama Bin Laden was unclear. What was clear, however, was that US military intelligence knew about these maneuvers ahead of time, which made the decision to order the SEALs on board the National Guard chopper even more foolish.

This stunning testimony was in Exhibit 89, pages 6 and 7 of the Colt Report, taken during an August 16, 2011, examination of the Task Force chief intelligence officer, a US Air Force Officer whose name was with-held for security purposes. The Air Force officer was being questioned by only one person in this case, the lead intelligence investigator for General Colt's investigatory team.

On page 6 the intelligence investigator asked about the threat to Coalition aircraft over the Tangi Valley in the ninety days leading up to the Extortion 17 shoot-down.

Q. Okay. Now, let's go even further back and, kind of, describe what the threat to aircraft or even coalition forces was in the Tangi Valley. Give us a snap shot of that up to the last six months or so.

A. Exactly. The last six months or you want to go 90 days?

Q. About 90 days. If you have got anything more past that, we will see where we are at?

A. And that actually puts some truth to this. It says Din Moham-mad, so we are just talking about Din Mohammad, who is objective Dunlap, was killed on 6 June [2011] in Tangi Valley, Sayyidabad District, by coalition forces after he was trying to attack coalition force helicopters in the Tangi Valley. So that's what we had coming out at that IIR.

At least one Taliban commander was killed on June 6, 2011, sixty days before Extortion 17 and five weeks after Bin Laden's death, for try-ing to lead attacks on Coalition helicopters.

But the intelligence reveals even more danger to US helicopters on page 7, stating that the Taliban had put increased effort into achieving its goal of shooting down a Coalition helicopter, by bringing in an additional one hundred fighters into the valley specifically for that purpose [author's emphasis].

A. The next piece of reporting that I have that fits within that time-frame comes from May 11 [2011] and it [sic] late May [sic] [2011] . . . . It's very brief. Again, it's out of Task Force. And it says some-thing to the effect that over 100 Taliban plan to travel from Prov-ince through Tangi Valley to possibly shoot down the coalition force aircraft.

Ten days after the Bin Laden killing, the Taliban seemed bent on retaliation in the Tangi Valley, so much so that they brought in an addi-tional one hundred insurgents with weapons into the valley to go hunting for an American helicopter.

The Army had the intelligence about the one hundred insurgents at its disposal, and it was aware of the concerns expressed by Special Forces operators about general forces aviation. The Joint Command knew about the other aforementioned CH-47 shoot-downs in the months lead-ing up to the Extortion 17 disaster. They knew pilot Bryan Nichols was inexperienced in combat situations, and yet Colonel Mattis called him "fully qualified" in the aftermath of the Extortion 17 incident, ignoring the kind but candid words of Nichols's former commanding officer Lieutenant Colonel Richard Sherman, who told the Associated Press that Nichols was a "young pilot" who was "getting better all the time" and was "going to improve." And yet someone still ordered that SEAL team on board a National Guard helicopter for their mission, putting them into an unconscionably dangerous environment.

CHAPTER 19

Chaos in the Air: The Lost Minutes

The CH-47D Chinook helicopter is a valuable tool in the US military arsenal and has been for over fifty years. It has been called the "helicopter version" of the workhorse C-130 fixed-wing cargo plane, and when operating within its proper role, the CH-47 has proven to be an invaluable asset.

The CH-47 is a twin-propeller, heavy-lift chopper that first saw action in 1962. It has been around a long time, and of course, has gone through upgraded designs over the years, increasing tremendously the chopper's lift capability, but the basic air platform remains the same, going back to the early 1960s.

The chopper can, for example, haul 19,500 pounds of cargo, or two Humvees, or thirty-three battle-ready soldiers for deployment. Its versatility as a cargo, heavy-lift, and transport chopper is invaluable.

The chopper was not designed, however, and never has been designed, for flying troops into a heated battle zone full of antiaircraft rockets or small weapons capable of taking it out, and especially not without pre-assault fire—a topic covered in later chapters.

But that is exactly what this CH-47, call name Extortion 17, was asked to do the night the SEAL team members died.

On the night that it was shot down, Extortion 17, with thirty Americans and eight Afghans aboard (seven Afghan commandos and one interpreter), was loaded to the max, and was flying into a very hot airspace, with no real antiaircraft protection.

The CH-47 was flying into "hot" airspace, meaning airspace where hostile rockets and RPGs were likely to fly, and one of the problems with the Chinook CH-47 as a battle wagon is that it is thunderous and loud upon approach. If the enemy is in the area, there is no surprise. Even in the dark of the night, the noise level alone provides a target for RPGs, small arms fire, and missiles. A Taliban insurgent, even if he cannot see the chopper, need only point toward the noise and fire. It is that simple to shoot it down, if the Taliban can get close enough, which is one of the many reasons Special Forces choppers should be selected for missions in high-risk areas.

In the dark morning hours of August 6th, as Bryan Nichols attempted to guide Extortion 17 toward the landing zone to unload, or "exfil" the SEAL team, there was a period of fourteen lost minutes in the air, when communication was lost with the chopper, when it did not call in to air traffic control on time, and when it was late for landing. The fourteen-minute period ended with the chopper being blown out of the air.

Had the mission been executed to razor-sharp precision by a Special Operations flight crew, the chopper would have been on the ground, would have unloaded the SEAL team, and would have been on its way back to Base Shank with fourteen minutes to spare.

But on the night of its destruction, there was an unexplained delay in the air and an unexplained lapse in radio communications.

And no one knows why.

———

The confusion in communications between the aircraft and military air traffic control started when Extortion 17 moved to within six minutes of landing. At that point, the chopper called in and announced that it was six minutes out from the designated landing zone, meaning that it should have been on the ground within six minutes from that call.

This recitation of the chronology of Extortion 17's last minutes will use Zulu time, because that is what was used in the Colt Report, but will also include local (Afghanistan) time to make it easier for civilian readers to follow the timeframe and sequence.

By protocol, the pilot was to call in at the six-minute mark before landing. As shown by Exhibit 50 of the Colt Report, that call came in from the chopper at 2156 Zulu time (2:26 a.m. local time). The mission appeared clearly on track, headed toward its last minutes before landing.

Based on the timing of that call, Extortion 17 should have been on the ground unloading the SEAL team at 2202 Zulu time (2:32 a.m. local time).

By protocol, another call was due from the helicopter at the three-minute mark before landing, at 2159 Zulu time (2:29 a.m. local time).

But there was no call from the chopper. Air traffic control could not raise the chopper by radio.

One minute passed. Still no three-minute call in.

Another minute passed. It was now 2201 Zulu time (2:31 a.m. local time) and still, there was no three-minute call.

By now, concern was setting in at military air traffic control. Why wasn't Extortion 17 calling in? What was going on up there?

The chopper was due to be on the ground in one minute, at 2202 Zulu time (2:32 local time), but in the early, moonless hours of the morning, over airspace where a hundred extra Taliban fighters had come to shoot down an American helicopter, it had not called in to announce "three minutes to landing."

Something wasn't right.

Another minute passed. Where was the three-minute call-in?

At this point, the tension level at base command rose to near-panic levels. The chopper appeared to be simply hovering in the air.

The slow speed and delay was a major concern. The chopper was simply hanging out there in the air too long, thundering in the night for the enemy to hear, making itself a target with its slow hover and high noise level.

Finally, at 2203 Zulu time (2:33 a.m. local time) the three-minute call came in.

It was still hovering in the air, at least three minutes from landing, when it was supposed to already be on the ground. The recalculated landing time would now be 2:36 a.m. local time, four minutes after the originally projected landing time of 2:32 a.m. local time.

Four minutes overtime in a loud, thundering helicopter is a long time, and, like an alarm clock going off early, gives the enemy extra reaction time to gather weaponry and be ready, eliminating any semblance of an element of surprise.

Extortion 17 was now in a dangerous race against the clock. For the mission planners back at flight control, monitoring the progress of the chopper and the SEAL team, the tension-filled atmosphere was not all that different from what had occurred at Mission Control in Houston, Texas, some forty-two years earlier, when NASA controllers nervously monitored the *Eagle's* descent to the lunar surface. On that night, with the tension already thick in the air, a sick feeling of near catastrophe had set in when Neil Armstrong suddenly overrode the lunar module's automatic pilot and took control when it became obvious that the spacecraft was about to land in an unsafe area with dangerous boulders.

Just as mission controllers in Houston in July of 1969 understood that delay in landing a spacecraft could mean certain death for their crew, the military controllers in Afghanistan tracking Extortion 17 knew that every second's delay in landing increased the chance the Americans aboard the chopper would never return alive.

In their battle against the clock, the enemies facing Armstrong and Buzz Aldrin, lunar boulders and evaporating fuel, were lifeless, natural conditions. But from the surface of the Tangi Valley, the enemies facing Extortion 17 were angry and belligerent. Every second of delay in the air would swing the momentum in favor of the enemy on the ground, giving them time to recover, giving them time to prepare, giving them time to load their rocket-propelled grenades and train them on the approaching chopper.

Perhaps the Taliban still wasn't aware of their presence. Despite the delay, perhaps the Taliban was not hearing the thundering rotors from the ground.

Now, t-minus three minutes and counting. Tensions back at flight control riveted up a notch, and then another notch, as controllers monitored their instruments and followed the progress of the aircraft.

Remember that the new updated landing time was 2206 Zulu (2:36 a.m. local). Under pre-established protocol, the chopper was to call in once more, at the one-minute mark before landing, at 2205 Zulu (2:35 a.m. local time).

As controllers nervously monitored the clock and the radar position of Extortion 17, one minute passed. It was now 2204 (2:34 a.m. local), two minutes from the readjusted landing time.

No one knew exactly what was going on aboard, but on radar, at times the chopper seemed to be in a hovering position.

Military flight controllers and mission controllers were anxiously watching the clock on the wall. There was no call from the chopper at the one-minute mark, 2205 Zulu time (2:35 local time). Moreover, the chopper was still hovering, making no meaningful move toward an actual landing.

The clock continued to tick, and now a feeling of panic was beginning to set in at flight control. Mission planners anxiously monitored their headsets, awaiting the one-minute call, hoping to hear news that Extortion 17 was on its final descent, that it would be setting down in a matter of seconds, unloading the SEAL team as planned.

Once again, there was nothing.

What's going on? Why the delays?

Another minute passed. Now the new readjusted landing time of 2206 Zulu Time (2:36 a.m. local time) approached. Remember that the originally designated landing time was 2:32 a.m. The chopper had now hung in the air four minutes after it should have been on the ground.

The next communication from the chopper, the one-minute call, would come thirty-nine seconds later, at 22:06:39 (2:36:39 a.m. local time). This call was not a "one-minute" call at all, but rather, was a request for one of the Apache helicopters to provide a "sparkle," that is to illuminate the ground with light. Testimony from the Task Force senior enlisted advisor (acronym TF-SEA) in Exhibit 48, page 23, gave insight into the state of mind of the flight controllers:

TF SEA: *Sir, I specifically remember going and I'm pointing with this green [Afghan military member], XO [executive officer] was there. I go, "That's the HLZ," [helo landing zone] he said, yes. And they were scanning the area. And I was like, it looks pretty quiet. We got the three-minute call, and then they were just—six minutes later, I was going, what's up with the infill, did they go in already.*

Some mission controllers wondered if the SEALs were rappelling down to the ground with ropes after the three-minute call, which might explain why the chopper had been hovering so long. The rappelling theory was a hopeful theory which, of course, turned out not to be true. But it does show how flight controllers were grasping, almost desperately, for a belief that something positive was happening aboard the chopper in its final few minutes.

In reality, delay and confusion marked the flight's final minutes. The request for a "sparkle" was Extortion 17's final transmission.

CHAPTER 20

The Chopper's Last Call

22:06:39 (2:36:39 A.M. LOCAL TIME)

Recall that the one-minute call did not take place on time and was delayed another one minute and thirty-nine seconds. The last communication from the helicopter, which came at 22:06:39 (2:36:39 a.m. local time) was not really a "one-minute" call at all.

It was not a "one-minute" call, because, alarmingly, the chopper still did not report that it was one minute from landing. As will be seen from the taped air traffic with one of the Apache helicopters accompanying Extortion 17, the old Chinook seemed confused, and made a premature request for a sparkle of the landing zone. That request raised questions with the Apache crew.

Simply put, to "sparkle" a landing zone, or to "put a sparkle" on a landing zone, means that one helicopter, generally an accompanying helicopter, will fire a laser beam from the sky, down to the ground, into the landing zone. Crudely defined, it's like turning on a giant laser flashlight to fire a light beam down into the landing zone. Sometimes, this process is referred to as "painting" the landing zone.

This is done for the purpose of helping the main helicopter, in this case, Extortion 17, to find the landing zone on the ground, and to fly to that landing zone.

Part of the problem is that if the sparkle comes too early, or if the sparkle lasts too long, it can alert the enemy on the ground of the visual position of the approaching helicopters. Even though an enemy might hear the thunder of chopper rotors, in the pitch-black of night, it is still difficult to always know from what direction that noise is coming. But the sparkle, if seen, can change that dynamic in favor of an enemy.

To see a laser sparkle, the enemy must ordinarily be equipped with night vision goggles, or a camera, and must be looking at the right time. So the sparkle should be used, if at all, very conservatively, in very short bursts, and ordinarily within one minute of landing, which is important to keep in mind in examining the final transmissions of Extortion 17.

The following dialogue was taken from the Full Motion Video (FMV) feed, known as "Gun Tape 5" and it comes from one of the two Apache helicopters that accompanied Extortion 17. The "Gun Tape," attached to the Colt Report as Exhibit 54, provided a twenty-nine-page verbatim transcript of communications between the two-man Apache crew and the ill-fated CH-47 crew.

Extortion 17's flight from base camp to the landing zone should have taken no more than eight minutes. The full gun tape begins at 21:44:33 Zulu (2:14 a.m. local time) and ends at 22:24:27 Zulu time . So the gun tape ran approximately one hour, basically from the launch of the mission.

The excerpt in question occurs on page 17 of 29, beginning at the 22:06:39 mark (2:36:39 a.m. local time).

Approximately two minutes later, on page 18 of the transcript, at 22:08:34 (2:38:34 a.m. local time) Bryan Nichols's voice is heard for the last time, with the words, "One minute. One minute." At least, it seemed to be Bryan Nichols's voice.

Then, seventy-two seconds later, the real-time description of the shoot-down begins at page 19 of 29, at the 22:09:46 (2:39:46 a.m. local time) mark.

Note the difference in time between these call-ins made by Extortion 17 and the actual time of the reported shoot-down. The Apache witnessed the shoot-down some three minutes after the odd request for an early sparkle, or some four minutes and forty seconds after the one-minute call was supposed to have been made.

What was going on inside Extortion 17? Why the delay?

Was the chopper hovering dangerously in the air?

CHAPTER 21

The Odd Request for a "Sparkle"

The next few chapters analyze the final three minutes of Extortion 17, beginning with an examination of the gun tapes referenced in the Colt Report at page 17 of Exhibit 48.

In the transcript, "EX17 PC" is the Extortion 17 pilot in command, Bryan Nichols. BS is the "back seat" pilot in the Apache, who is the lead pilot of the apache. "FS" is the gunner and navigator, in the front seat of the Apache helicopter.

For purposes of analysis, the final three minutes of the flight are broken up into three segments over a final three-minute period. The first forty-nine-second segment involved Extortion 17's odd request for a premature sparkle of the landing zone.

The second segment, coming two minutes later, was the final "one minute" call from Extortion 17.

The third and final segment, coming approximately one minute later, featured the Apache pilots' description of witnessing the shoot-down, with the sad declaration of "Fallen Angel," the universal, emergency, call sign that a US military aircraft has gone down.

Final Segment 1 (49 Seconds)—
The Request for the Sparkle (2:36:39 a.m. Local Time)

22:06:39	EX17 PC:	Could you guys sparkle, please?
22:06:42	BS:	And roger. You one minute?

22:06:46	EX17 PC:	Negative, but our lane direction isn't matching up just give them a little better idea where we're landing.
22:06:51		[INAUDIBLE]
22:06:51	FS:	, could you sparkle LZ?
22:06:56	:	*23/2 burn is on [INAUDIBLE]* [author's emphasis here and below]
22:07:01	FS:	Do we have burn in sight?
22:07:19	:	.
22:07:28	BS:	*Not even a minute out and you're requesting a damn sparkle.*

The first communication, "could you guys sparkle please," was from the pilot in command of Extortion 17, Bryan Nichols. Although there is nothing to positively identify the voice as Bryan's, the transcript designated the caller to be "EX17 PC."

When he asked "Could you guys request a sparkle please," he was asking that the Apache helicopter, one of two Apaches escorting Extortion 17 to the landing zone, make a request to the US Air Force AC-130 gunship flying 7,000 to 8,000 feet above them.

The Extortion 17 was accompanied through the dark night skies by three US aircraft with tons of offensive firepower that was never used, until after the fact. The two Apache attack helicopters code-named Gun 1 and Gun 2 and the US Air Force AC-130 gunship had been circling almost directly overhead.

As will be discussed later, the AC-130, prior to the shoot-down, had requested permission to attack enemy insurgents on the ground in the vicinity of the Extortion 17 shoot-down, *but was denied permission to fire ahead of time.* These insurgents, according to the aircraft commander, were only about 600 meters (just over 630 yards) away from the CH-47, and one of them could very well have fired the RPG that minutes later would bring down the helicopter. Had the AC-130 been allowed to pour fire into that area, there is a good chance that the area would have been cleared of enemy insurgents and Extortion 17 could have landed safely.

As a side note for those not familiar with military aircraft, an AC-130 is a fixed-wing aircraft, with four propellers—two on each wing. It can be used primarily as a heavy-load cargo plane, the C-130 variant, or it can be configured as an attack aircraft, heavily armored to provide fire support for troops on the ground.

Having been denied permission to conduct any pre-assault fire prior to Extortion 17's landing, the AC-130's mission, circling high overhead, was now to coordinate communications with the aircraft in the area, and to track enemy positions on the ground and report on those positions. It also had the capability to deliver devastating firepower to the ground if permitted by the rules of engagement.

Furthermore, it had the ability to "paint" the landing area with high-powered laser beams. So when Extortion 17 opened this exchange by asking "Could you guys request a sparkle please," they were asking the Apache helicopters to relay a request up to the AC-130 gunship to hit the landing zone with a powerful laser beam.

That gathers this response from the lead pilot of the Apache helicopter (BS for "back seat"—remember the pilot sits in the back seat of an Apache helicopter and the gunner sits in the front). "And roger. You one minute?"

The Apache pilot was asking Extortion 17 if they were one minute away from landing for two reasons. First, Extortion 17 had already made its three-minute call, and its one-minute call was now overdue by a minute and thirty-nine seconds. Second, as was emphasized in earlier communications to Extortion 17, the request for a sparkle should come at the one-minute mark, in part to keep the enemy guessing for as long as possible about where the chopper will be coming in. Moreover, the burn or sparkle should be as short as possible to avoid the possibility of being seen by the enemy utilizing night vision.

With all this in mind, the Apache pilot was trying to verify with the Extortion 17 Pilot that he was now one minute from landing, and presumably, the sparkle would be short.

Note, however, the surprising reaction from Extortion 17, when asked if they were one minute out. "Negative, but our lane direction isn't matching up just give them a little better idea where we're landing."

First off, Extortion 17 was saying that he *was not one minute from landing.* So this sparkle was being requested prematurely.

Second, the words "lane direction not matching up" and "a little better idea where we're landing" suggest that there was confusion aboard Extortion 17. At a time when they were supposed to be making their one-minute call on final approach, they couldn't seem to find the correct "lane direction" and they didn't seem to even know where they were landing.

CHAPTER 22

The Final Seconds: Who Is "Them"?

The Extortion 17 pilot said he was requesting the sparkle to "give *them* a better idea of where we're landing."

Who was "them?"

Perhaps "them" was the SEAL team inside the chopper. But the statement is odd. It's odd in part because the SEAL team would be sitting in jump seats, inside the cargo bay, facing inward, waiting for exfil. The SEAL team would not be crowded around the three windows on each side of the back of the chopper, looking out to see what's down there. First off, there aren't enough windows in the back of the CH-47, and there's not enough room for that sort of thing. It's not like there are windows by every seat, like a commercial airliner. The SEAL team would be at this point facing inward, readying their weapons to storm out the back of the Chinook once it touched down.

Perhaps "them" was someone else. Could "them" have been the seven unidentified Afghans who illegally infiltrated the chopper, and whose bodies were later apparently cremated, thus destroying DNA evidence to make their identification next to impossible?

Was the Extortion 17 pilot, Bryan Nichols, trying to tell us something here? Could "them" have been someone on the ground? Could there have been another "them" with an interest in knowing where that chopper was about to set down?

Maybe the use of "them" was not significant. But given the odd circumstances already surrounding this mission, from the infiltration of seven unidentified Afghans, to Extortion 17's seemingly strange and odd confusion over finding the landing zone, something that should not be that difficult, the very odd word choice here should be examined.

Overhead, the AC-130 pilot realized that Extortion 17 was confused. In Exhibit 40 of the Colt Report, the AC-130 pilot said (on page 22), "it seemed from our perspective a little confusion on exactly where the HLZ [Helo Landing Zone] was going to be."

After Nichols asked for the "sparkle," he explained that he was off-center and was asking for the sparkle to "show them the landing zone."

Why did Extortion 17 seem to have such a hard time finding the landing zone? Why all the delays? Why the confusion? In this age of GPS technology, there should have been absolutely no confusion as to the precise location of the landing zone.

If we have that kind of precision in commercial airliners, then why couldn't Extortion 17 find the landing zone?

Neither the Apaches nor the AC-130 had any problems locating the landing zone. Why, then, was Extortion 17 having the problems that it was having?

Yes, Bryan Nichols was a young pilot. But he had been flying for three years, and even a young pilot should be able to find a landing zone using GPS navigational systems. Besides, he had a more experienced co-pilot, David Carter, sitting beside him in the cockpit, and they were certainly able to find the landing zone earlier in the evening, when they dropped off the Ranger team several clicks outside the battle zone.

Pinpointing the landing zone should have been the simplest of tasks. The confusion aboard Extortion 17 does not seem like pilot error; it smacks of something else going on in the aircraft. The question is, "what?"

In the transcript the Apache co-pilot and gunner, designated in the transcript as "FS" for "Front Seat," asks, "could you sparkle LZ?"

Here, LZ is, of course, the acronym for landing zone, and the co-pilot of the Apache helicopter is radioing up to the AC-130, requesting that the "sparkle," that is the high-powered laser beam, be flashed down into the landing zone.

Next we hear, "23/2 burn is on [INAUDIBLE]." This was a communication from the AC-130 overhead, and the phrase "burn is on" means that the laser is now burning, and the sparkle has begun.

It's important to note the time that the sparkle begins. It's 22:06:56, or 2:36:56, just four seconds before 2:37 a.m.

By this time there had already been a considerable delay in landing, and officers at flight control were concerned that the helicopter was stalled in the air. One of the Apache pilots flying alongside Extortion 17 was also perplexed, as detailed in the next chapter.

CHAPTER 23

Extortion 17's Bizarre Behavior

The Apache pilot seemed disgusted that Extortion 17 was requesting the sparkle prematurely. He chided the Extortion 17 pilot in no uncertain terms: "Not even a minute out and you're requesting a damn sparkle."

Based upon a review of the flight transcript, there seemed to be a certain disgust in the Apache pilot's tone here, because he understood that a sparkle requested prematurely and outside of a minute from landing could alert the enemy on the ground and prove unnecessarily dangerous.

Even Brigadier General Colt raised this question himself, at Exhibit 53, in the transcript of his team's interview with both Apache pilots after the shoot-down. The general's comments were captured at page 32 of Exhibit 53, as follows:

> **BG COLT:** . . . *sparkle? I believe that there was commentary about "I don't know why he's asking for it so soon."*
>
> *. . . it sounded like [it] was an incredulous comment that he just asked for the burn at three, why did he do that? I mean normally, he calls at one. We're not even clear if there was even a one-minute call, or if that was the moment that he was struck.*

The AC-130 pilot, in his testimony at Exhibit 40, page 22, noted that, "We had coordinated with the Helos that we were going to the burn down at H minus one so we had one of our sensors on the HLZ." This testimony confirmed the original plan to do a brief burst or "burn down" at less than one minute before landing.

Why does Extortion 17 request the premature sparkle, more than one minute from landing? Perhaps to help the pilot visibly find the landing zone if, in fact, he was not able to find it. But that doesn't make a lot of sense, because with GPS navigation, Extortion 17 should have been able to fly directly to the landing zone, without confusion. The AC-130 overhead was able to sparkle it with a laser beam with no problem. In fact, per the testimony of the AC-130 aircraft commander, it was able to keep sensors on the landing zone the whole time.

The next chapter explores the second segment of the final three minutes of the life of Extortion 17, with the next transmission coming some two minutes later.

CHAPTER 24

The "Two-Minute Burn" and the "One-Minute Call" That Wasn't

Extortion 17's confusing and contradictory actions in the air were compounded not only by the odd request for a sparkle, when that was never part of the battle plan, but also in continuing to make targeted timeline calls that never materialized. There was apparently an odd and long two-minute burn from the AC-130, perhaps even longer. If that happened in response to the sparkle request, and it apparently did happen, the chopper could have been painted, or "lit up" with ultraviolet light, making it a target for any Taliban within range with night vision goggles. That odd, "two-minute burn" was followed up by a "one-minute call," from the chopper, indicating that it was one minute from landing.

But Extortion 17 was not one minute from landing. It still hung in the air beyond the one-minute call, when it should have been on the ground, and was then blown out of the sky by the enemy.

The sequence on the gun tape is as follows [author's emphasis]:

Second Segment

22:08:34	PC:	, 1 minute. 1 minute.
22:08:37	BS:	Copy 1 minute. 1 minute. *Burn's out.*
22:08:39	:	[INAUDIBLE] — the grid you can get it from or .

22:08:43	:	, copy.
22:08:46	:	
22:08:56	BS:	. LZ is still ICE.
22:09:16	BS:	—Current LZ looks like it's still on the green zone. I do see little fields. It's probably new crops in, looks like mild to light dust and winds at altitude are currently

At thirty-four seconds past 2:38 a.m., local time, Bryan Nichols (or someone pretending to be him) said "One minute. One minute."

The actual one minute call, which was the call saying, essentially, that "we are one minute from landing," was over three minutes delayed. The last communication from the chopper had been over two minutes before the one minute call, at 22:06:39 (236:39).

Once the one-minute call was made, the pilot of the Apache, Gun 1, acknowledged with, "Copy 1 minute. 1 minute."

The next transmission was the most significant in the sequence.

At 2:38:37, three seconds later (three seconds after the one-minute call), the Apache pilot said "burn's out."

That's significant, because this apparently marked the end of the duration of the infrared burn that had been shooting down on the landing zone from the AC-130.

Remember in the first of the three transmissions, the announcement that "burn's on" came at 22:06:56. Now at 22:08:37, "burn's out."

That meant that for a period of one minute and forty-one seconds, there was not only a sparkle, but *a continuous burn on the landing zone.*

Understand the difference. A sparkle is a brief nighttime flash that is turned on for a second, and then turned off. But a burn is more of a continuous illumination, like taking a giant flashlight and leaving it on for almost two minutes, and then turning it off.

However, despite the Apache pilot announcing that "burn's out" at the 22:08:37 mark, there was testimony from the AC-130 gun crew, circling overhead, that the burn was not out before the shoot-down, but in fact, that the burn was still on at the time of the shoot-down!

There was a bright burn from the sky to the ground, illuminated from the AC-130 overhead, which was nineteen seconds short of two minutes, if the "burn's out" call by the Apache was accurate. Or if the testimony of the AC-130 gun crew, the aircraft initiating the burn, was accurate, the burn was still on at the time of the shoot-down, making the Apache's announcement that "burn's out" apparently in error.

If the burn was still on at the time of shoot-down, this would mean that the burn actually exceeded two minutes, and put Extortion 17 in the enemy spotlight, making it an easy, visible target, up to the very moment of the shoot-down.

So just how large of an area was being illuminated? And just how bright was the burn?

Colt and his team examined these questions when they interviewed the four Apache pilots from Gun 1 and Gun 2 on August 18, 2011, Exhibit 53 in the Colt Report.

At page 18 of Exhibit 53, the co-pilot of Gun 1 explained the difference between a short-burst sparkle which illuminated only for a brief second or so, and a longer-term burn.

The co-pilot went on to explain that a burn was better for a landing zone—as opposed to a sparkle to follow enemy combatants on the ground—because "a burn is better because it allows them to see a whole lot more."

General Colt then asked about the size of the ground area being illuminated: "And how big is the box when they are doing that?"

To that, the co-pilot of Gun 2, the second Apache, replies, "A football field." And then the pilot of Gun 1, the first Apache, chimes in. "I would say 500 meters or so. It's pretty big."

So both the co-pilot of one Apache and the pilot of the other Apache testified that a very large area of ground was being illuminated on the ground at the landing zone.

Moreover, at page 33 of the same exhibit, Colt came back to the difference between the use of short-burst sparkles and the "burn that is placed on the landing zone." Both co-pilots explained that the AC-130 was using periodic sparkles to illuminate the movement of enemy insurgents, called "squirters," on the ground.

General Colt then asks if a sparkle had been placed on the landing zone where Extortion 17 was trying to set down. The answer given by the co-pilot of the second Apache helicopter, Gun 2, is significant. The co-pilot's acronym is "PB70FS."

PB70FS (Co-Pilot Gun 2): I couldn't tell you if the sparkle hit it. The burn was so bright.

In other words, the co-pilot of the second Apache was saying that the two minute burn was "so bright"—i.e., blinding—that it would have flooded out any sparkle that was shot into the landing zone.

So an area the size of a football field or larger was lit for an extraordinarily long period of two minutes, showing the precise spot that the chopper was about to land, right before it landed.

The length, duration, and size of that illumination were more than enough to scream to the enemy, especially if the enemy had NVGs, "get ready, here we come." In the weeks after the shoot-down, military briefers told family members that the Taliban might have seen dust that was being blown up from the ground, dust generated by the Chinook's powerful twin rotary blades. Under the theory proffered by the military briefers, as the dust was blown up off the ground on approach to landing, a dust cloud swirled up around the rotary blades, which could have cast a glow, making a visual target for the Taliban firing RPGs.

This theory is plausible, but most likely, the "glow" from the dust swirling around the blades came from the burn being lit from the AC-130 circling 7,000 feet above.

With the landing zone having not been cleared out by pre-assault fire, dust or no dust, anyone in the area with night goggles and an RPG, and within range, needed to do nothing more than wait and aim, because the long, bright burn marked the exact spot where Extortion 17 was about to land. And that is exactly what happened.

It appears that when the request for "sparkle" was initiated by Extortion 17, the AC-130 thought the chopper was about to land, and consequently flooded the area.

When the actual "one-minute" call came almost two minutes later, the gunship realized that the chopper was still in the air and cut the burn.

This brings us back to the question: Why did the request for the sparkle come so prematurely, and not within the one-minute timeframe according to the plan? Also, why did the AC-130 burn the landing zone, instead of only briefly sparkling it?

The air traffic transcripts between the Apaches, the AC-130, and the Chinook (Extortion 17), in the minutes leading up to this request for a "sparkle," repeatedly made it clear that the operational plan called for a burn and not a sparkle at the one-minute mark prior to landing.

A sparkle is a brief flash, far more difficult for an enemy to track to its source than a longer burn.

The transcript for Exhibit 53, page 17 showed that all pilots, including the Extortion 17 pilots, had been briefed to expect a burn—not a sparkle—and this was drilled into them during pre-flight briefings.

Here, the questioning was being conducted by an officer on Colt's staff who was part of the Airworthiness Directive Support Action Team. The acronym for this officer in the transcript was "ADSAT4."

This officer was an expert whose job was to explore any airworthiness issues, or lack thereof, of the aircraft. Although the military obviously is not part of the FAA, this officer—one of at least four expert advisors Colt used—was on the team to ask questions similar to what the FAA mandates during investigations of crashes—i.e., was something wrong with the aircraft? Or was there pilot error? Or both?

The ADSAT advisor questioned the Apache pilots about whether they expected a pre-landing burn or a pre-landing sparkle.

Remember that PB70FS was the co-pilot of Gun 2, the second Apache, and PB65FS is the co-pilot of Gun 1, the first Apache:

ADSAT4: *Going into, what was the interpretation between your crews and 17? How were they expecting the LZ to be marked?*

PB70FS (Co-pilot Gun 2): *is the one [inaudible] going to the crash. It marked by burn.*

ADSAT4: *I understand what it was marked by. What did they believe how it was going to be marked?*

PB65FS: (Co-pilot Gun 1): *Every brief we do, now that we've—with being able to burn, we have always told them that we had preferred they take burn rather than illume. So we have talked to them every time.*

It seems from this excerpt, that for nighttime landing ops involving the CH-47 that the Apache pilots prefer to see a final burn on approach to landing rather than an illume [sparkle], and that they had communicated this preference to the CH-47 flight crew. Remember that Extortion 17 was not requesting a burn, but was requesting sparkles, which meant that the doomed chopper was, oddly, in contradiction to the normal, preferred procedure. This is one of several factors suggesting that something abnormal was happening aboard the CH-47 prior to its shoot-down.

CHAPTER 25

Was Bryan Nichols Trying to Tell Us Something?

Based on the clear testimony of the two Apache co-pilots who were in the air with Extortion 17, the plan all along was not to sparkle, but to burn the landing zone within the one-minute mark.

Why did Bryan Nichols ask for a sparkle instead of a burn? He very clearly knew that the plan was to burn within the last minute of landing, because he had been briefed on it.

Was it possible that Nichols simply got confused, and mixed up the terms "sparkle" and "burn," and the AC-130 commenced the burn because that was the predetermined battle plan?

That is possible, but because there is a double-oddity about this request, that is, both the premature timing of the request and the request for the sparkle instead of the burn, the "Bryan Nichols was confused" theory does not seem plausible. Nichols may have been a younger National Guard pilot, but it seems unlikely that he would make such a (1) premature timing mistake and (2) a nomenclature mistake, all wrapped together, and especially not with a more experienced pilot, CW04 David Carter, sitting in the cockpit beside him.

We do not hear a follow-up call from Extortion 17 stating, "correction requesting burn not sparkle." Nor do we hear a follow-up call even when the Apache pilot seemingly chided Extortion 17 with his comment of incredulity, "Not even a minute out and you're requesting a damn sparkle."

Could it be that (a) Bryan Nichols actually wanted a sparkle instead of a burn, because of information he had received from someone inside the chopper that the chopper would be targeted on the ground, knowing that the sparkle would make him a more elusive target?

Could it be that (b) he was being ordered by someone inside the chopper to prematurely request the burn so that the landing zone would be pinpointed by the enemy?

Could it be that (c) someone else had taken control of the helicopter and was flying it at this point, and that whoever was flying the chopper as it approached the landing zone did not know that all pre-flight briefings had repeatedly called for a burn and not a sparkle?

Could it be that (d) someone else had taken control of the helicopter and was flying it at this point, and that whoever was flying the chopper did not know the difference between a sparkle and a burn?

Could it be that (e) by requesting such a premature illumination of the landing zone and by using the wrong phrase, which didn't match the pre-mission planning, that Bryan Nichols was trying to tell us something?

The questions being raised herein are not to suggest one scenario over the other. Rather, these questions are being raised because General Colt's team should have raised them, and did not raise them.

One thing seems indisputable. Something odd was happening inside that helicopter.

The third and final segment of the transcript breaks down the last three minutes of the flight of Extortion 17.

In this section, there weren't any broadcasts from the helicopter.

Still, timing is crucial in analyzing this section. Remember the "two-minute burn" from the second segment, referring to the beam flashed down onto the landing zone from the AC-130 gunship, which actually lasted 22:06:56 to 22:08:37, or a period of one minute and forty-one seconds.

Pay attention to the ending time of the burn in the second segment 22:08:37 (2:38:37 a.m.), and the beginning of the shoot-down at 22:09:46 (2:39:46).

There was a period of one minute nine seconds (22:08:37 to 22:09:46) between the ending of the "two-minute burn" and the beginning of the shoot-down sequence—that is if the "burn's out" call from the Apache was correct at the 22:08:37 mark. But if the burn was not out, as was suggested by the AC-130 gunship crew in testimony at Exhibit 40, this effectively means the chopper was spotlighted from the burn initiation point, at 22:06:56, all the way up to the shoot-down, at 22:09:46.

In that case, if the burn did not go out until after the RPGs started flying, then the burn would have lasted ten seconds short of three minutes, illuminating the chopper all the way up to shoot-down! This would in effect have made it a three-minute burn instead of a two-minute burn.

CHAPTER 26

A Three-Minute Burn? The Chopper in the Spotlight?

Although not directly addressed in the Executive Summary of the Colt Report, the danger of using a burn instead of a sparkle was that Taliban with night vision goggles could potentially see exactly where the chopper was flying, simply by following the burn down to the ground, and be ready with their RPGs.

In looking at the air traffic transcripts (also called "gun tapes") in conjunction with the testimony of the AC-130 crew, there appears to be some confusion as to the actual length of the burn.

The air traffic transcripts alone suggest a burn lasting approximately two minutes. The air traffic transcripts combined with the AC-130 testimony suggest an even longer burn, of approximately three minutes.

Either way the infrared burn was entirely too long, giving the Taliban ample time to put the CH-47 in their crosshairs on the ground, and then simply wait.

So which is the more credible explanation? That the burn was cut at the 22:08:37 mark (as reported by the Apache and supporting the two-minute burn theory), or that the burn lasted up through the shoot-down and was cut only after the firing started (as reported by the AC-130)?

The more credible explanation seems to be that the burn illuminating the chopper lasted through the moment of shoot-down, and was not cut at the 22:08:37 mark, but, rather, continued until after the RPGs started flying. But why? There are several reasons.

First, multiple witnesses on board the AC-130 testified *that the burn lasted through the shoot-down*, versus only one co-pilot who called "burn's out." So the greater weight of the evidence suggests that the burn lasted through shoot-down. Remember also that the recording on the gun tape was not sworn testimony, only a spontaneous observation of the co-pilot's perceptions at a given moment in time. In this instance, the weight goes to the sworn testimony.

Second, the AC-130 was the aircraft actually initiating the burn. That flight crew was in the very best position to know whether they were initiating the burn, or not. They testified that the burn lasted through the shoot-down.

How, then, do we reconcile the Apache co-pilot calling "burn's out" at the 22:08:37 mark? Remember that there were four different aircraft moving in the sky, probably not in exactly the same direction: the two Apaches, the AC-130, and Extortion 17. It is possible that the Apache co-pilot may have temporarily lost track of the burn and inadvertently called, "burn's out." Also, bear in mind that the burn was only visible through night vision goggles, which increases the possibility that the co-pilot may have momentarily lost track of it. Either way, there seems to be an indisputable inconsistency on a crucial point here, notably the time at which the burn actually went out.

Interestingly, the Colt Report does not even acknowledge the inconsistency in the evidence on the time of "burn's out," let alone attempt to resolve it. But this is an area that needs to be looked at, and needs to be resolved, because elongated burn times can pose a threat to US helicopters seeking to insert troops.

One thing seems certain. With the confusion demonstrated by the chopper in the minutes before the shoot-down, including the delays, the inexplicable ability to find the landing zone, the strange request for a sparkle minutes before landing, and the conclusion by some individuals at flight control that the Chinook was stalled in the air, Extortion 17 was acting like an aircraft whose crew may not have had full control over it. This brings us back to the original question about the pink elephant.

Who are the seven Afghans, and why won't the military talk about them?

CHAPTER 27

Fallen Angel:
The Final Seconds of Extortion 17

In reading the transmission describing the shoot-down in real time, keep two things in mind. First, Extortion 17, per the testimony of the Apache pilots at Exhibit 53, page 37, was between 100 and 150 feet off the ground when hit by an RPG. At page 52 of that same exhibit, the transcript noted that the chopper had slowed her airspeed to "80 knots or less."

Eighty knots is 92 miles per hour. We don't really know what "or less" means, except that it's less than 92 miles per hour. But it seems doubtful that the chopper would be flying 92 miles per hour as it entered the landing zone. Helicopters slow and feather as they are about to set down. So that part (92 mph) is not believable. The "or less" part is believable. The question is, "How much less?" Probably considerably less.

Also keep in mind reports from flight control that the chopper was not moving at all. So the chopper was very low at this point, was truly about to land, and was so close to the ground that the RPG shot had to have been a point-blank shot.

Remember that on the tape at thirty-four seconds past 2:38 a.m. local time, Bryan Nichols (or someone impersonating him) said "One minute. One minute."

Sixty-eight seconds later, at 22:09:46 (2:39:46 local time), the aircraft had already been delayed, eight seconds behind the pilot's latest estimate. But strangely, it's still apparently hovering in the sky, just hanging there as a target, for reasons that remain a mystery.

In this portion of the transcript, "BS" is the backseat pilot in the Apache helicopter, or the lead pilot of Gun 1. "FS" is the front seat pilot, or co-pilot, of Gun 1.

The sequence begins with the lead pilot of Gun 1 (BS) announcing, "I just saw a flash."

Note the tragic announcement of "Fallen Angel," the military distress code announcing that a US military aircraft has gone down.

Final Segment 3

22:09:46	BS:	I just saw a flash. Did you see a flash?
22:09:48	FS:	Yeah, they're being shot at.
22:09:52		H17 traffic. CH-47 transitioning south [INAUDIBLE]
22:09:55	BS:	What is that?
22:09:58	FS:	Dude, I think they just got shot.
22:10:01	BS:	Are you shot?
22:10:03	FS:	Are you on that?
22:10:05	FS:	I'm on it, sir! [Extortion 17] is down.
22:10:12		Roger.
22:10:13	BS:	Coalition traffic; we have a Fallen Angel. Fallen Angel. It's [Extortion 17].
22:10:26	BS:	[EXPLETIVE].
22:10:33	FS:	.
22:10:39	BS:	We pushed
22:10:41	:	s go ahead.

22:10:42	FS:	Roger. We have a Fallen Angel. [Extortion 17] was shot down in the Tangi Valley [INAUDIBLE]
22:10:45	BS:	Coalition traffic, anybody out there? We have a Fallen Angel CTAF
22:10:50	:	[Gun 1], H-17. Say location.
22:10:53	BS:	Location Tangi Valley. Tangi Valley and we're up on 338.45 on in the green plain text.
22:10:58		[INAUDIBLE].
22:11:01	FS:	Roger, what we're remaining [INAUDIBLE] 33/45
22:11:04	BS:	Roger. Roger. Right now, currently it's one Chinook down. How copy?
22:11:08		Roger. [Extortion 17] is down.
22:11:11		That's a good copy. We're already made on SATCOM [INAUDIBLE].
22:11:21	BS:	1 this is 2. Do you have anything?
22:11:24	BS:	We got nothing at this time. We got a wreckage on fire.
22:11:28	FS:	Alright, the calls been made to X.
22:11:31	BS:	I have [Extortion 17] right now down in the Airborne Valley by Hotel coming in on CTAF.
22:11:38	FS:	Right, I'm going stay up here and develop things. Where are you at?

22:11:43	FS:	Roger, we are circling overhead. I saw where the [EXPLETIVE] explosion came from, man. I'm searching the buildings. If I see [EXPLETIVE] anybody with a weapon, I'm firing.
22:11:52	:	. Helo common.
22:11:58	FS:	.
22:11:59	BS:	[Call sign deleted], it's . Go.
22:12:11	BS:	[Call sign deleted], this is [Call sign deleted] on Helo common. Go.
22:12:17	FS:	Did you see any survivors down there?
22:12:19	BS:	I'm not seeing any.
22:12:20	BS:	No, I'm not seeing anything right now. It is a ball of fire. It looks bad.
22:12:24	FS:	Okay.
22:12:26	BS:	Another explosion.
22:12:28	FS:	I got secondary's. Are they shooting them still?
22:12:34	BS:	No. I got secondary. I think that's fuel.

The sudden, almost panic-like reaction in the voices of the Apache pilots marked a very sad and dramatic moment for the Americans aboard Extortion 17. Their deaths, here, are recorded in real time. Indeed, this was a difficult passage to read. It's at this point, as precisely reflected on the gun tape, in a horrible flash at a moment frozen in time, that lives, American lives, were changed forever.

Braydon Nichols lost his father and Kimberly Vaughn lost her husband. Billy and Karen Vaughn lost their son. The two Vaughn children, Reagan and Chamberlain, in the horrible instant of a blinding moment, were forever fatherless.

Charles Strange, a blue-collar worker from Philadelphia, lost his son Michael, who was a Navy cryptologist supporting the SEAL team, and Candie Reagan lost her longtime fiancé, Patrick Hamburger.

Young Payton Hamburger, just two years old, would never see her father again.

Before dissecting specific timeframes, it's important to note that this shoot-down was not just witnessed by the Apache pilots, who were discussing it here in real time. It was also witnessed by the AC-130 pilot, along with several of his crewmembers. The pilot testified that three shots were fired, and that either the first or the second shot appeared to strike the chopper.

Meanwhile, another member of the AC-130 Crew, the Left Scanner, testified that the second RPG hit the chopper.

The first excerpt, taken from Exhibit 40, page 25, was the aircraft commander's testimony describing that he saw three shots fired at Extortion 17. Remember that the AC-130 was circling 7,000 to 8,000 feet overhead.

> **AC-130 Aircraft Commander:** *Shortly after the burn came on we saw—I saw three RPG shots, kind of just ripple—one, two, three—coming from the south to the north, I was in the southern part of the orbit and I saw, what I saw was either the first or second one make an initial hit, and just a massive explosion, and it just seemed to be stationary and it just dropped.*

Now here is the Left Scanner's testimony, at page 27 of Exhibit 40:

> **LEFT SCANNER:** *I was sitting left scanner, I have a single monocle that I look out of—NVGs so I had like one eye that's just looking*

normal, and one eye looking through the NVG. From my perspective the second RPG did hit directly. It made direct contact with the helicopter.

IO-DEP: *The first RPG?*

LEFT SCANNER: *The second RPG.*

IO-DEP: *The second RPG; I'm sorry.*

LEFT SCANNER: *I think the first RPG went underneath the helicopter, from my perspective. The second one did make a direct hit with the helicopter and there was a fairly large explosion in the air, but it was split seconds between the time the helicopter was hit. There was that explosion, and then it hit the ground and then there was an explosion.*

This testimony was highly relevant for two reasons. First, the aircraft commander revealed that three shots were fired at Extortion 17. But the second revelation, as alluded to earlier, is significant. The commander said, "Shortly after the burn came on we saw—I saw three RPG shots, kind of just ripple—one, two, three—coming from the south to the north."

Note the testimony here was not "shortly after the burn went out," but rather "shortly after the burn came on, we saw three RPG [rocket propelled grenade] shots." So the pilot of the AC-130 testified that the burn was *on* at the time of shoot-down. This is inconsistent with the Apache gun tape recording of "burn's out" at the 22:08:37 mark.

Now, remaining for the moment in Exhibit 40 of the Colt Report (interviews of AC-130 crew), take a look at a series of questions asked by the deputy investigating officer, beginning at page 27. These questions were directed at two AC-130 crewmembers, namely the television sensor operator and the left scanner.

On the question of how long the burn lasted, the television sensor operator's testimony was most crucial, because he was the airman who actually operated the burn.

TELEVISION SENSOR OPERATOR: *When he called that he saw RPGs come up, I turned off the burn, slid over to him, and that's* *when I saw the third RPG. And, the third RPG had already started coming out of the tube when the Helo was already on the deck—it was already on the ground—impacted with the ground. And, at that point, I mean, the first or second one had to have hit it, and it was a massive fireball. I mean, it just lit up.*

On the question of when the burn ended, the television sensor operator's testimony is compelling. "When he called that he saw RPGs come up, I turned off the burn, slid over to him, and that's when I saw the third RPG." He turned the burn off *after* the RPGs were launched. This means that the landing zone, and perhaps even the chopper, were being spotlighted by the bright, wide burn at the moment of shoot-down. This also means that the enemy on the ground, with a relatively inexpensive set of night vision goggles (NVGs) had plenty of time to focus on the spot-lit landing zone, to ready his RPG, and to fire as the helicopter descended through the ultraviolet light.

It's clear that the possibility of the "burn" illuminating the chopper and making it a more visible target became a concern, at least to members of the AC-130 gun-crew.

The navigator of the AC-130, at page 48, testified and verified other testimony that the burn size was roughly the size of a football field, but also noted that he didn't believe the burn could have highlighted the aircraft.

NAVIGATOR: *"Our burn is probably roughly the equivalent to the size of a football field and we're down here to the south on HLZ. I don't believe there's any way that our burn could have highlighted the aircraft."*

A couple of points about the navigator's comments. First, it's clear, at least at this point, that there was a concern about the burn lighting the helicopter. That's why the navigator says, "I don't believe there's any way that our burn could have highlighted the aircraft."

Of course, it really doesn't matter whether the burn highlighted the aircraft, because the burn put a big bright spot, the size of a football field, on the ground at the exact spot that the helicopter (Extortion 17) was fly-ing to. All the Taliban had to do was get their RPGs, run to the edge of the big bright spot on the ground, stay back just behind the bright lights, wait until the helicopter flew in toward them, then point in the air, and aim toward the noise.

Pay close attention to the navigator's testimony regarding directions. He said because "we're down here south of the HLZ," in other words the AC-130 was spotting the HLZ (acronym for helicopter landing zone) from an aerial position almost over the landing zone, but just south of it.

Compare that with the AC-130 commander's testimony on direc-tions, found at page 40 of Exhibit 5:

AC-130 Commander: *And they're changing their run-in heading it sounded like, they are coming from the Northwest now and so there was that delay and then we heard the one-minute out call, put the burn on. Shortly after the burn came on we saw—I saw three RPG shots, kind of just ripple— one, two, three—coming from the south to the north, I was in the southern part of the orbit and I saw, what I saw was either the first or second one make an initial hit, and just a massive explosion, and it just seemed to be stationary and it just dropped.*

A couple of relevant points from this portion of the AC-130 pilot's testimony: First, Extortion 17 was coming, that is converging on the landing zone, from the northwest. Because the gunship was converging from the south, the gunship was firing down its light beam at a slightly different angle from the helicopter's approach.

Because the chopper and gunship were approaching the landing zone from slightly different angles, the plane from the south, the chopper from the northwest, the gunship's navigator assumed that the light did not clip the helicopter.

Maybe the light did not clip the chopper. Maybe it did.

Again, it doesn't matter, because the target stage was painted with the AC-130's powerful light. This long illumination gave the Taliban time to know where to stand and shoot.

To better understand where the AC-130 was flying in relation to the landing zone, turn to Exhibit 83 of the Colt Report, the transcript of the second day of testimony from the AC-130 gunship. Exhibit 40 included the first day of testimony of the AC-130 crew, conducted August 18, 2011, and Exhibit 83 was the continuation of that testimony, taken on August 19, 2011.

In his opening statement on August 19, at page 3 of Exhibit 83, the AC-130 aircraft commander explained that the gunship was actually flying in a tight, circling pattern over the landing zone.

AIRCRAFT COMMANDER: *[I was] the aircraft commander on that night. We were on (the) southern part of the orbit, and we were essentially [performing a] 1.5 nautical mile radius wheel, counter clockwise around the helicopter landing zone (HLZ) at the point when I saw the rocket propelled grenade (RPG). Now the helo was calling one-minute out and we set up a contract to put down our burn, which is actually just a football (field) size flash light, infrared flashlight that you can see on NVGs.*

So the AC-130 was basically flying a tight, counterclockwise orbit around the landing zone, with a radius of only 1.5 nautical miles, shining down its burn on the landing zone. The aircraft commander noted that the burn could be seen with NVGs, or night vision goggles.

Remember, the Taliban would need NVGs (night vision goggles) for the ultraviolet burn from the AC-130 to have been a fatally defective mistake. Without NVGs, the ultraviolet burn would have been invisible to the naked eye.

But did the Taliban have access to NVGs? The next chapter examines that question.

CHAPTER 28

Taliban Access to NVGs and Other Weapons

Did the Taliban have access to night vision goggles (NVGs) that would have enabled them to see the ultraviolet burn being fired down by the AC-130 gunship?

Yes. Of course they did.

This leads to the next question: Where did the Taliban get NVGs?

Pakistan.

The *Express Tribune* is the major English-language newspaper published in Pakistan, and it is affiliated with the *International New York Times*, the global edition of the *New York Times*.

On June 15, 2011, less than sixty days before the Extortion 17 shoot-down, the *Express Tribune* ran an article entitled "Welcome to the 'American Market'— On sale: Night-vision goggles, RPGs." That article, authored by Pakistani reporter Nadir Hassan, revealed the extent of the arms market in Pakistan, where American weaponry was sold, often stolen from neighboring Afghanistan, not just in the city of Peshawar, but in several cities through Pakistan.

Consider the following excerpts from the *Express Tribune*'s article.

PESHAWAR: For people who openly sell night-vision goggles, grenades and even the occasional RPG, the dealers at the American Market in Peshawar are remarkably reluctant to talk about their clientele. . . .

Most of the arms here will end up with the Taliban. Some people come to buy these weapons for themselves but mostly they are bought by militants," he [the laptop dealer] says.

He explains that the area has come to be known as the American Market because it sells US goods that have either been stolen and transported from Afghanistan or captured from NATO trucks being transported from Pakistan to Afghanistan.

The laptop dealer says the American Market is only the third largest of its kind in Pakistan, and similar markets in Bara, Jamrud and Dara Adam Khel offer a greater variety of weapons, although he adds that there has been an army clampdown in Dara Adam Khel.

Despite the abundance of arms available in these markets, this is only the tip of the iceberg for the Taliban.

"The Taliban are the United Nations of weaponry," says Lee Wollonsky, an arms-smuggling expert who has worked with various think-tanks in the US.

The article verified that US weapons, including NVGs, were plentiful to the Taliban, and that a good portion of those weapons came through Pakistan. But perhaps the most sobering and indeed chilling excerpt revealed in the article was the very last paragraph.

Ultimately, though, the greatest provider—though inadvertently—of weaponry to the Taliban based in Afghanistan may be its greatest target: the US. As the laptop dealer at the American Market in Peshawar says, "The US gives weapons to people in Afghanistan to fight the Taliban and they just go and sell it to people here who then sell it to the Taliban."

Remember that this article was written in June of 2011, less than two months before the shoot-down. Recall also the testimony from Exhibit 89 from military intelligence officials that more than one hundred Taliban insurgents had been moved into the Tangi Valley for the purpose of shooting down a Coalition helicopter.

To think that those insurgents would not bring NVGs to accomplish the task would be quite absurd.

After all, American helicopters fly at night.

CHAPTER 29

A Point-Blank Shot: Clues from Exhibit 60

The Executive Summary of the Colt Report grossly exaggerated the distance between the helicopter (Extortion 17) and the Taliban insurgent who fired the RPG that brought the chopper down, noting that a "previously undetected group of suspected Taliban fighters fired two or three RPGs in rapid succession from the tower of a two-story mud brick building approximately 220 meters south of the CH-47D."

Aside from the fact that 220 meters (720 feet) is outside the effective range of the RPG weapon that brought the chopper down, a fact also proven by internal evidence in the Colt Report, it can be mathematically proven from evidence presented by the Combat Assessment Team investigating the shoot-down that the "distance-to-shooter" as set forth in the Executive Summary was wrong.

Why do this? Why grossly exaggerate the distance-to-shooter?

Here's why.

If it can be shown that the shot was fired from a much longer distance away, outside the landing zone, this takes the heat off the military and off the Obama Administration for its foolish rules of engagement that prevented pre-assault fire in the landing zone to begin with. In other words, they can say, "Hey, the shot didn't even come from anywhere near the landing zone, so our decision not to pour pre-assault fire into the landing zone didn't have any effect on the shoot-down." In other words, they could plausibly say that "the shoot-down had nothing to do with the rules of engagement."

That argument, however, is malarkey, and the internal evidence, which the military probably did not expect to be leaked out so quickly, proved it.

One of the most crucial exhibits from the Colt Report was Exhibit 60. This was the report of the Joint Combat Assessment Team (JCAT) at Bagram Air Base. It should be noted that at the time of the release of the Executive Summary, which established the military/government narrative of "don't look at us, we did nothing wrong," it's doubtful that either Brigadier General Colt, or General Mattis, or CENTCOM, or the Obama Administration counted on the JCAT report or sworn testimonies within the investigation ever seeing the light of day.

Look at the role of the Joint Combat Assessment team, as defined at page 2 of Exhibit 60:

The Joint Combat Assessment Team (JCAT) investigates battle damage and shoot-downs to determine the threat weapon system used in the attack and the enemy TTP employed, enabling the commander to determine the best counter-tactics to defeat the threat. Additionally JCAT cooperates with the acquisition and test community, and the Survivability Information Analysis Center to share lessons learned, archive survivability data, and reduce future aircraft vulnerabilities.

Thus, it was JCAT's job to examine forensic evidence from the crash, including the rotary blades to determine the angle-of-strike, analyze the statements of witnesses and chemical evidence where available, and serve as the one unit on the ground physically sifting through the wreckage and having scientific tests run on fragments of the aircraft to piece together what happened. Their job was to report back with a no-holds-barred, no-bull assessment of what went wrong, given whatever evidence they compiled.

This does not mean that they were privy to everything. There is no evidence, for example, that they were privy to knowledge about the Joint "Lima Bravo" unit that arrived at 3:04 a.m. (more on that in a later chapter), moments after the shoot-down, nor is there any evidence that they knew anything about the seven mysterious Afghans who illegally entered the aircraft prior to takeoff. They did, however, sift through the aircraft wreckage for structural, engineering, chemical, and electrical forensic evidence regarding the shoot-down. The helicopter, after being shot down, was cut up, put on trucks, and physically removed, piece-by-piece from the shoot-down site, and taken to the Bagram Air Base in Afghanistan, where the JCAT unit did most of its work.

While Exhibit 60 still did not include any clues as to the identity of the seven mysterious Afghan invaders, it did prove some crucial forensics information and was frank in its assessment at times.

The JCAT report covered altitude, speed, the weapon used to bring down the chopper, and point of origin of the attack. All JCAT-compiled evidence suggested that Extortion 17 was about to land when it was shot down.

At page 6, and this evidence is crucial, the report noted that the chopper was between 100 and 150 feet above the ground, and that it had slowed its air speed to "less than 50 knots." Converted to miles-per-hour, 50 knots is approximately 57 miles per hour. Less than 50 knots could be 40 knots. It could be 30 knots. It could be 10 knots.

It should be noted that the evidence at page 6, noting air speed to "less than 50 knots" is even slower than the estimate, previously referred to at page 52 of Exhibit 53, where one of the Apache pilots testified in the transcript that the chopper had slowed her airspeed to "80 knots or less."

It's possible that the Apache pilot's moment-in-time observation of "80 knots or less" may have occurred seconds before the chopper continued her deceleration to "50 knots or less."

It's also possible that eyeball estimations of speed may not have been critically accurate.

Nevertheless, whether we go with "80 knots or less" from Exhibit 53, or the "50 knots or less" estimate, the somewhat common phrases among the two estimates are the phrases "or less" and "less than," making it apparent that the aircraft during this timeframe was flying at a relative slow rate of speed and was probably decelerating.

The report did not say how much slower than fifty knots Extortion 17 was flying, but we know that it was slower than 57 miles an hour at this point. Even given the fastest estimate within the "less than 50 knots" estimate, the chopper was flying slower than most cars travel on interstate highways.

In another part of the report at page 60, the JCAT team reported that Extortion 17 was 50 meters (54 yards) from FA site (Final Approach Site). This down-and-distance finding is crucial in understanding why the RPG was fired when it was.

Go back to the testimony on the size of the spotlight being shot down on the landing zone. Remember that General Colt asked the Apache crews about the size of the ground area being illuminated: "And how big is the box when they are doing that?"

The co-pilot of the second Apache replied "A football field." And then the pilot of Gun 1, the first Apache, chimed in. "I would say 500 meters or so. It's pretty big." And the navigator of the AC-130 said, at page 48 of Exhibit 40, "Our burn is probably roughly the equivalent to the size of a football field."

Do the math. A football field is 100 yards. Based on this, if a player were to stand on the 50-yard-line of a 100-yard football field (the midpoint), he would be 50 yards from one end zone, and 50 yards from the other end zone.

Likewise, if the Taliban insurgent was standing at the midpoint of the landing zone, right in the very center of the burn being flashed down by the AC-130, that means he would have to walk at least 50 yards in either direction to walk out from under the spotlight.

At the time it was struck, the chopper was 54 yards from the midpoint landing zone. That's an approximation, of course, and the estimate might be slightly off either way by a few yards.

That means the chopper, at 54 yards out, if that estimate were exactly correct, would be 4 yards from entering the perimeter of the spotlight being shone down from the AC-130.

Of course if the calculation is repeated with the second co-pilot's estimate about the size of the burn zone, at 500 meters (546 yards divided by 2 = 273 yards from center point of landing zone) that means the chopper was now clearly inside the landing zone and under the bright infrared spotlight being beamed down.

But based on the 54-yard estimate, and given approximately 50 yards of light to the center point of the landing zone, the evidence suggested that Extortion 17 was probably just breaking into the spotlight at the time the RPG was fired. This explains why the RPG was fired when it was fired. The chopper had just broken into the lights, and the Taliban insurgent started firing away the second it became visible, which would have been at least 50–54 yards from the center of the spotted landing zone.

Now a Chinook doesn't have a tail rotor blade like most helicopters. Instead, it has twin main rotor blades, one in the front and one in the back. Looking at the Chinook from above, it is easy to see that there are three rotor blades in the front, all conjoined at a fixed, spinning axis, like a three-bladed fan, and the same is true for the back.

So from the top, the blade configurations, in both the front and back of the big helicopter, look almost like a "Peace" symbol, as can be seen in this diagram of the rotor blade configuration system of the Chinook.

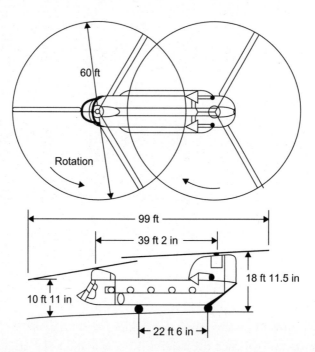

That means the chopper, at the instant of its demise, was going very low, and very slow. Reports show that the second rocket-propelled grenade struck the black rotary blade of the helicopter, a blade that is about 30 feet long.

The wingspan of each blade system is about sixty feet across the swirling circle, and the distance from the front tip of the front blade to the back tip of the back blade is about one hundred feet.

This means that if the Taliban was shooting with a RPG, and no one in the military has claimed that anything but an RPG was used, the terrorist was firing at a target of 99 feet long (front blade-tip to back blade-tip) and 60 feet wide (side blade-tip to side blade-tip).

If the shooter was up-close to the target, say at point-blank range, that's a pretty good-size target. But if he backed off a half-mile or more, hitting 99 feet by 60 feet would have become more like hitting a needle in a haystack.

The fatal shot that brought down the chopper struck in the back blades and blew up, destabilizing the aircraft, breaking her apart into three parts, sending it quickly to the ground below. The diagram below, showing the angle at which the RPG struck the back rotor blade of the chopper, was taken from page 14 of the JCAT report (Exhibit 60 of Colt Report). The JCAT was able to determine this angle because they examined the blade and ran tests on it.

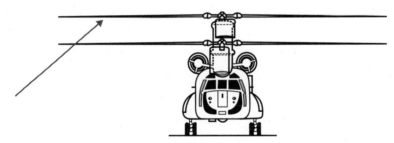

Now just how close was the Taliban attacker to Extortion 17? Imagine being up in the air, looking straight at the front of the helicopter, and it's approaching at eye level at the time it's struck by the fatal RPG.

CALCULATION WITH CHOPPER 100 FEET ABOVE GROUND WHEN STRUCK

Remember that the JCAT report (Exhibit 60, page 6 of the Colt Report) estimated that at this point the chopper was, when struck by the RPG, between 100 and 150 feet above the ground.

The blades in this diagram are 60 feet from left to right. If you double the blade length, it becomes 120 feet. To get an idea for the approximate distance the attacker was from the helicopter, and for greater simplicity of calculation, assume the arrow was striking the blade at 100 feet off the ground.

Here, apply some simple geometric principles, using the Pythagorean theorem to get some ballpark estimates.

Take a look at the right triangle shown below.

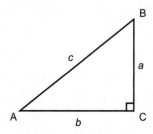

Now compare this to the diagram shown in the Colt Report. By analogy, point "B" would be the point at which the RPG struck the helicopter blade.

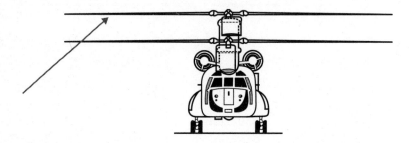

Point "C" is the ground, which is 100 feet below point "B."

From the diagram in the report itself, the tip of the arrow represents capital "B," the point of attack.

POINT OF IMPACT – "B"

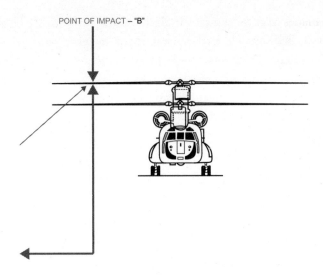

Here the triangle comes together as shown on page 14 of Exhibit 60. The ground under the chopper is capital "C," called "ground zero," because this is the point directly under the chopper at the moment of impact.

By extrapolation, and based on the angle of attack shown in the JCAT report, Point "A" would mark the position from which the shots were fired, based upon the angle that the RPG struck.

SHOTS FIRED

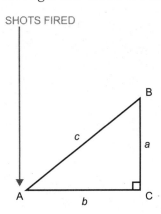

The distance between Point "A" (origin of shot) and Point "B" (point of impact) runs along the hypotenuse of the triangle. Remember from high school geometry class that the hypotenuse is the longest side of a triangle.

Remember also there's a formula for calculating the distance of the hypotenuse. That's the old Pythagorean theorem, which is $a^2 + b^2 = c^2$, with c as the hypotenuse and a and b as the two shorter sides of the triangle.

In this case, the hypotenuse is going to be the actual distance that the RPG traveled in the air before it struck the blade of Extortion 17.

Look at the model triangle again:

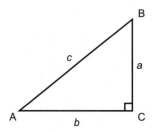

The capital "B" represents the position of the helicopter (Extortion 17). The small "c" is the hypotenuse, and represents the angle and distance that the RPG traveled to strike the helicopter. Also remember that the three interior angles of a triangle must add up to 180 degrees.

Again, the position at capital "C" (ground zero) marks the position on the ground just below Extortion 17 the moment it was struck by the RPG.

The small "a" and the small "b" are the "legs" of the triangle, and the small "a" represents the distance between the helicopter at the point of impact and the ground, *which the Combat Assessment Team determined to be between 100 and 150 feet* (Exhibit 60, page 6).

All triangles have 180 degrees total. In this triangle, the interior angle at Point "C"—ground level under Extortion 17 (ground zero), is 90 degrees (a right angle).

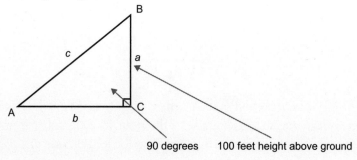

90 degrees   100 feet height above ground

That leaves a total of 90 degrees to work with using the remaining interior angles, which are the key to determining the length of leg "b" (distance from shooter to ground zero) and the hypotenuse "c" (distance from shooter to blade of helicopter).

In the diagram provided at page 14 of Exhibit 60, it appears that the interior angles at "A" (position of shooter) and "B" (point of impact) are each about 45 degrees.

Actually, that's not far off. On page 28 of exhibit 60, the interior angle at the point of impact "B" was given as approximately 50 degrees. The report showed that the *"(S) Weapon angle of impact was approximately 40° relative to the bottom surface of the blade"* [author's emphasis].

In other words, from the bottom surface of the blade to the line of attack by the RPG (the hypotenuse of the triangle), there was an angle of 40 degrees.

Now the blade, which was spinning horizontally, and the line down to ground zero intersect and form a right triangle of 90 degrees, mirroring the right triangle at ground zero (point "C").

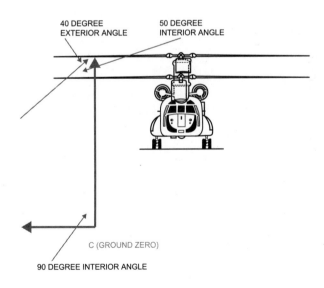

Let's look at our triangle again.

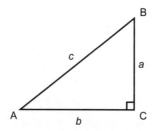

So to review, the interior angle at "B" (point of impact) is 50 degrees. The interior angle at C (ground zero) is 90 degrees, because it's a right angle. The interior angle at A (position of shooter) is by deduction 40 degrees, because we've already used up 140 degrees (90 at ground zero plus 50 at point of impact) leaving only 40 degrees.

With the length of "a" and the interior angle of "B" (50 degrees), the distance from the shooter to the chopper can be computed using the basic trigonometric principles of sine, cosine, and tangent.

The tangent of 50 degrees is 1.19. Remember that the known height "a" from ground zero (Point C) to the point of impact (Point B) is 100 feet.

To determine distance from ground zero to the shooter (line "b"), multiply 1.19 by 100 (length of "a"). 100 x 1.19 = 119 feet.

So now we know that the shooter was lurking only 119 feet from ground zero, at the time he fired the RPG that brought the chopper down.

Stop and consider this for a moment. Remember that the blades on that chopper were 120 feet all the way across, so that means they extended 60 feet out from the axis.

The shooter, assuming Extortion 17 was at a height 100 feet above ground, was on the ground 119 feet away from ground zero. But the choppers' blades extend 60 feet each way out from the spinning axis being driven by the rear engine. That means that the shooter was so close to the chopper's flight path that he could have been as close as 59 feet to being directly under the rotation of the blade!

That math is easy to calculate. 119 feet distance, shooter to ground zero minus 60-foot radius of the blade, leaves you with 59 feet. That's how close the shooter was to being almost directly under the chopper as it landed.

On August 10, 2011, four days after the shoot-down, the UK *Daily Mail* quoted an Afghan governmental official as saying that the Taliban was tipped off as to the mission, that the Taliban knew the flight path, and that the chopper was lured to the landing zone.

> He (an Afghan government official) said that Taliban commander Qari Tahir lured US forces to the scene by tipping them off that a Taliban meeting was taking place.
>
> He also said four Pakistanis helped Tahir carry out the strike.
>
> "Now it's confirmed that the helicopter was shot down and it was a trap that was set by a Taliban commander," said the official, citing intelligence gathered from the area.

That same report, that the Taliban had knowledge of the flight of Extortion 17, followed in one of the other major British dailies, the UK *Telegraph*.

Bear in mind this is not the Taliban crowing. It's the British press quoting the Afghan government.

If the chopper were lured in by baited information on Tahir's location, that would explain how the Taliban got off such a point-blank shot. And the math above shows that the shot was about as point-blank as you can get, which proves that (a) the *Daily Mail* report that the Taliban was tipped off on Extortion 17's flight plan from the inside was probably correct, and (b) that the position in General Colt's Executive Summary later adopted by the Defense Department, that the RPG was fired from a tower 220 meters (720 feet) away, is mathematically impossible.

Now moving on in our calculations, there's still one number missing, and that's the length of the hypotenuse, or "c," which will show the actual distance between the shooter and the helicopter. Remember that General Colt claimed 220 meters or 720 feet (beyond the effective range of the RPG).

But now apply the Pythagorean theorem, $a^2 + b^2 = c^2$, to get an idea of just what a point-blank shot this was.

The small "a" is the distance from the helicopter blade to ground zero. Using 100 feet, because the JCAT estimated between 100 and 150 feet above the ground at the moment of attack, a^2 is 100 times 100 or 10,000.

Now the small "b" is the distance from the ground (directly under the helicopter) where the terrorist fired the RPG. Based upon the earlier calculations using the tangent of 50 degrees, this distance is 119 feet.

Therefore, since b is 119 feet, b^2 is 14,161.

Now adding a^2 (10,000) plus b^2 (14,161) yields c^2 (24,161).

To get the estimated distance of line c, the hypotenuse of the triangle, take the square root of 24,161. The square root of 24,161 is about 155!

Therefore, if Extortion 17 were 100 feet off the ground, given the approximate angle as diagrammed by the JCAT team, the Taliban insurgent was probably about 155 feet (51 yards) away when he fired.

Remember, General Colt claimed the distance at 220 meters or 720 feet. But the math, assuming 100 feet off the ground as determined in the JCAT report, shows a distance of one-fifth that at 155 feet. The figure in the Executive Summary was a gross exaggeration.

CALCULATION WITH CHOPPER 150 FEET ABOVE GROUND WHEN STRUCK

Assuming the chopper was 150 feet off the ground, the other end of the range, applying the same tangent and applying the Pythagorean theorem, the ground distance between the shooter and ground zero is 178 feet, and the actual distance, along the hypotenuse, is 227 feet.

That means the maximum distance that the shooter could have been from Extortion was 178 feet, not 720 feet as Brigadier Colt suggested.

Again, the gross exaggeration of distance-to-shooter is important to supporting the "we did nothing wrong" narrative, which in fact may have a larger purpose, not only to defend foolish rules of engagement, but also to hide the truth about Taliban infiltration of this mission.

So these calculations show an approximate range of distance-to-shooter between 155 feet (51 yards), if the chopper were 100 feet off the ground, to 227 feet (75 yards), if the chopper were 150 feet off the ground.

Just as significant is the shooter's even closer distance to ground zero. The math showed that the shooter was only 119 feet to ground zero (assuming the chopper was 100 feet off the ground) to 178 to ground zero (assuming the chopper was 150 feet off the ground).

This super-close distance will become more relevant in later discussions of the military's failure to clear out the landing zone with pre-assault fire, something it easily could have done.

What would be the chances that Extortion 17 would just happen to fly within 75 yards of a Taliban insurgent waiting with an RPG, unless the Taliban insurgent knew in advance exactly where Extortion 17 was going to land?

About as likely as finding a needle in a haystack.

Clearly, the Taliban shooter was waiting at or near the landing zone, most likely tipped off by someone who knew Extortion 17's flight path, as the UK *Daily Mail* reported.

Remember also that it's mathematically impossible that the shot could have come from some building 220 meters away, not only because the math doesn't add up, but because the military's own JCAT (Exhibit 60, page 37) report shows that the maximum effective range of the RPG is 170 meters. Also even if the insurgent had night vision goggles, the range on those goggles is limited. In fact, under the limited lighting circumstances that night, and given that the chopper was operating with its lights off, it would be virtually impossible for him to have seen Extortion 17 from 220 meters (720) feet away, let alone get off an accurate shot with an RPG already out of range.

CHAPTER 30

Testimony of Apache Pilots and Pitch-Black Conditions

The testimony of the two Apache gunships accompanying Extortion 17 underscored just how dark conditions were at the time of shoot-down, and how difficult it was even for US helicopters with night vision goggles to keep track of Extortion 17.

In examining this interchange between the Apache pilots, it's important to understand that the Apache call signs were Pitch Black 65 (Gun 1), and Pitch Black 70 (Gun 2). PB65FS is the Front Seat Pilot in the Apache referred to as Gun 1. PB65FS is the acronym for "Pitch Black 65 Front Seat." PB65BS is the Back Seat Pilot in the Apache referred to as Gun 1. PB65BS is the acronym for "Pitch Black 65 Back Seat."

The first testimonial exchange, at page 34 of Exhibit 53, was between the co-pilot of Gun 2, call sign Pitch Black 70, about the dark conditions:

BG COLT: *Right. What was 17's light configuration when he came inbound?*

PB70FS: *He was dark. He was really hard to see. I think they would have the pink light on in the Chinooks or something like that. And they would have their IR strobes on bright. So they were always easy to pick up.*

Well, (Extortion 17) doesn't fly around like that. They were actually—they were real hard for us to find.

More testimony is presented at page 53 of Exhibit 53, this time from the co-pilot of Gun 1, call sign Pitch Black 65 [author's emphasis].

PB65FS: *Where the point of impact was, Juy Zarrin [an Afghan village] was directly to the north. And, yes, that could have silhouetted them. We were literally under goggles. It was red alone.* We were having a hard time seeing them due to the fact it was dark and they were dark.

A third exchange appears at pages 54-55 of Exhibit 53, this time from the lead of Gun 1, call sign Pitch Black 65 [author's emphasis].

PB65BS: *Based on where it was, there might have been enough light to silhouette the helicopter to give whoever the shooter was a better idea of the area to aim at.* But at least unaided, it never appeared that there was a significant light source of any kind that would silhouette a perfect shape of an aircraft.

Note the consistent theme: Extortion 17 was blacked out to the point that even the American pilots accompanying them, wearing night vision goggles, were having a difficult time seeing the aircraft.

How could some Taliban insurgent, way off at a distance of 220 meters, see the helicopter well enough to aim a RPG launcher at it, fire, and have that RPG strike at a distance beyond its maximum effective range?

THE LINE OF SIGHT PROBLEM

The aerial photograph on page 174 shows the terrain between the point of attack and the alleged origin of the shot to be full of trees.

There was a field of trees between the "qualat," the building from which General Colt claims the shot was fired, and the shoot-down point. Additionally, there was a line of trees along the "wadi," beyond the tree line, separating the low-flying chopper from Colt's proposed position for the origin of shots. So there was zero visibility, and there was a field of

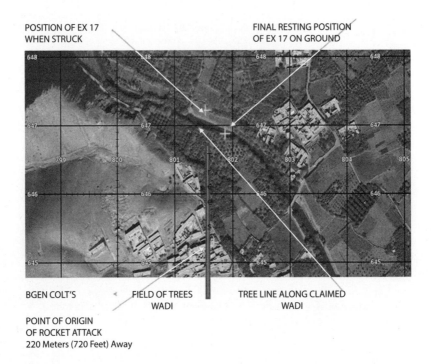

POSITION OF EX 17
WHEN STRUCK

FINAL RESTING POSITION
OF EX 17 ON GROUND

BGEN COLT'S

FIELD OF TREES
WADI

TREE LINE ALONG CLAIMED
WADI

POINT OF ORIGIN
OF ROCKET ATTACK
220 Meters (720 Feet) Away

trees in between the shooter and the chopper, which was only 100 to 150 feet off the ground.

The trees in the field were not extremely tall trees, but they were tall enough to provide not only an additional visual obstruction, especially under pitch-black conditions, but also to make it impossible for the RPG to have come in and struck the blade at a 50-degree angle.

The photograph on page 175 is found at page 21 of the Exhibit 60, and was taken later in the day following the shoot-down. If the RPG had been fired from where Brigadier General Colt claims, some 722 feet beyond this tree line, then the grenade would have cleared the tops of these trees, then would have had to strike the chopper at a 50-degree angle, which as noted earlier is mathematically impossible given an above-ground altitude of 100 to 150 feet.

Remember, the chopper was 100 to 150 feet above the ground. These trees were not that tall. But they were much taller than a man,

and therefore, were tall enough to create an additional visual obstruction for the shooter standing 722 feet away, and create an additional aiming obstruction, even if the conditions were not pitch-black outside.

It's not like the shooter, under the Colt claim, would have been aiming across the wide-open space of a desert, or across flat, open water with no obstruction. There were plenty of visual obstructions.

To get a better idea of the obstruction that the trees created, imagine for a moment that you're looking through these trees, out in the other direction, in pitch-black darkness, trying to see a helicopter about 720 feet (two-and-a-half football fields) away, flying from left to right, only 100 feet off the ground.

It would be impossible to see that chopper, or even aim at it, given the distance, the obstructions, and the dark conditions, even with a weapon that would effectively shoot that far.

Remember, here again is the diagram of the angle of attack, taken straight out of the military's JCAT report.

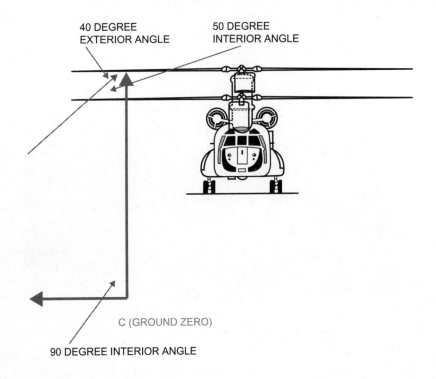

Again, it's plain from this angle, even without doing the mathematical calculations, that the RPG could never have cleared the trees, and especially not if the chopper is only 100 to 150 feet off the ground.

❦

Now to recap the evidence proving that General Colt's distance-to-shooter claim of "220 meters from a building" was clearly false. First, the effective range of the RPG, per the JCAT report (Exhibit 60) was only 170 meters. So the RPG was not in range of the chopper at 220 meters, even if the Taliban had been able to see the chopper and get a shot off from that distance.

Second, light conditions were pitch-black, so dark, in fact, that not even the US pilots in the Apache helicopters accompanying Extortion 17 could easily see it, even with sophisticated night vision goggles.

Third, the principles of mathematics work against Colt's claim. Flying at 100 to 150 feet above the ground, with the RPG striking its blade from a 50-degree angle, approximate range of distance-to-shooter along the hypotenuse of that triangle ranges from 155 feet (51 yards), if the chopper were 100 feet off the ground, to 227 feet (75 yards), if the chopper were 150 feet off the ground.

Just as significant is the shooter's even closer distance to ground zero. The math showed that the shooter was only 119 feet to ground zero (with the chopper 100 feet off the ground) to 178 feet to ground zero (with the chopper 150 feet off the ground).

Fourth, trees on the ground and along the wadi, located between the "building" from which Colt claims the RPG was fired and the helicopter, would have made the chopper even more difficult to see from 220 meters, and a straight line-of-fire even more difficult to attain at 220 meters (720 feet).

Fifth, the JCAT report, after assessing all the data on the issue, concluded, "Point of origin was never positively identified or actioned" (Exhibit 60, page 42). In fact, the JCAT report, on the very same page, also concluded that "Participating aircrews were not aware EX 17 was being fired upon until it was hit."

All of this undercuts Colt's claim that the RPG was fired from 220 meters away. That dubious claim was being made, most likely, to try and deflect criticism against the military and the Obama Administration for the foolish rules of engagement that prevented pre-assault fire that could have saved Extortion 17.

This leads to the question—where was the RPG fired from?

Given the tight angle, probably along the tree-lined banks of the wadi. Under pitch-black conditions, the Taliban would have to have been that close to get off a point-blank shot, and the math suggests that they were in fact that close.

CHAPTER 31

Extortion 17 and the Earlier Ranger Mission

After reviewing Extortion 17's odd and repeated delays, the sparkle vs. burn confusion, and its apparent stall in the air, one thing seems clear: the helicopter's odd behavior does not add up.

Isn't it interesting that just prior to its shoot-down, Extortion 17 was the only aircraft in the sky over the Tangi Valley that could not locate the landing zone? The Apache helicopter gunships knew exactly where the landing zone was. The AC-130 fixed-wing gunship circling 7,000 feet overhead knew exactly where it was.

Of course those other aircraft knew where the landing zone was. In an age of guided-precision GPS that allows smart bombs to find their targets with absolute accuracy and precision when launched from a thousand miles away, landing on the eye of a needle, it is impossible to envision a realistic scenario under which Extortion 17 should have had difficulty finding the landing zone.

Yet Extortion 17 indicated that it was having trouble lining up with the landing zone, claiming that "our lane direction isn't matching up" and the sparkle was to "give them [whoever 'them' is] a little better idea where we're landing."

None of this makes sense in the computerized GPS era, and suggests the aircraft had been infiltrated. It smacks of a pilot trying to stall, perhaps for self-preservation purposes.

Recall that this final, fatal flight was not Extortion 17's only mission that night. Earlier in the evening, before its mission with the SEAL team, the chopper dropped off a platoon of US Army Rangers several clicks (kilometers) outside the battle zone, meaning that it did not fly over "hot" air space where Taliban RPGs posed a direct threat.

So naturally, one might wonder, "Did Extortion 17 have all those problems finding the landing zone when it dropped off the Rangers earlier in the evening?"

The answer: absolutely not. The chronology of the earlier flight showed the chopper approaching the Rangers' landing zone with no problems finding it. The pilot radioed his approach on time, executed the landing on time, infiltrated the Rangers, then took off and flew back to Base Shank to await his next mission, which, unfortunately, would be his last.

Here is the chronology from Extortion 17's earlier mission (the Ranger mission), laid out in Enclosure H, at page 2 [author's emphasis]:

> *2253 EX 17 depart Sayyid Abad for*
> *2254 EX 17 reports 6 minutes to infill (3)*
> *2256 EX 17 reports 3 minutes to infill (3)*
> 2258 EX 17 wheels down at (3)
> *2259 EX 17 infill complete (3)*
> *2300 EX 17 depart, en-route FOB (3)*
> *2308 EX 17 arrival FOB, assume casualty alert posture (19)*
> 2323 1/B reports arrival at CP1 (19)
> *2327 While ground force conducts movement toward Objective area, positively identifies (PID) eight (8) insurgents with RPGs and AK-47s (3)*

Note that Extortion 17 made timely call-ins, and there are no unexplained delays, nor any requests for sparkles.

Extortion 17, under the command of Bryan Nichols, had absolutely no trouble locating the landing zone for the Rangers. The pre-landing calls were radioed in on time.

On Extortion 17's first mission of the evening, there were no delays. There was no indecisiveness on the part of the pilot. There were no requests for a sparkle. There were no radio transmissions from Bryan

Nichols requesting the sparkle to "give *them* a better idea of where we're landing." There were no odd comments from Bryan Nichols indicating that "Lane direction not matching up."

As a matter of fact, Extortion 17's first mission, infiltrating the Army Rangers, *ran so smoothly that the landing took place one minute ahead of schedule.*

How could Nichols have displayed such crisp precision on the first mission of the evening with the Rangers, then showed such odd indecision, and what appears to be borderline incompetence during the second mission involving the SEALs?

As mentioned earlier Nichols and Carter were not Special Forces pilots, and they were not trained in the same way as the aviators of the 160th Special Operations Airborne Regiment out of Fort Campbell, Kentucky. They did not have the same type of training for low, fast-speed approaches as did Special Forces pilots, nor did they pilot the Special Forces helicopters that would have allowed them to pull off this type of mission.

But the ability to simply find and approach a landing zone, using GPS navigation, is not an ability that is unique just to Special Forces aviators.

Bryan Nichols clearly possessed the ability to land his aircraft on target, in a timely manner, and with crisp precision, as he proved in the first infiltration that night involving US Army Rangers.

So logic dictates that the second mission—involving the SEALs—shows a pilot that for whatever reason did not have full control of his aircraft. Nichols had proven himself earlier in the evening, and the more experienced co-pilot David Carter could have put that helicopter down on the head of a dime in his sleep.

Something went terribly wrong inside that helicopter, and whatever went wrong was most likely beyond the pilots' control.

This draws our attention right back on the pink elephant in the room—namely the seven unidentified Afghans who infiltrated Extortion 17, and whose names have not been released.

Did Bryan Nichols suddenly forget how to fly? Did he forget how to find a landing zone?

Of course not.

Frankly, the bizarre behavior exhibited by Extortion 17 on its final, fateful mission was the behavior of an aircraft that was under siege from forces within.

Could this be the reason that the Executive Summary of the Colt Report does not mention the seven Afghans at all? Or, could this be the reason that the Joint Special Operations Task Force commander abruptly cut off the J3 (operations officer) mid-sentence when he attempted to offer more information on the unidentified Afghans? Could this be the reason that the sergeant major, sitting in Billy and Karen Vaughn's Florida home, in the presence of Admiral McRaven, told the Vaughns that the Afghans getting on that aircraft without being properly identified on the manifest was a "very big deal"?

Were they trying to hide the politically embarrassing fact that this flight was, or could have been, compromised by Taliban infiltrators determined to help sabotage it from the inside, or to communicate with Taliban forces on the ground about the choppers approach to coordinate the timing of a point-blank shot?

The military's attempted secrecy on this matter, combined with the inexplicably erratic behavior of the helicopter in the air on its final mission, suggest that there is a cause-and-effect relationship here, and that the presence of the seven Afghans may have been a cause of the chopper stalling, delaying, and making odd requests (for a sparkle) and comments ("Lane direction not matching up") just before the shoot-down.

Bryan Nichols and David Carter were not blind mice flying in the dark. They could have, and should have, been able to land that helicopter on time, had they not been interfered with.

Moreover, the chronology on the first flight of Extortion 17 (the Rangers flight) underscores another important point about where the Rangers were infiltrated when the helicopter landed. Remember, at paragraph 3 of his Executive Summary, Brigadier General Colt stated, "The aircrew, having flown into the valley only hours before to insert the initial force, was the most familiar aircrew available to effectively carry out this mission."

With this statement, Colt implied that the flight path taken by Extortion 17 in both its first and second missions was the same, and that the level of danger was the same in both flights.

But this is not accurate. In fact, the second mission involved a far more dangerous flight path than the first. Look at Enclosure H, beginning at 10:59 p.m. (2259), the moment the Rangers had completed exiting the aircraft.

> *2259 EX 17 infill complete (3)*
>
> *2300 EX 17 depart, en-route FOB (3)*
>
> *2308 EX 17 arrival FOB, assume casualty alert posture (19)*
>
> *2323 1/B reports arrival at CP1 (19)*
>
> *2327 While ground force conducts movement toward objective area, positively identifies (PID) eight (8) insurgents with RPGs and AK-47s (3)*

The Rangers "infiltrate" (step off the chopper and onto the ground) at 10:59 p.m., and one minute later, at 11:00 p.m. (2300), Extortion 17 took off and headed back to Base Shank. Translated, "EX 17 depart" means Extortion 17 had taken off, and "en-route FOB" means that the helicopter was en route to Forward Operating Base Shank, where it would soon pick up the SEAL team.

Now take a look at the last entry from this section, at 11:27 p.m. (2327), twenty-seven minutes after Extortion 17 has dropped off the Rangers and taken off and headed back to Base Shank.

Note that the ground force, the same ground force of Rangers that Extortion 17 just put on the ground, was conducting "movement toward (the) objective area." What does that mean? Well if the ground force was moving "toward (the) objective area," that means that the ground force had been moving for nearly thirty minutes on foot, and they still hadn't reached the objective area yet. That's because Extortion 17 on this mission (the Ranger mission) did not fly into or over the objective area, but in fact, dropped the Rangers off several clicks (kilometers) behind the battle zone (objective area), and left the Rangers to move into the danger zone on foot.

Note too, that the Rangers had moved on foot for twenty-seven minutes before they even spotted enemy forces, as noted in the language stating, "positively identifies (PID) eight (8) insurgents with RPGs and AK-47s (3)." That means that Extortion 17, on its earlier "Ranger mission" did not fly the Rangers over a hot zone occupied by RPG-bearing Taliban as later happened with the SEALs, *but dropped the Rangers off several kilometers behind the lines.* It took the Rangers half an hour before they had even seen a Taliban fighter with an RPG.

So, Colt was either intentionally obscuring the truth (likely) or was woefully uninformed about the earlier mission (highly unlikely) when he implied that the same degree of danger applied to both the first and second missions.

The SEALs were later flown over a hot valley, where Taliban forces were waiting with RPGs to shoot down a US helicopter, and the Army knew this at the time the mission was ordered. Put another way, the Rangers' flight path was a flight into the park. The SEALs' flight path, later in the evening, was a flight into a buzz saw.

To make matters worse, they ordered Extortion 17 to carry these SEALs into a buzz saw, but set rules of engagement to prevent the aircraft accompanying the SEALs from attacking Taliban on the ground—a subject covered in more depth in the following chapters.

CHAPTER 32

The Rules of Engagement: Groundwork for the Death of Thirty Americans

For those unfamiliar with the military, the rules of engagement are the rules under which US military forces are authorized to use force against an enemy.

Almost always, commanders have standing rules of engagement to fire if fired upon. But in other circumstances, US military forces are not allowed to fire against an enemy unless given permission from higher-ups in the military chain of command.

One sub-element in the rules of engagement is an option called "pre-assault fire." When pre-assault fire is authorized, it is usually designed to clear the ground for an American landing force and minimize loss of life. Put another way, a lack of pre-assault fire often creates the most danger-ous situation for American forces attempting to land in hostile zones. The pre-assault fire can (a) kill enemy insurgents who are waiting to kill Americans about to land, or (b) drive enemy insurgents away from the landing zone, far enough away so that their guns are not within reach of American forces.

Perhaps the most famous example of pre-assault fire in American military history occurred on D-day, June 6, 1944, when Allied naval forces began bombarding the beaches at Normandy to soften the beachhead, to make way for amphibious and infantry forces about to hit the beaches.

In helicopter assaults, such as the one attempted by Extortion 17, often other aircraft will begin firing into the landing zone prior to the arrival of the helicopter carrying the landing force, for the purpose of, again, (a) killing enemy insurgents who are waiting to kill Americans about to land, or (b) driving enemy insurgents away from the landing zone, far enough away so that their guns are not within reach of American forces.

Put simply, these SEALs and the aircrew were probably killed because the rules of engagement set down by the US military did not allow for pre-assault fire to protect the SEAL team as it approached the landing zone.

There were three aircraft accompanying Extortion 17 that were capable of delivering pre-assault fire. But these aircraft were not allowed to do so, because of the self-imposed American rules of engagement. These aircraft included the two AH-64 Apache helicopters, referred to collectively as the "Air Weapons Team," or AWT.

The third US aircraft capable of delivering pre-assault fire was the AC-130 gunship, which was orbiting about 7,000 feet above the landing zone. Both the Apaches and the AC-130 were denied by the rules of engagement of the ability to use pre-assault fire to clear the landing zone. In fact, the C-130 asked permission to fire against enemy forces on the ground, and was denied.

Enemy Taliban forces were all over the ground, in the vicinity of the landing zone. On the night of the attack, Extortion 17's mission was in support of a military operation code-named Operation Lefty Grove.

This operation was executed with the purpose of killing or capturing a Taliban terrorist leader named Qari Tahir. Two groups of US Special Forces were designated as part of the operations plan to capture or kill Tahir.

The first group, a platoon of US Army Rangers, was designated as the Initial Assault Force (IAF), and was the principal Special Forces group, and if things went well, the only Special Forces group that would be involved in the operation. The two CH-47D Chinooks, Extortion 16 and Extortion 17, had flown the Ranger group, the IAF, to the edge of the combat zone earlier in the evening. Then, the Chinooks flew back to Forward Operating Base Shank, where they remained on standby.

The second group, the Navy SEAL group that died on Extortion 17, was designated as an Immediate Reaction Force (IRF). The Immediate Reaction Force was designated as "reactionary" because it was not planned to be part of the operation. It was to be called into action to "react" if something went wrong. The reactionary force was on the ground to bail out the Rangers if the Rangers got into trouble.

Indeed, during the first couple of days after the shoot-down, the American press reported that the SEAL team had been deployed aboard Extortion 17 to "rescue" the Ranger team that according to their erroneous reporting had been "pinned down." In other words, numerous press outlets reported a story that would have fit the SEALs' planned role on this mission. But as it turns out, the press's initial reports that the SEALs were deployed to save the Rangers were not true.

In fact, the SEALs were deployed to find Qari Tahir, and in doing so, Extortion 17 flew right over the top of enemy forces on the ground moving north, actually moving away from the Ranger platoon, toward a "compound" in which the terrorist leader, Qari Tahir was believed to be near the landing zone that was targeted.

CHAPTER 33

Enemy "Squirters" on the Ground Prior to Shoot-Down

There were enemy insurgents all over the ground prior to the shoot-down, and those enemy insurgents posed a grave concern to the aircraft accompanying Extortion 17.

The word "squirters" appeared throughout Exhibit 1 (initial interview of Joint Task Force commander, operations officer, and others), Exhibit 40 (interview of AC-130 aircrew), Exhibit 54 (helicopter gun tape) and other exhibits.

Basically, a "squirter" in Afghan war parlance means an enemy combatant (Taliban) on the ground. In fact, at pages 97–98 of Exhibit 1, the J3 officer, the operations officer of the Joint Special Operations Task Force, defined squirters as "enemy combatants based on hostile intent that they assessed."

Remember that this same officer, the J3, was the guy who started to provide an analysis of why seven unidentified Afghans were allowed to board Extortion 17, and then was abruptly cut off by his boss, the Joint Special Operations Task Force commander.

A good portion of the conversation on the Apache gun tape (Exhibit 54) leading up to the shoot-down of Extortion 17 involved keeping track of squirters on the ground.

As Extortion 17 was attempting to fly into landing position, all three other aircraft with offensive capabilities, the two Apaches and the AC-130 Gunship, were talking constantly about the position of these enemy combatants, aka squirters, moving all over the ground.

At Exhibit 53, page 29, General Colt asked the Apache crews about their surveillance of the landing zone and whether they were actually watching Extortion 17 as it approached the Landing Zone. The co-pilot of the Apache helicopter known as Gun 1 testified that he was watching squirters on the ground and, even up to the time Extortion 17 was attempting to land, was concerned about safety considerations on the ground right up to landing [author's emphasis].

General Colt: *And that point you had already made a definitive LZ (Landing Zone) reconnaissance. Just tell us about, in your eyes, what you felt you saw. We, obviously, have the gun tape, so we captured that. But in your own thoughts now, what do you think about the posture of in the surrounding area? What did you observe?*

PB65FS (Apache Co-Pilot): *From Gun 1—I will let Gun 2 speak. But Gun 1, my biggest threat was the squirters. So I never put eyes on [Extortion 17]. I was more worried about finding the squirters that would pose a threat to our guys when they were landing or when they were infilling the aircraft. Gun 2 had made COMMs, and had eyes on the LZ. But I was still trying to get eyes on the threat. I mean, that was up until they started giving 6, 3, and 1-minute calls.*

The co-pilot's concern continued at page 34 of exhibit 53:

PB65FS (Apache Co-Pilot):—*because we were inside the valley, and we knew that they were outside the valley. Honestly, they were outside our area. And we were so worried about the squirters and lead that it wasn't that important for us to know exactly where they [Extortion 17] were holding.*

Incredibly, despite the dangers that these enemy combatants on the ground posed to the approaching helicopter and despite the grave concern of the US pilots in aircraft accompanying Extortion 17 on its final mission, American military officials denied permission to the AC-130 gunship to attack them from the air and did not allow pre-assault fire into the landing zone, all of which might have saved the lives of the Extortion 17 crewmembers.

In the minutes leading up to the Extortion 17 shoot-down, the AC-130 *requested permission* to fire on enemy squirters on the ground. In this exchange from Exhibit 40, page 6 and 7, the question was being asked by the SME-JSOAC, who is the Special Missions Expert—Joint Special Operations Air Command. This officer was interviewing both the navigator and the pilot (commander) of the AC-130 gunship, *who both testify that they were prohibited (by the rules of engagement) from firing at the enemy on the ground* [author's emphasis]:

> **SME-JSOAC:** *So just to be able to provide fire support if needed. Is this your standard TTP? [TTP stands for Tactics, Technique, and Procedures]*
>
> **AIRCRAFT COMMANDER:** *Really quick an important point I think at this juncture is,* we had requested to engage those two individuals and we were denied—

Two pages later, at page 9 of Exhibit 40, the navigator of the AC-130 testified that the gunship was not allowed to fire on the enemy combatant squirters, but instead, was told to watch them on the ground and report their positions [author's emphasis]:

> **NAVIGATOR:** *Basically like we said we were passing periodic updates to the first one we passed was when the squirters were 200 meters away. . . .* They said they didn't want us to engage; what he passed to us was that they wanted to follow those guys and figure out where they stopped. *And then find out exactly where they were and then basically use that as follow-on after they were done clearing and securing the actual Lefty Grove site.*

Further evidence of the rules of engagement preventing pre-assault fire appeared at Exhibit 53 of the Colt Report. In this exhibit Colt and his team were interviewing five men, including the pilot and co-pilot of each of the two Apaches that were in the air with Extortion 17, and also

CALL SIGN EXTORTION 17

the Helicopter Task Force commander, the immediate boss of the four pilots being interviewed.

Consider this testimony from the co-pilot of one of the Apache helicopters (Gun 1), at pages 14–15, in response to a question from Brigadier General Colt about pre-assault fires:

Apache Co-Pilot: *"We have to take the 47s in on all the LZs . . . We are not cleared for pre-assault fires or anything like that . . ."*

The Ground Force Special Missions Expert then asked a follow-up question at page 69 of the exhibit, which generated this response, first from the helicopter task force commander at page 70: "And to get back to your question about pre-assault fires, the ROE and the tactical directorate are pretty specific about what we can and can't do." To this comment, the Ground Force Special Missions expert immediately responds, "From my experience, pre-assault fires are next to impossible."

In other words, even though the AC-130 gunship specifically requested permission for pre-assault fire, the rules of engagement prevented US military aircraft from clearing out the landing zone to ensure a safer landing for Extortion 17.

The purpose of this ludicrous rule, by the way, prohibiting pre-assault fire, was to appease the Afghan government, which had launched protests to the Obama Administration about the practices. The Administration acquiesced to that demand and ordered the US military to refrain from pre-assault fire, which was ultimately why the landing zone was not cleared of hostile RPG-toting Taliban insurgents, and why Bryan Nichols, David Carter, and the SEAL team members lost their lives that day.

CHAPTER 34

Hypocrisies and Inconsistencies in the Rules of Engagement

To further illustrate the ludicrousness of the US rules of engagement as set down by US military planners in Washington, and the haphazard application of those rules, the record shows that on two occasions, within two hours after the shoot-down, US helicopters were in fact firing rounds into the ground in the area of the attack. The first chopper provided post-assault fire that came seconds after the shoot-down (see below), and a second chopper poured pre-suppression fire into the landing area before US Army Pathfinders, dispatched to secure the wreck scene, landed on the ground (see next chapter).

In the emotional and adrenaline-charged seconds following the shoot-down, one of the Apache helicopters broke protocol, broke the rules of engagement, and opened fire into the ground, attempting to fire in the area of the RPG attack. This burst of fire came at 0240:18, just thirty seconds after the shoot-down at 0239:48 (Enclosure H, page 5).

In the exchange below, note what the pilot said, and note also, how in the aftermath, Brigadier General Colt seems to put the pilot on the defensive in his questioning of that decision to open fire.

At 22:11:43 Zulu time (2:41:43 a.m. local time), seconds after the shoot-down, the gun-tape (Exhibit 54) reveals the co-pilot of the Apache helicopter closest to Extortion 17 making these comments.

Roger, we are circling overhead. I saw where the [EXPLETIVE] explosion came from, man. I'm searching the buildings. If I see [EXPLETIVE] anybody with a weapon, I'm firing.

These comments on the gun tape were made one minute and twenty-five seconds after one of the Apaches first fired at 2:40:18 AM. The record isn't clear which of the Apaches fired first, and which fired second. All that is clear is that the Apaches did not fire until after the shoot-down.

But with Extortion 17 in flames on the ground, that Apache helicopters, either on or both of them, did, in fact, almost immediately open fire in the aftermath of the shooting. For that, the pilot was treated to a thorough cross-examination by Brigadier General Colt.

First off, note that Colt tried to frame his questions in a way that suggests that the squirters (enemy Taliban) who were spotted on the ground from overhead aircraft were not close enough to Extortion to pose a threat.

That supposition is rebuffed by the co-pilot of Apache 1, who testified that the squirters could have been at the landing zone site for Extortion 17 (Exhibit 53, pages 73–74).

BG COLT: *For clarification, you said "that's where the threat was." You are still referring to the Alpha and Bravo. But in your assessment from Alpha and Bravo, those forces at the time could not have applied effective fires against the aircraft on its approach to the LZ?*

Apache Co-Pilot: *Not the approach. But when they would have been at their LZ, they would have been within—from Bravo, I believe it was close to 600 meters . . . But those guys—the reason why we saw them as such a threat is because they had squirted from a place where [they] had just engaged six individuals that were heavily armed moving in a very military manner.*

So we assessed that these guys were trained military. They weren't just five guys that picked up a weapon for a weekend of fun. These guys were legitimately, to me, the real thing, and that's where we saw the threat.

It's very clear that the Apache crews viewed the squirters as mortal danger to Extortion 17.

Two points: First, neither the Apaches nor the AC-130 were allowed to fire against Taliban insurgents on the ground considered to be a threat to Extortion 17. These insurgents, by the way, were all over the ground, posing a threat to Extortion 17. They were not in some building 220 meters away.

Second, when the Apache fired immediately after Extortion 17 was shot down, General Colt grilled the Apache pilot as if the pilot were under cross-examination, asking the pilot if it was generally the pilot's procedure to engage a point of origin without positively identifying a target:

Consider this exchange, from page 40 of Exhibit 53:

BG COLT: *Is it a general TTP [tactics, techniques and procedures] of yours to engage a POO—or suppress, I should say, a POO without PIDing the target?*

   PB65FS: (Apache Co-Pilot): *Sir, I wouldn't say it's a TTP. I saw when they went down. And if there was any survivors, I wanted suppression fire to be placed where I thought the POO was.*

The Apache co-pilot's testimony went on to say that the Apache fired between seventy and one hundred rounds in the area near the downed chopper to prevent anyone from approaching it. The co-pilot testified that they believed that the RPGs might have been fired from a qualat, which is a primitive Afghan compound made of a mud-brick substance.

The implication from General Colt here was, "look, you shouldn't have fired unless you positively identified your targets as the enemy." Also, it was in the military's best interests to suggest that the RPG was fired some 220 meters away from a building. In this way, they can argue that their failure to allow pre-assault fire did not contribute to the SEAL team's deaths. In other words, "pre-assault fire wouldn't have helped because the shot was fired from out yonder." If the Apache pilot fired into the ground after the shoot-down, that suggests the shot might have been fired from somewhere other than the building 220 meters away. The military brass couldn't have that.

Again, there were contradictory reports from multiple witnesses about the true point of origin of the attack. The Combat Assessment Team at Bagram Air Base concluded that the "Point of origin was never positively identified or actioned" (Exhibit 60, page 42).

Regardless, the absurd point here is that the Apache was allowed to, or rather got away with, firing *after* the shoot-down, i.e., post-assault fire, but wasn't allowed to protect the SEALs by firing pre-assault rounds before the shoot-down.

CHAPTER 35

Indefensible Inconsistency: Pathfinders Get Pre-Assault Fire but SEALs Don't

Adding insult to injury, the US Army's Pathfinder team, the team that goes in to help secure the area on the ground after a crash or shoot-down of a US military aircraft, was, unlike the Navy SEAL team, protected with pre-assault fire before it landed. This occurred less than two hours after the shoot-down of the SEAL team, at 4:14 a.m. This was revealed in the interview of the Pathfinder commander, at Exhibit 65 of the Colt Report, and also at Enclosure H.

Remember that the shoot-down takes place at 239:48 a.m. (Enclosure H to Colt Report).

At 4:14 a.m., with the US Army Pathfinders unit now in helicopters approaching the landing zone adjacent to the downed Extortion 17, the UH-60 Black Hawk helicopters accompanying the Pathfinders poured pre-assault fire into the landing zone prior to the Pathfinders setting down (Enclosure H, page 7).

Then, one minute later, at 4:15 a.m., after Black Hawk helicopters have strafed the landing zone with machine-gun fire, the Pathfinders set down, approximately 600 meters southeast of the downed Extortion 17 (Enclosure H, page 7).

The Pathfinder commander reported that the Black Hawks put a few rounds in the ground to make people scatter prior to landing. Here's that testimony from Exhibit 65, page 6 of the Colt Report.

SME-MH47: *And they did pre-assault fires into that HLZ?*

TF CDR: *Roger, this time they did. Again for what we talked about earlier put a few rounds down in the field to make people duck their heads and I spoke specifically to the crews that were doing it, one of them which was our company SIP, we told him look we are coming in here we are doing it fast, deliberately, controlled, and putting him down and getting them out.*

This exchange demonstrates a radically inconsistent application in the rules of engagement, all within a matter of ninety minutes. The SEALs were denied pre-assault fire, which led to their deaths but the Pathfinders were given pre-assault fire prior to landing, allowing them to land safely to secure the Extortion 17 crash site.

Common sense prevailed and the Pathfinders received pre-assault fire before their landing at 4:15 a.m. But if common sense had prevailed earlier, and pre-assault fire had been allowed at 2:38 a.m., the SEALs could have landed safely, and there would have been no need to deploy the Pathfinders to the scene.

Remember, the math showed the shooter was between 119 feet and 178 feet from ground zero (the ground under the chopper when it was struck by the RPG). This is significant, because either one of the two Apache helicopters flying with Extortion 17 or the AC-130 gunship could have easily sprayed that area with gunfire to clear it out, which most likely would have saved American lives. But the rules of engagement for this mission foolishly prevented pre-assault fire.

The US Navy SEAL team was not given the same protection as the US Army Pathfinder team, and the US military has given no cogent explanation for the foolish and inexcusable decision to deliberately deny pre-assault fire for the SEAL team and the Americans aboard Extortion 17.

As long as the US military remains in Afghanistan, or in any area where known insurgents are on the ground with RPGs and other weapons capable of shooting down US aircraft, as was clearly the case with the Tangi Valley on the morning of this shoot-down, the rules of engagement should be changed to always allow pre-assault fire into a landing zone to save American lives. Political correctness should not come into play when it comes to saving American lives.

CHAPTER 36

The Disappearing Black Box:
Further Evidence of
Inconsistencies and Cover-Up

One of the most disturbing aspects of the Extortion 17 mission involved the disappearance of the flight data recorder, otherwise known colloquially as the "black box." As previously pointed out, Exhibit 65 of the Colt Report, which contains testimony of US Army Pathfinders, was labeled by the military as the Black Box exhibit and outlined the efforts made by US Army Pathfinders to locate the helicopter's black box.

Exhibit 65 discussed the Pathfinder's attempt to find the black box in the midst of the wreckage of Extortion 17, a search that extended over a period of two days and resulted in "the first time," per the Pathfinder commander's testimony, that the Pathfinders had been unable to recover a black box. If discovered, the black box could have provided clues, maybe even the absolute answer to what happened aboard Extortion 17.

The black box is the box (actually orange in color) which typically contains an aircraft's (1) flight data recorder and (2) cockpit voice recorder. In virtually every aircraft mishap in commercial or military aviation, the first question asked is, "what about the black box?"

Not only does the black box record crucial data concerning the function of the aircraft systems recorded in the flight data recorder, in real time, but often the pilots' voices are recorded and preserved, which can help investigators determine what happened to a flight.

What if, for example, the seven unidentified Afghans had attempted to either disrupt or sabotage the flight? Had that happened, there is a good chance that some clues would have been found on the cockpit voice recorder (one of the components of the black box). Or, if other problems had arisen, there is, again, a reasonable chance that the cockpit voice recorder would have recorded these problems.

THE ARMY'S ORDERS TO THE PATHFINDERS: "FIND THE BLACK BOX!"

When the Pathfinders arrived on the ground to comb through the Extortion 17 wreckage, one of the first instructions given to the entire Pathfinder team was "Find the black box."

However, it's important to realize that although the Pathfinders were on the scene within an hour-and-a-half after the shoot-down, they were not first on the scene. A Special Operations group known as "Lima Bravo" had beaten them there, by well over an hour. The Chronology at Enclosure H showed that the first forces arrived at the crash site at 3:04 a.m. Also, an unidentified coalition group entered the crash zone, examined the area, "surveyed the aircraft," and then left along an unidentified road. *All this occurred before the Pathfinders arrived, and all this is mysteriously and without explanation omitted from the Executive Summary of the Colt Report.* This crucial point will be examined in more detail later.

But first, look at the testimony of the Pathfinder Commander on the team's search for the black box.

At page 11 of Exhibit 65, a member of the Aviation Shoot-Down Assessment Team (ASDAT3) was questioning the officer who was in charge of the Pathfinders on the ground, the Pathfinder Commander (PF CDR).

ASDAT3: *How about a play book for the [inaudible], the maintenance recorders in the aircraft, by different airframe w[h]ere those locations are so in the event you find a few slides you've got some pretty significant damage, you guys know a focal point on the aircraft what to get and what's classified, what's going to help us paint the picture? Do you guys have a book like that? Was that fed to you?*

Pathfinder Commander: *We actually do have a standardized list with pictures for a CH-47 with the radar detection, ATIRCM, everything in the radio suite in the back, and how to get it out.*

So in response to the questions about the recorders located on the helicopter, the Pathfinder commander said that the Pathfinders were equipped with photographs for the radar detection, ATIRCM (Advanced Threat Infrared Countermeasures) and the radio suite in the back.

Later the Pathfinder platoon leader testified directly about the efforts to locate the black box, at page 13 of Exhibit 65 [author's emphasis]:

ASDAT3: *Does anybody brief the follow-on forces that come in behind you on what to look for on that site?*

PF PLT LDR: *Sir, in this case the first night we went—we* looked for the flight recorder, *but because the way the fire had burned down* we were told to look for the flight recorder—*I think this is actually the only time we hadn't been successful in recovering that—by the cockpit near the pilot seat on the left hand side and we got as much as we could, but it was still smoldering at that point. And then, after the flood came in, we looked again and we also—we briefed the human remains team and the downed aircraft assessment team as well as everyone else who was working on the stretchers to look for the flight recorder in any of the wreckage, but to my knowledge no one— we had a couple, I guess, false alarms, but we could never actually find the actual flight recorder.*

The testimony revealed several things about the search for the flight recorder. First, it implied that the Pathfinder team might actually have seen the flight recorder, were unable to initially recover it, and when they came back, it was gone: *"We were told to look for the flight recorder—by the* cockpit near the pilot seat on the left hand side and we got as much as we could, but it was still smoldering at that point."

Second, it appears that the Pathfinders got part of the recorder ("we got as much as we could") but could not get all of it because it was still smoldering. However, there is enough ambiguity in this portion of the testimony that "we got as much as we could" could be referring to something other than the flight recorder.

Third, after a flooding rain, they came back to look for the rest of the flight recorder, but couldn't find it: "And then, after the flood came in, we looked again and we also—we had a couple, I guess, false alarms, but we could never actually find the actual flight recorder."

Fourth, the search for the flight recorder expanded beyond just the Pathfinders, and included the human remains team.

So there was an all-out effort committing considerable military resources to looking for the now-lost flight data recorder after the "flood." But all the manpower dedicated to the search turned up nothing.

Fifth, and this point will become crucial later, the Pathfinder platoon leader testified that this was the first time they had never recovered the flight recorder from a crashed helicopter.

Keep in mind most downed helicopters in Afghanistan, in fact, half of the helicopters shot down, were CH-47 Chinooks. But the Pathfinder platoon leader said this was the first time ever they had failed to recover the voice recorder from a downed helicopter.

So there is evidence suggesting that the recorder was possibly spotted, that part of it might have been recovered, that they came back, after the "flood," and it was gone. Again, the Pathfinders had always been successful in recovering black boxes before, many from the exact same model of helicopter, the Chinook CH-47D that as noted earlier had been involved in roughly half the helicopter shoot-downs in Afghanistan. So what went wrong there? And how did the recorder mysteriously disappear between the time the Pathfinders apparently spotted it and apparently, retrieved part of it? Or, could it have been removed earlier, before the Pathfinders arrived on the scene? Could the flight recorder have somehow disappeared during the "flood" mentioned in the testimony?

When Extortion 17 hit the ground, it broke into three main pieces, scattered into a triangular debris field with each part of the destroyed helicopter separated by just over 100 meters . The three parts included the forward pylon (containing the forward rotor blade), the aft pylon (containing the aft rotor blade), and the fuselage.

The fuselage itself, including the cockpit and the main body of the helicopter, fell into a small, shallow muddy creek known as a wadi. This wadi is also known as the "Logar River bed." In the hours after Extortion 17 was shot down, heavy rains moved into the area, apparently causing a rise in the level of the wadi (referred to as "flooding" in the testimony). When the Pathfinder team returned after the initial rain and was unable to locate the black box, there was speculation that it might have washed downstream with other debris—realistically an unlikely scenario because of its weight and because it would have been bolted into place (assuming that it did not become displaced in the crash).

At page 17 of Exhibit 65, a third Pathfinder team member testified to the problems created by the flooding of the wadi: "Once the rain and the flash flood came in, we had to go searching the Wadi looking for the pieces that had floated down with the current."

But the wadi, in reality, is nothing more than a narrow, shallow, muddy creek, as shown in photographs in Exhibit 60 of the Colt Report.

Which raises the question again, where is the black box?

The notion that the black box just disappeared in the wadi is a fantasy. As is commonly known, black boxes emit low-frequency electronic pings, which make them immediately traceable. Black boxes, because of the pings, are often pulled off the bottom of the ocean floor.

One flight recorder, the one on South African Airways Flight 295, a Boeing 747 that went down in the Indian Ocean in 1987, was recovered off the ocean floor from a depth of over 16,000 feet. Likewise, the black box for Air France 447, an Airbus 330 that crashed in the Atlantic in 2009, was also recovered, this time in over 13,000 feet of water. In August of 2013, a British company recovered the black box of a Super Puma helicopter that went down in the North Sea off the Shetland Islands.

A black box submerged in water in a muddy wadi with depths ranging from knee-deep to a little over waist-deep should present no serious challenges. Yet, in spite of the fact that the Army committed a team of soldiers specializing in aircraft recovery to searching for the black box, who fanned out and walked in and along the wadi, they came up with nothing.

Moreover, it's significant that not one question was asked, anywhere in the Colt Report, about the low-frequency signals that the black box emits. Instead, the Pathfinders testified about their unsuccessful efforts to find the black box, and not one investigator asked, "Did you try and find it in the water by homing in on its electronic pinging signal?"

It's as if the black box was being intentionally ignored by the investigators, and questions that were asked weren't followed up on to determine the whereabouts of this, the most crucial piece of evidence, nor was there any clarification placed on the record about its absence or presence at the wreck scene.

It's clear that the Pathfinders committed considerable assets to finding it, and the Pathfinder platoon leader said this was the first time they hadn't recovered one in a crash in Afghanistan.

So what happened to the black box?

That cannot fully be determined from the record, except it appears to have gotten lost between the Pathfinder's first approach to the smoldering wreckage, and sometime later that day, after a heavy rain "flooded" the wadi. At least that was the narrative first pushed by the military.

However, there is additional evidence to be considered.

First, while the Pathfinders have provided most of the information about the search for the black box, it's crucial to understand that the Pathfinders were not the first unit on the ground to secure the chopper, nor were they the only unit on the ground.

UNIDENTIFIED JOINT SPECIAL OPS TASK FORCE UNIT ON GROUND BEFORE US ARMY PATHFINDERS

It's important to know that another unidentified unit, whose identity is blocked in the Colt Report, but a unit attached to the Joint Special Operations Task Force, was also on the ground along with the US Army Pathfinders.

We see this in testimony at page 115 of Exhibit 1, given by the J3 (operations) officer from the Joint Special Operations Task Force:

Based on our assessment of the time it was taking, you know, the decision was made to infill the Task Force element into an HLZ, you can see reflected there at item Number 10. But, really, what had ended up happening was our guys, ended up getting there prior to the path finder element.

Who was this unit? And how much sooner were they on the ground? There is no way to know for sure. But remember, the Pathfinders were on the ground at 4:15 a.m. That means that the unidentified task force had to have arrived on the ground prior to 4:15 a.m. (with the shoot-down having occurred at 2:39:40 a.m.). In fact, the official chronology, which was attached to Enclosure H, states that the unidentified Task Force arrived at 3:04 a.m., over an hour before the Pathfinders arrived.

ENCLOSURE "H" Chronology

0239:48 P states "There's an explosion, there's another . . . explosion." Further states: "Extortion is down." (3/4)

0240:17 makes "Fallen Angel" NET call to all elements in the Objective area indicating EXTORTION 17 has been shot down (4)

0240:18 [Apache Helicopter . . . Gun 1] suppresses suspected enemy positions IVO the suspected point of origin (POO) (3)

0240:18 [AC-130] establishes security orbit over crash site (3)

0240:36 notifies TOC that EXTORTION 17 has been shot down (4)

0242:59 [Gun 1] P 5 relays to (AC-130) suspected POO of RPG attack (3)

0243 TOC initiates downed aircraft procedures (7)

0243 TF [unidentified unit] element notified of downed aircraft (15)

0245 PB reports secondary explosions at crash site (1)

0245 TF [unidentified unit] duty log reports crash site IVO (2/7)

0245 10th CAB (Combat Air Battalion) Duty Officer notifies Division of downed aircraft (10)

0248 EXTORTION [16] remains in a holding pattern 3 miles from crash site (1/7)

0250 1/B reports they are leaving all detainees on Objective LEFTY GROVE and moving to crash site ASAP (19)

0252 Additional AWT (Air Weapons Team) at FOB (Forward Operating Base) assumes REDCON level 2 (1)

0254 EXTORTION 16 arrives at [Forward Operating Base] (1)

0254 10th CAB Fire Support Officer (FSO) reports [unidentified unit] (B1-B) nine (9) minutes away from crash site (10)

0255 10th CAB intelligence section reports N (MQ-1) UAV O/S over crash site (10)

0256 (AC-130) assumes role as On-Scene Commander (4)

0304 10th CAB FSO reports [unidentified unit] O/S at the EXTORTION 17 crash site.

* * *

0321 AWT (Air Weapons Team) conducting containment fire (7)

0327:43 element identifies possible FKIA IVO crash site for first time (3) **Refuted after viewing gun tapes and crew statements; coroner finds injuries invalidate the initial report**

* * *

0347 [Unidentified unit] reports insurgents have identified that coalition elements had entered a field, surveyed the aircraft, and then headed back to an unspecified road (14)

* * *

0350 TF (unidentified Task Force) approves the launch of the [Pathfinder] element to crash site (10)

0359 Pathfinder element (20 pax) (20 personnel) depart FOB (Forward Operating Base Shank) en-route crash site on GALLANT 40/44 (2 x UH-60) (7/10)

* * *

0405 TF (task force) reports there is one friendly spotted 10-15 meters outside of crash site (10) **Refuted after viewing (apache) gun tapes and crew statements; coroner finds injuries invalidate the initial report**

0407 TF (task force) reports one coalition service member recovered from Crash site by (10) **Refuted after viewing gun tapes and crew statements**

* * *

0414 [Air Weapons Team Black Hawk helicopters] initiates suppressive fires IVO (in vicinity of) Pathfinder HLZ (helicopter landing zone)

0415 with Pathfinder element lands in HLZ approximately 600m southeast of crash site. (1/4/7)

0415 reports visual contact of Pathfinder element, but has not established radio communications (7)

There is considerable detail in the chronology, quite a contrast with the strange lack of detail in General Colt's Executive Summary, which created a different impression of what happened on the ground in the aftermath of the crash.

Recapping some key points in the chronology: By 2:50 a.m. the unidentified unit (Lima Bravo) is abandoning its Lefty Grove position and heading to the crash site.

At 2:55 a.m., the Predator drone is overhead, providing close aviation supervision of the site. Remember that the Predator drone can provide fire support from the air.

At 3:04 a.m., an unidentified unit (presumably Lima Bravo) is on site.

At 3:47 a.m., "insurgents have identified that coalition elements had entered a field, surveyed the aircraft, and then headed back to an unspecified road." Note that "coalition elements" entered the field, surveyed the aircraft—whatever that means—and left. It's odd that there was no follow-up and no clarification on this point. No questions were asked in the transcripts along the lines of "who were these coalition elements?" Or "what does it mean that they *surveyed* the aircraft and then left?" All that is ignored.

Three minutes later, at 3:50 a.m., the Task Force (presumably Lima Bravo on the ground) *approves the launch* of the Pathfinder element. So all the activity described so far has taken place on the ground before permission is granted for the Pathfinder element to take off. Nine minutes later, at 3:59 a.m., the Pathfinder element, with two members aboard, takes off headed for the crash site.

Stop and think about the timing of the Pathfinder launch. Extortion 17 was fatally attacked at 2:39 a.m. The principal unit that typically searches wreckage sites was not even launched until one hour and twenty minutes after the shoot-down.

Then at 4:14 a.m., the Air Weapons Team delivered pre-assault fire on the landing zone, and one minute later the Pathfinder team landed on the ground, 600 meters from the crash site, or 656 yards (1,968 feet) from the crash zone. To put that in more perspective, the Pathfinders have landed a little less than one half mile away.

Testimony from exhibits 65 and 84 helps explain what both the Pathfinders and Rangers found when they landed.

Here is what the Pathfinder leader said (Exhibit 65, page 3).

PF PLT LDR: *Just when we touched down and LZ was just starting to get light sir, so we were still moving [in a] period of limited visibility. I think it was 560 meters from our LZ to the crash site just would have been to the southeast, we moved parallel in the Wadi up to the khalat the Lima Bravo element was already on scene, I think they beat us about 30 minutes.*

Here's what the Army Ranger Platoon Leader said at page 5, Exhibit 84.

We got a few hours of sleep, probably four hours of sleep or so, and then at a point somebody came and got me and woke me up and said you guys have been notified you are going to be the element to go and relieve 1/B at the crash site. You need to get up and get spinning on this.

From this testimony, we know the Ranger unit was actually deployed into the crash site to relieve this Lima Bravo unit. This is corroborated by the brief exchange at page 8 of Exhibit 84.

SME-GFA: *And correct me if I'm wrong, but the element had some outside security is that true?*

RANGER PLATOON LEADER: *Roger sir, they still had the outer cordon, they didn't have any folks right on top of the wreckage or just outside for security purpose.*

So we know, not only from Enclosure H, but also the testimony from Exhibits 65 and 84, that this "Unit 1/B" or "Lima Bravo" was on the ground considerably sooner than the Rangers.

But that's not how it's portrayed in Brigadier General Colt's Executive Summary. General Colt made it appear that the Rangers first arrived at 4:12 a.m. Nothing was mentioned of anything happening on the ground before then.

Here's how the Executive Summary described the first moments on the ground after the shoot-down:

6. Recovery Operations, *Following the shoot-down, the Ranger-led assault force began a rapid foot movement to the crash site. At 04:12. The assault force was the first element to arrive at the crash, established a security perimeter around it, and began searching for survivors. The assault force initially discovered twelve friendly remains, but could not immediately continue recovery efforts due to secondary explosions from within the wreckage. Within minutes, the 20-man Pathfinder element (downed aircraft rescue and recovery unit) joined the assault force to assist in site security and recovery of remains.*

So the question here is "Why?" Why no mention in the Executive Summary of the Predator drone securing the airspace? Why no mention of the Unit "1/B" arriving at 3:04 a.m.? Why no mention of Coalition elements "surveying" the aircraft at 3:47 a.m.?

Did General Colt not want this important data in the official report? If not, why not? Did something happen in that period of time that the military does not wish to focus upon? Perhaps the removal of the black box?

"Lima Bravo" a Joint Special Operation Unit?

Just who was this mysterious Lima Bravo unit, apparently also known as "1/B," that appears to have been the first unit on the ground, but whose presence was mysteriously not mentioned in the Executive Summary?

The unit appeared to be part of the Joint Special Operations Task Force. The testimony of the JSOTF operations officer confirmed this (Exhibit 1, pages 115–116) when he called the infiltrating team "our guys."

> **JSOTF J3:** *Immediately after the crash happened, you know, obviously, the battle space owner element, they offered up their Pathfinder element, which is a quick reaction force they have standing by primarily for aviation incidences like this. They said they're ready to go and they wanted to infill them.*
>
> *Obviously, we were very hesitant to put in any additional aircraft. So we were weighing the time it was going to take to get there because it was about a 3.9 kilometer movement. By the time it was going to take them to get there with—you know, they needed to get that site secure and the additional risk, the rotary wing aircraft getting them there. Based on our assessment of the time it was taking, you know, the decision was made to infill the Task Force element into an HLZ, you can see reflected there at item Number 10. But, really, what had ended up happening was our guys, ended up getting there prior to the Pathfinder element.*
>
> *They secured the site, and the Pathfinder element linked up with on the ground about 0027 Zulu there.*

Joint Special Operations is a joint unit, meaning the unit could have been composed of several branches of the military—possibly Navy SEALs, possibly US Army Rangers, possibly US Army Delta Force, possibly Marine Recon. They were not regular US Army. This unit arrived much earlier than the regular Ranger unit, based upon the Ranger unit leader's testimony at Exhibit 84, indicating that the "1/B" unit *and* the Pathfinders were already on the ground when the regular Ranger unit arrived.

There appears to be a distinction between Lima Bravo, apparently under the Joint Special Operations Task Force for this mission, and the Ranger unit referenced in their unit leader's testimony at Exhibit 84.

General Colt's Executive Summary does not mention members of the Joint Special Operations Task Force arriving on the ground.

Also, it should be noted that Lima Bravo, per the J3's testimony, was approximately 3.9 kilometers (2.4 miles) away at the time of the crash at 2:39 a.m.

At average walking speed of 4 mph, it would take about thirty-seven minutes to walk 2.5 miles. The Special Ops unit would most likely have been moving on foot faster than the average civilian.

Because Enclosure H shows elements of the group arriving at 3:04, or twenty-five minutes later, it is safe to assume that they were deployed to the site immediately after the shoot-down and moved with some speed and urgency.

By contrast, General Colt said in his Executive Summary that the Rangers arrived at 4:12 a.m. (one hour and thirty-two minutes after shoot-down), which would imply lollygagging of over an hour in trying to make a decision on whether to send the Special Forces unit to the crash site by foot (if he's implying that the Joint Special Forces and Rangers were one in the same). A one-hour time lag is not believable. That decision would have been made and, in fact, was made *immediately*.

Note the J3's testimony. In describing the timeframe for making a decision to send guys in on foot, he uses this phrase: "Immediately after the crash happened."

Once again Colt's summary does not match the facts.

So why omit the actual arrival time of the Lima Bravo team and instead make it appear that the Ranger unit was first to arrive at 4:12? Ordinarily, showing the earlier arrival time would be a feather in the military's cap, by showing the almost immediate movement of forces into the crash area to search for possible survivors and clear the area.

It seems odd that the actual arrival time would be omitted, unless, of course, the military did not want questions asked about what happened in the crash zone during that timeframe between 3:04 a.m. and 4:12 a.m.

Could activity that occurred during this timeframe provide a clue as to what happened to the black box?

Remember that the activities described by the Pathfinder leader, in searching for the black box, occurred *after* whatever undocumented activities took place in the crash zone between 3:04 a.m. and 4:12 a.m.

The Pathfinders, who were not part of the Joint Special Operations force that was on the ground effective 3:04 a.m., had been told that the chopper had a black box (flight data recorder) and were told to go look for it. They even spent considerable time looking for it.

Could the black box, unbeknownst to the Pathfinders, have been removed between 3:04 a.m. and 4:12 a.m.? Could the black box possibly have been removed by special ground forces who were ordered to remove it from the cockpit because it contained data revealing evidence of Taliban infiltration of Extortion 17? Could it have been removed because it contained information embarrassing to the military and/or the Obama Administration?

There is no direct evidence that the box was removed during that time period. But something happened to it.

It's equally disturbing that no one from the Lima Bravo unit that arrived at 3:04 a.m. was interviewed in the Colt investigation, and it's also both disturbing and suspicious that their presence was not even noted in the Executive Summary.

Why not?

Also disturbing and suspicious is the fact that neither the Executive Summary nor the congressional "hearing" delve at all into the reference to Coalition elements "surveying" the wreckage at 3:47 a.m.

Here's that notation from Enclosure H again, where, twenty minutes after Lima Bravo arrives at the crash site, at 3:47 a.m., "insurgents have identified that coalition elements had entered a field, surveyed the aircraft, and then headed back to an unspecified road."

Just what does that mean? Does it mean that "insurgents" (the enemy) saw Coalition forces approaching the wreckage?

What does it mean that coalition elements "surveyed the aircraft"? Could this "survey" of the aircraft, out in the field, have anything to do with the missing black box?

And what's this "unspecified road" that Coalition forces headed back to?

And why would these "Coalition elements" have a need to head back up an "unspecified road" *prior* to the arrival of the Pathfinders on the scene at 4:15 a.m.?

It seems, logically, that in the minutes following the shoot-down, this would be the time to be reinforcing troops on the ground, not pulling them out already. Is it possible that these "coalition elements" retreated back along this "unspecified road" because they had something in their possession that they didn't want the Pathfinders to find? Perhaps a black box?

None of this makes any sense.

No questions were asked about any of this in the Colt investigation—as if the military didn't want any of this on the record. Moreover, congressional investigators, who had access to all this data, asked not a single question about any of it. Why not?

The failure of anyone to ask any questions seeking clarification of this documented sequence is unbelievable—unless, of course, there is data and evidence in connection with this sequence that the military and the government were intent on covering up, information that might be embarrassing to the military and/or the Administration.

CHAPTER 37

Disconnect: The Pathfinders vs. the Task Force

Based upon the evidence underlying the Colt Report, there appears to have been a wild disconnect between the Pathfinders, who arrived on scene at 4:15 a.m., and the Joint Special Operations Task Force. The two groups seemed to be operating based on a different set of assumptions, and reported to different officers in the chain of command.

The biggest disconnect appears to be this: the Pathfinders were told, "Go find the black box." Yet everyone else, from General Colt on down, is cagey at best about the black box.

Recall that the Pathfinders arrived one hour and nine minutes after the mysterious unit "1/B," which appears to be a military unit from the Joint Special Operations Task Force.

It is clear, based upon the testimony provided by the Pathfinder leader at Exhibit 65, that the Pathfinders were told to go find the black box and, in fact, committed considerable resources over a couple of days to find it.

During the course of the Pathfinder leader's testimony, General Colt, who was there listening, never corrected the Pathfinder leader by saying, "wait a minute, there was no black box in this helicopter." Not once was there such a correction or comment, even after there had been considerable testimony about the search for the black box.

General Colt's failure to say anything is odd, especially because just before the testimony of the Pathfinder leader, General Colt made this comment at page 11 of Exhibit 5: "We do need to talk VADRs though, because it's critical. This one didn't have one."

If by his odd comment at page 11, General Colt was trying to say, at least peripherally, that there was no black box on this helicopter, it's interesting to note that two pages later, following the Pathfinder platoon leader's extensive comments about searching for the black box, Colt remained silent. Neither Colt nor members of his staff ever asked the platoon leaders, "Why were you searching for a black box, when you know there was not one?" There was no language like that whatsoever.

It appears that the Pathfinders, whose standing orders had been to first search for the black box and had done so every time a helicopter went down in Afghanistan, were not informed whether or not the black box had been removed from the aircraft, and committed time and man hours searching for it. Did the Special Forces unit remove the box, and if they did, why not inform the Pathfinders?

CHAPTER 38

The Black Box Absent from
the Executive Summary

The black box did not just disappear from the wreckage of Extortion 17. It also disappeared, mysteriously, from the Executive Summary of the Colt Report.

As the black box would have provided key information about the shoot-down, it is odd that the Executive Summary would not address it. The Executive Summary didn't say that there was no black box. It didn't say the black box could not be found, nor did it say there was no black box. It simply ignored the issue.

This glaring omission, in and of itself, is enough to raise suspicion. How can you simply ignore, and not mention, the presence or absence of the most important forensics clue in any aircraft shoot-down investigation? Yet Colt's Executive Summary did just that—ignored any mention of the black box. If there was no black box on the aircraft, why not report that crucial fact in the Executive Summary? Or if the black box couldn't be recovered and just washed down the wadi, as appears to be the theme of the first narrative put out by the military, why not report that in the Executive Summary?

Could it be that this crucial evidence was left out of the Executive Summary because they were still trying to get their story straight on what to say about it?

When Colt was asked about the black box by family members at Little Creek, Virginia, in October 2011, he was equally vague in his answers, telling the family members to refer to his report—which, of course, featured the Pathfinders testifying that they had searched for the black box, but could not find it. To confuse matters even further, he is reported to have told one family, the family of deceased Navy cryptologist Michael Strange, that the black box disappeared in the flood.

The first narrative that the military pushed was that the black box disappeared in the "flooding of the wadi," the shallow, muddy riverbed. Of course it's extremely hard to believe that the US military would lose a black box from one of its helicopters in a shallow, muddy creek in a Third World country, no matter how much it rained the night before.

CHAPTER 39

The Crash Site:
Before the Pathfinders' Arrival

What happened on the ground before the arrival of the US Army Path-finders? First, at 3:27 a.m., just twenty-three minutes after arriving on scene, the unidentified mystery unit began to identify FKIA, which means "friendly killed in action." In other words, they were already identifying Americans killed on Extortion 17. There had been a report of survivors earlier, but a military coroner on site with the unidentified unit refuted that.

Then, twenty minutes later, at 3:47 a.m., as documented in Enclosure H, the unidentified unit (Lima Bravo) reported that Coalition elements (meaning US forces or a US ally) "had entered a field, surveyed the aircraft, and then headed back to an unspecified road."

So who were these Coalition elements? Why did they come in and "survey the aircraft"? Did they remove anything from the aircraft? Could they have removed the black box from the aircraft? Where did they go? They just disappeared to an "unspecified road"?

What road?

Why is nothing else said about this group of "coalition elements" that entered the field and "surveyed" the aircraft? Why weren't members of this group of coalition elements interviewed in the Colt Report? Now keep in mind that this group of "Coalition elements" was the *second unidentified* group (this group plus the unidentified task force that landed at 3:04 a.m.) to arrive before the Pathfinders, who would not even take off for the site until 3:59 or 4:00 a.m. Naturally, not only were these "Coalition elements" not identified in the Colt Report, but they weren't interviewed. Neither was the unidentified unit from the Joint Special Operations Task Force. Nothing else was mentioned about them.

The next sequence is equally interesting. Why did the Pathfinders wait so long to take off? Only after these unidentified "coalition elements" conducted their "survey" of the aircraft and then disappeared onto an "unspecified road" at 3:47 a.m. were the Pathfinders permitted to launch.

In fact, the unidentified task force on the ground actually had to approve the launch of the Pathfinders helicopter, which they did at 3:50 a.m., three minutes after these "coalition elements" had finished their "survey of the aircraft."

Here, again, is the notation directly from the official chronology at Enclosure H, showing the Task Force approving the Pathfinders' launch: "0350 TF [Task Force] approves launch of the [Pathfinder] element to crash site."

Each bit of information revealed in the timeline raises more questions. Why, for example, would they wait until after the "survey of the aircraft" by this unidentified group before calling in the Pathfinders? Was there any reason to delay the Pathfinders arrival? Was the goal to intentionally keep them away?

According to the chronology, the Pathfinders did not arrive until 4:15 a.m. That's a gap of one hour and eleven minutes in which the unidentified Special Forces unit, often referred to as the "task force," is on the ground *before* the arrival of the Pathfinders.

But who exactly was this group on the ground first? And why didn't they testify in the Colt Report? And why did Colt omit them from his Executive Summary?

CHAPTER 40

The Mystery Unit First on the Ground

The testimony of the Pathfinders' platoon leader generated some more clues about the group that was already on the ground when the Pathfinders arrived. At page 3 of Exhibit 65, the Pathfinder platoon leader testified that when his element finally landed (approx. 4:15 a.m.), the landing zone was already starting to get light, and that his group was met by a group called the "Lima Bravo" element.

Here's part of that testimony [author's emphasis].

> **PF PLT LDR:** *Just when we touched down and LZ [landing zone] was just starting to get light sir, so we were still moving [in a] period of limited visibility. I think it was 560 meters from our LZ to the crash site [which] just would have been to the southeast. We moved parallel in the Wadi up to the khalat. The* Lima Bravo element was already on scene, *I think they beat us [by] about 30 minutes. So . . . from there I talked to [name deleted] [who] was the GFC [ground forces commander] at the time. Establish security with them. We [Pathfinders] took security on the north end of the Wadi. They [Lima Bravo] took it on the south and also had an OP [outer perimeter] set up on the high ground to the Southwest of the crash site.*

When the Pathfinder platoon leader speculated, "I think they beat us about 30 minutes," his estimate was way off. This unidentified element had already been on the ground for one hour and eleven minutes, had already begun to identify American bodies, and had already permitted a "coalition element" to conduct a "survey of the aircraft" in the field, and then disappear on an "unspecified road," all before the Pathfinders arrived.

Once again, it should be emphasized that no one from this mysterious Lima Bravo element was interviewed in the Colt investigation and there was no testimony from anyone associated with that unit in the Colt Report.

Why not? Why would Brigadier General Colt not want to interview the first element on the ground after the shoot-down?

Only the Army can answer that question.

CHAPTER 41

The Executive Summary: Whitewashing the Real Chronology

In view of the very clear chronology as laid out in Enclosure H, which shows the Predator drone securing the site from overhead at 2:55 a.m., and then the unidentified unit (presumably Lima Bravo) arriving at the crash site by 3:04 a.m., and then considerable other activity taking place on the ground, including identifying potential Friendly Killed in Action and the "coalition elements" who entered the field to "survey" the craft, it is surprising that General Colt's Executive Summary (Enclosure C) simply left all that out. Instead, Colt's summary dated September 9, 2011, curiously omitted all that.

Nothing was mentioned about the Predator drone securing the airspace over Extortion 17 at 2:55 a.m. Nothing was mentioned at all about Lima Bravo arriving at 3:04 a.m. Nothing was revealed about identifying dead American service members, or Coalition forces entering the field and surveying the aircraft at 3:04 a.m.

The revisionism of the Executive Summary at subchapter 6, Recovery Operations, is perplexing. The fact that Colt would (1) leave out the Predator drone's early arrival, thus securing the airspace minutes after the shoot-down, (2) omit the mysterious Lima Bravo group arrival by 3:04 a.m., and (3) omit that "coalition elements" entered the field and "surveyed" the aircraft at 3:47 a.m., makes no sense. These crucial omissions smack of cover-up.

CHAPTER 42

The Little Creek Briefing and Other Reports: More Questions on the Box

In October of 2011, a little over sixty days after the shoot-down, and just over thirty days after the completion of the Colt Report, the Joint Special Operations Task Force conducted a briefing of SEAL team family members at the US Navy's Amphibious Base in Little Creek, Virginia. That meeting was presided over by Brigadier General Jeffrey Colt.

After confirming that Extortion 17 was flying 100–150 feet above the ground at the time of the shoot-down, General Colt started getting questions from family members about the black box.

General Colt did not directly answer these questions. Curiously, he did not say, "we could not find the black box," nor did he say, "There was no black box on the chopper. Instead he referred families to "the report."

Of course, at that time, "the report," which we are referring to herein as the "Colt Report," had just been released to several families of the fallen. It appears, however, that very few families had actually read the report at the time of the Little Creek meeting. One would have to know exactly where to go to look in the voluminous report to find the Pathfinders' testimony about the black box.

One Extortion 17 parent, Mr. Charles Strange of Philadelphia, put the question even more bluntly to Brigadier General Colt. Mr. Strange recounted his exchange with Colt from 2011 at a press conference that several Extortion 17 families gave on May 9, 2013, in Washington. Mr. Strange's recollection of that event is set forth below:

In October (2011), we went down for General Colt's assessment of the investigation. We get there. They have a projector screen. The families are there. He's going over what happened. He said it went through a chain-of-command for this landing site.

I raised my hand, and I said "sir? Can I have the names of that chain-of-command?"

His neck snaps, and he said "It's in the book, sir."

I said "How about the black box?"

He said, "The black box got blown away by the flood."

In Afghanistan? Come on. You can't find the black box? I looked it up in Google. T[hose] black boxes don't go away. They lose black boxes in the swamp in Florida, and they find them. And you're telling me you can't find the black box? Not acceptable.

Therefore, according to Mr. Strange, the "flood theory" was introduced by Colt himself in October of 2011 at the Little Creek, Virginia, briefing with families.

Other families do not have specific recollection of General Colt mentioning the flood, at least not in public, when asked about the black box in October of 2011. But all the families interviewed for this book recall him (Colt) pointing them to the report, in response to their questioning.

According to witnesses, at no time during that meeting did Colt ever say that the Chinook did not have a black box from the beginning.

Even if Mr. Strange's recollection is faulty and General Colt did not specifically mention the flood to explain the disappearance of the black box, he certainly pointed families in that direction by directing families to the report. In the period between October 2011 and February 2014, various articles were written concerning the disappearing black box. Diana West, writing in the online magazine townhall.com, reported on May 17, 2013, in an article entitled "Afghanistan's Benghazi: The Shoot-Down of Extortion 17" that "The black box was never recovered, the military insists."

On July 23, 2013, in an article in *The Hill* written by Bob Cusack and entitled "Congress to Probe Lethal Crash that Killed SEAL Team 6 Members," the paper reported that, "Their bodies were later recovered, but the helicopter's black box was not. Pentagon officials have said that it could not be recovered, citing a flash flood that happened soon after the assault."

The Hill's account seems consistent—this *the flood got the black box* narrative—with the sworn testimony of the Pathfinders, who talked about searching extensively for the black box, then returned after the flood, and found themselves unable to find the black box "for the first time."

CHAPTER 43

February 27, 2014: The Congressional Hearing

For two-and-a-half years the Department of Defense stuck to their position that the black box was lost, or "washed away." There was no apparent shift in that claim until February 27, 2014, when under tremendous pressure from families, congressmen granted a very short, one hour and forty-five minute hearing. This hearing took place before a sparsely attended National Security Subcommittee, part of the House Oversight and Government Committee.

The subcommittee, chaired by Representative Jason Chaffetz, a Utah Republican, called a panel of five witnesses (three military officers and two DoD civilians), none of whom were in Afghanistan on the night in question, and none of whom had any firsthand knowledge of what happened in the early morning hours of August 6, 2011.

Chaffetz opened by assuring the families that the committee had questioned Department of Defense officials on the full spectrum of the mission, including *extremely sensitive and highly classified information*, in an effort to fully understand the events of the tragedy that unfolded that fateful day. "It is extremely sensitive. There are things that we cannot and will not be discussing given the classified nature," Congressman Chaffetz expounded. It is clear from the congressman's opening statement alone that information *was* and is still being withheld from the public.

This begs the question: Is the true identity of the seven Afghan infiltrators "extremely sensitive and highly classified"? Is information concerning the fate of the bodies of the men of Extortion 17 "extremely sensitive and highly classified"? Is information concerning how the Taliban infiltrated the flight "extremely sensitive and highly classified"? Is information about the tip-off of the Taliban possibly coming from inside the American camp because of our policy of bringing the Afghans on each and every mission "extremely sensitive and highly classified"?

The congressman's brief and pointed comments were yet another piece of evidence that the truth of Extortion 17s fate is being withheld from the public.

Congressman Chaffetz has by all accounts been a friend to Extortion 17 families, making himself accessible to the press in answering questions, and helping to keep this case in the forefront, at least to a degree, as long as unanswered questions remain.

All that said, and while acknowledging Congressman Chaffetz for his sensitivity to Extortion 17 families who lost loved ones, the congressional hearing itself was nothing but a dog-and-pony show aimed at appeasement, mostly because of who the Pentagon offered up to testify, and who was not allowed to testify.

Not one US military officer who was on the ground in Afghanistan was allowed to testify. Not one officer who served as a member of the Colt investigation was allowed to testify. There was no one who was a part of either planning for or executing this mission. No one was present who could provide any substantive expertise—not one US Navy SEAL, not one US Army Ranger, not one National Guard aviator.

Instead, the panel served up by the Pentagon included two civilian bureaucrats and three mortuary affairs officers, none of whom had any direct involvement with the planning or execution of Extortion 17.

Most of the testimony at the hearing came from an Obama Administration Department of Defense appointee, Gary Reid, bearing the title of "Principal Deputy Assistant Defense Secretary for Special Operations and Low Intensity Conflict." Mr. Reid was appointed to his post in June of 2012. Reid was joined by another Pentagon official, Ms. Deborah Skillman, the Defense Department casualty and mortuary affairs director. In addition to Reid and Skillman, three military officers, an Air Force colonel, Army colonel, and Navy commander, appeared and testified. The Air Force representative was Colonel John Devillier, US Air Force mortuary affairs operation commander. The Navy was represented by Commander Aaron Brodsky, the US Navy casualty services director, and the Army by Colonel Kirk Brown, the director of Army mortuary and casualty affairs.

All of these officials who appeared at the hearing have important roles and functions within the Defense Department. But if we look more closely at the makeup of the five-member panel scheduled to testify, not only were all five witnesses either military officers or DoD officials stationed in Washington who had nothing to do with the operation itself, but four of the five, excluding Mr. Reid, were mortuary affairs representatives from each of the services involved in the shoot-down. In other words, the panel was stacked with military body-handling and funeral experts.

These experts each played a vital role in the US military, and their service was important to the family members whose loved ones were killed in action. But at the same time, *the notable absence of any officer, any military member, any SEAL, or anyone who was involved in the operation in Afghanistan on August 6, 2011, made it clear from the beginning that the subcommittee hearing was designed to constitute a one hour forty-five minute whitewash to avoid dealing with anything of real substance.*

Most of the panel would have no reason to know, for example, the identities of the seven Afghans who penetrated the chopper, or the whereabouts of the black box, or why there was a delay in landing.

Although the hearing revealed very little, as is the case with many congressional subcommittees, the testimony wound up further calling the government's explanation into question.

CHAPTER 44

The Military's Changed Tune: "There Was No Black Box"

The only stab at substantive testimony at the February 2014 hearing was presented, very briefly, by the deputy assistant defense secretary, Gary Reid, an Obama Administration appointee, whose testimony left more questions than answers.

Reid's testimony raised even more questions and left gaping holes concerning (a) the location of the Taliban insurgents who fired the RPGs, and (b) the mysterious explanation about the missing "black box."

Reid said "Taliban fighters, hidden in a building, fired two or three rocket-propelled grenades at close range, leaving the pilot no chance to perform evasive maneuvers." However, this reference to "Taliban fighters, hidden in a building," directly contradicts the Combat Assessment Team at Bagram Air Base. It also contradicts indisputable mathematical principles. At an altitude above ground of 100–150 feet, the distance between the chopper and the shooter would range from 155 to 227 feet, as previously established.

There were no buildings within 155 to 227 feet of Extortion 17 at the moment of shoot-down.

Recall Exhibit 60, page 42. There were contradictory reports from multiple witnesses about the true point of origin of the attack. The Combat Assessment Team at Bagram Air Base concluded that the "Point-of-origin was never positively identified or actioned." In fact, Exhibit 60, page 42 goes even further, by revealing that, "participating aircrews were not aware EX17 was being fired upon until it was hit." Again, these are the final "Tactical Observations" from the Combat Assessment Team at Bagram Air Base. Not only could the point of origin not be positively identified, but when pressed, no one could even say they saw the shots until the helicopter was struck.

Mr. Reid perpetuated the false narrative, started in the Executive Summary, that the RPG was fired from a building 722 feet away (outside the RPG range of 150 meters).

Why would Mr. Reid and Brigadier General Colt try to change this narrative about the point of origin, when the CAT (Combat Assessment Team) in Afghanistan, investigating this claim, concluded that the point of origin of the RPGs was "never positively identified" and that none of the pilots in accompanying aircraft were aware that Extortion 17 was even under fire until it was hit?

No one can read their minds.

However, the narrative appears to be a butt-saving maneuver to make people believe that "it wouldn't have done any good to fire into the landing zone, because the shooter was somewhere off yonder, outside the zone."

If the shots came from a building, as opposed to the field, or the creek bed, or the landing zone, then the argument that pre-assault fire into the landing zone could have saved the lives of the SEAL team becomes less meritorious, in effect, shifting criticism away from the rules of engagement that did not allow pre-assault fire to protect the chopper.

Reid and Colt should have shot it straight on this matter, that the point of origin for the RPGs could not be positively identified, rather than spinning the narrative in a way that did not fit with the findings of their own Combat Assessment Team. Their attempt to bend and spin calls their conclusions into question.

After contradicting the Combat Assessment Team's conclusion that the point of origin for the RPGs "could not be positively identified," Reid went into a seemingly new narrative, after two-and-a-half years, on the whereabouts of the black box.

Reid opened the subject by saying, "Contrary to some unofficial statements, there was no flight data recorder, no so-called 'black box.' This equipment is not standard on this aircraft.

"An investigation was launched immediately, and completed within 30 days. And I'd just like to highlight some of the results and conclusions of that investigation," Reid continued.

Q: From Congressman Chaffetz: "The idea that the black box washed away. Was there a black box?"

Note the form of the question from Congressman Chaffetz here. He starts his question by stating, "The idea that the black box washed away." The congressman prefaces his question with this observation, because this was precisely the narrative that the military had been pushing for two-and-a-half years, that the "black box washed away."

There had been no change in the military's position on this, until Reid's answer to this question on February 27, 2014—yet another about-face.

A: (from Reid) "No sir. As I indicated, there is a device attached to the engines that records engine performance. The engines are new. In fact the same engines that were on the other Chinooks. The modern engines.

"But the airframe itself is an analog aircraft. There is no source of digital data. There is no traditional black box."

It seems that not a single member of the subcommittee was sufficiently familiar with Exhibit 65 (Pathfinders' testimony) to ask Mr. Reid any questions about the extensive search for the black box detailed in the report.

No one asked Mr. Reid, "If there were no black box, sir, then why did the Pathfinders devote so much time and resources on the ground looking for it?"

No one asked Mr. Reid, "If these helicopters don't have black boxes, then why did the Pathfinders' testimony indicate this was the first time they had failed to recover a black box from a downed helicopter?"

And of course, nobody dared ask, "What did the Lima/Bravo Unit, or whoever they are, do on the ground from 3:04 a.m. until the Pathfinders arrived at 4:15 a.m.?"

No one asked, "Who were these Coalition elements who entered the field and surveyed the aircraft, and what road did they disappear on?"

No one asked, "Mister Reid, why did they survey the aircraft?"

No one asked, "Mister Reid, why didn't Brigadier General Colt's Executive Summary reflect any of the events that occurred on the ground before the arrival of the Pathfinder elements at 4:15 a.m.?"

No one asked, "Mister Reid, why did the Pathfinders get the benefit of pre-assault fire at 4:14 a.m., when the SEALs on Extortion 17 were not provided pre-assault fire in the moments leading up to 2:39 a.m.?"

No one asked, "Mister Reid, what happened to the bodies? Were they cremated or not?"

No one asked, "Mister Reid, what are the names of the seven Afghans who infiltrated this aircraft prior to its takeoff?"

No one asked, "Mister Reid, isn't it true that having unauthorized persons entering the aircraft, who are not pre-approved and whose names are not on the flight manifest, was a major security breach and a major breach of protocol?"

No one asked, "Mister Reid, what follow-up did the government take on the reports in the UK *Daily Mail* and the UK *Telegraph,* citing sources in the Afghan government that the Taliban was tipped off on the mission and flight path of Extortion 17?"

No one asked, "Mister Reid, how is it mathematically possible that an aircraft, flying only 100 to 150 feet off the ground, could be struck at an angle of 50 degrees from a building 722 feet away?"

No one asked, "Mister Reid, why are you and Brigadier General Colt sticking to this 'the shot was fired from a building 220 meters away' story, when the Joint Combat Assessment Team concluded, 'point of origin was never positively identified or actioned.'"

No one asked, "Mister Reid, do we know whether the seven Afghans who entered Extortion 17 were Taliban sympathizers?"

No one asked, "Mister Reid, why did General Colt not interview a single Afghan in his investigation?"

No one asked, "Mister Reid, what are we doing to vet the Afghans who fly with US Navy SEALs to ensure that the Afghans are not Taliban sympathizers?"

No one asked, "Mister Reid, when the AC-130 flying above Extortion 17 requested permission to fire on enemy insurgents on the ground, why was that request denied?"

Not a single, hardball question was asked of Mister Reid by a single member of that subcommittee on February 27, 2014. Why not? Because the committee hearing amounted to fluff, from the beginning, to whitewash the specifics. Instead, all the contradictory underlying evidence from the investigation, subverting his claim that "there was no black box," was ignored by the congressional subcommittee, making the hearing largely a meaningless exercise for public relations purposes.

CHAPTER 45

Black Box Black Magic: The "Analog" Ruse

Reid tried to convince the committee members, who did not know any better, that an aircraft with analog instruments either can't have a black box or doesn't have a black box.

That notion was a red herring to get the committee off track and get their heads nodding out of ignorance. The assertion that an aircraft with analog instruments can't have a black box is absolutely incorrect.

Here are those comments from Mr. Reid again: "But the airframe itself is an analog aircraft. There is no source of digital data. There is no traditional black box."

Soon after this statement was made, the author spoke with a veteran US Navy helicopter pilot, who pointed out that Mr. Reid's statement was misleading.

Why? Because whether the cockpit has analog or digital instruments has nothing to do with the presence or absence of a flight data recorder.

Mr. Reid implied that analog-heavy aircraft or analog instruments do not work in conjunction with a black box. But this is not the case at all. As the Navy pilot explained, both analog instruments and digital instruments feed data into the cockpit data recorder (black box).

In fact, the Boeing aircraft website contains basic information corroborating the Navy pilot's observation [author's emphasis]:

1 Purpose of Flight Data Recorders
The purpose of an airplane flight data recorder system is to collect and record data from a variety of airplane sensors onto a medium designed to survive an accident. Depending on the age of an airplane, the FDR

system may consist of (1) an analog or digital flight data acquisition unit *(FDAU) and a digital FDR (DFDR) that may have a*
tape or solid-state memory, or (2) simply an FDR.
http://www.boeing.com/commercial/aeromagazine/aero_02/tex-
tonly/s01txt.html

A flight data recorder may consist of an analog unit, or a digital unit,
with either tape memory or solid-state memory. That the Chinook may
have had analog instruments has nothing to do with whether there was
a data recorder.

Of course, none of the members of the congressional committee
possessed the technical expertise to press Mr. Reid on this issue They
simply nodded their heads in agreement, as if they knew what Mr. Reid
was talking about, and proceeded with a well-intentioned dog-and-pony
show to "honor the heroes" of Extortion 17. Nice window-dressing, but
no answers, and typical of most congressional hearings.

Based upon the Colt report and the congressional testimony ignoring the events on the ground at the crash site at 3:04 a.m. and 3:47 a.m.
(Coalition unit "surveying" wreckage then disappearing), and based upon
both General Colt and Mr. Reid ignoring the Pathfinders' testimony, the
late change in the government's position on the black box to "there never
was one" was not credible.

Either way, the military's position here is a lose-lose proposition. If
they actually put a highly trained, valuable US Navy SEAL team onto an
old aircraft, so old and antiquated that it did not even have a flight data
recorder, then the mission planning was callous and irresponsible. If, as
appears to be the case, they could not find the flight data recorder in a
shallow, knee-deep creek, or if the flight data recorder was removed from
the aircraft, a possible scenario, then those scenarios are also inexcusable.
And of course, there is a strong third possibility—that the black box disappeared after the shoot-down but before the arrival of the Pathfinders.

Based upon the inconsistent stories about the black box, and based on
other inconsistencies and implausibilities as well, many Extortion 17 families weren't buying the government's "we did nothing wrong" narrative.

As Doug Hamburger, the father of Pat Hamburger said after the hearing, "We're still very positive that they could have been set up—that this was an inside thing, that they knew they were coming."

Hamburger's concerns are well taken, and his instincts are probably on mark. One thing seems certain. The inconsistencies, sleight-of-hand, and lack of forthrightness with the families and the public lead to one inescapable conclusion: Something is being covered up. The question is what?

Clearly, the National Security Subcommittee's performance on February 27, 2014, showed little results in getting to the bottom of anything. The widows and the children and parents of the brave Americans killed aboard Extortion 17 deserved better.

CHAPTER 46

Chaffetz on Fox: The Pink Elephant Lives

Later that day, following the congressional hearing, Congressman Chaffetz appeared in a five-minute interview with Fox News about the hearing. A review of that interview shows how little the hearing accomplished and, in fact, how nothing was accomplished on the biggest pink elephant question looming over the mission: "Who were the seven Afghans?"

> **Shannon Bream, Fox News:** *Doug Hamburger, whose son, Staff Sergeant Patrick was killed in this crash, said he wanted to know why Afghans were not interviewed as part of the military's post-crash investigation. Did you get any answers on that point today?*
>
> **Congressman Chaffetz:** *I asked that specific question, in the hearing, of the Pentagon. They did not have a good answer on that. They agreed to get back to us on that. But we did not get a clarifying answer on that particular point.*

The congressman asked the question about Afghans not being interviewed by the Colt team, and got no answer. The lack of response that Congressman Chaffetz got was unacceptable and showed the military, again, doing all it could to avoid the "A" word (Afghan).

But an even larger question still looms. Who were the Afghans who boarded that chopper?" That question was not asked and, of course, there was no answer. Here is another key exchange. ·

> **Shannon Bream, Fox News:** *Charles Strange, the father of one of the Navy SEALs, Michael Strange, said he didn't believe the explanation*

*from the Pentagon that the Taliban wasn't tipped off to this mission—
the Extortion 17 mission—And there are many of these families who
say they feel in some way that the Taliban had gotten certain information—from somebody who leaked information, and that's how they
knew this particular Chinook was coming. Any discussion of that?*

Congressman Chaffetz: *I think it was a legitimate question.
But if you look at the operation itself, there was actually a Ranger
team that went in first, and then this SEAL team. Primarily SEALs.
There were Army involved in this. Air Force as well. But this team
was actually not . . . they were the backup. And when they were called
into service, they didn't know exactly where they were gonna go until
they actually went and took off. I don't think there was even an opportunity to tell the Taliban. It's horrific. It's awful. These people are going
to the most dangerous places in the world. But I don't see any evidence
that somehow the Taliban was tipped off and they were prepared, and
that's what took out this helicopter.*

The congressman's response seems inadequate here. He seems to
proffer the theory that because this was a contingency mission, designed
to back up the Rangers, that there was no way the Taliban could have
been tipped off in advance.

But there are numerous holes in the congressman's assumption—
emphasizing the word "assumption"—that the Taliban was not tipped.

First, Chaffetz should not have ruled out the possibility the seven
Afghans who infiltrated the chopper were Taliban infiltrators. The military has remained suspiciously mum about them on every front. Could
they have been carrying communications or tracking devices that would
have allowed them to either talk to their comrades on the ground or communicate GPS positioning data?

Knowing the immense problem of well-documented Green-on-Blue
violence, one simply cannot come to an objective, intellectual conclusion
that the Taliban was not tipped off until ruling out that the seven unidentified Afghans were Taliban operatives or sympathizers.

Moreover, Congressman Chaffetz did not even address the British
press reports from the *Telegraph* and the *Daily Mail*. Here's the relevant

portion, again, of that August 10, 2011, *Daily Mail* report quoting an Afghan government official that the Taliban had been tipped.

> *He (Afghan government official) said that Taliban commander Qari Tahir lured US forces to the scene by tipping them off that a Taliban meeting was taking place.*
>
> *He also said four Pakistanis helped Tahir carry out the strike.*
>
> *'Now it's confirmed that the helicopter was shot down and it was a trap that was set by a Taliban commander,' said the official, citing intelligence gathered from the area.*

What steps were taken to ensure that these reports in the British press were not accurate? Wouldn't that be important? Instead, the pink elephant in the room was ignored again.

Congressman Chaffetz didn't mention these reports. Deputy Assistant Defense Secretary Reid didn't mention them. And General Colt, as previously reported, certainly didn't cover this issue in his questions.

Is this why the Afghans weren't interviewed, because they could have confirmed exactly what the British press quoted them as saying, that the Taliban had been tipped? Or does the military establishment not want it out in the open that Qari Tahir had set a trap by putting out information that this meeting was taking place?

If Qari Tahir had, in fact, floated this information to lure the chopper, as the British press reported, then the Taliban would know the flight path of the chopper, and all they would need to do would be to surround the meeting area with men with RPGs and wait for the sound of the rotary blades.

Moreover, if they had sympathizers aboard Extortion 17 with communications or tracking devices, then the trap becomes more executable. For the congressman to simply come to the conclusion that the Taliban was not tipped was a premature conclusion, based upon speculation and not enough information.

According to Doug Hamburger, father of guardsman Pat Hamburger, who died in the shoot-down, his son had reported that one of the biggest problems with Afghan forces flying aboard US helicopters was that the Afghans were often insistent upon carrying their cellphones aboard. This often created a bone of contention between the Afghans and the Americans.

With the cellphones, the Afghans could text, they could call, and many of these cellphones had tracking features, which would, in theory, make it relatively simple to track the position of an approaching helicopter.

The congressman might not have seen any evidence of an inside job, but he wouldn't have the evidence unless he asked the right questions—unless, of course, the predetermined goal was to wind up with no evidence. Another excerpt from the Fox News broadcast:

Shannon Bream, Fox News: *So the families say they've got inconsistent stories. They've been told things and there are discrepancies that don't line up. Do you think they're getting any closer to having any kind of closure? Not that you can when you lose a loved one like this. But at least to get some answers that make sense for them?*

Chaffetz: *Well Shannon, that's really the reason we held the hearing today. I think we clarified things about the black box. About the operation itself. About the so-called flash flood.*

With all due respect to Congressman Chaffetz, absolutely nothing was clarified about the black box. If there was no black box, then why did the Pathfinder team spend considerable time and effort looking for a black box? Why did the Pathfinders testify under oath that this was the first time they had never found a black box?

Moreover, why weren't the families informed that there was "no black box" way back in October 2011, at the meeting between General Colt and Extortion 17 families in Virginia? The black box was very much on the minds of family members then, and they specifically asked Brigadier General Colt about it.

The families interviewed by the author say that Colt never told them that there was no black box. Billy and Karen Vaughn, parents of fallen Navy SEAL Aaron Vaughn, say when Colt was asked about the black box, he was cagey and told them to read the report.

Charles Strange, father of Navy cryptologist Michael Strange, was blunter. When he asked Colt about the black box, according to Mr. Strange, Colt informed him that the black box had been "blown away by the flood."

So Mr. Reid's new claim on February 27, 2014, that there was no black box was a major shift in the story that the military had floated—no pun intended—up to that point about the box disappearing in the flood.

Why wait so long to make this claim? Why the apparent shift? None of it rings true. And none of these questions were pressed by congressional committee members. Instead, there appears to be a willingness on the part of Congressman Chaffetz to simply buy into the military's "there was no black box theory," without questioning prior contradictions.

CHAPTER 47

Cremation and the Destruction of DNA Evidence

The congressional subcommittee not only did not touch on the issue of what happened to the bodies of the Americans killed, but just as important for purposes of getting to the truth, they did not explore what happened to the bodies of the seven Afghans who infiltrated the aircraft.

Many family members were upset about the handling of the bodies after Extortion 17 was shot down. Much has been said, and rightly so, about a joint "ramp ceremony" at Bagram Air Base, on August 8, 2011, just two days after the shoot-down, when all thirty Americans, and all eight Afghans (the seven unidentified Afghans plus the Afghan translator) were flown to Bagram, where their caskets were removed from Air Force jets, and words were spoken over their bodies by a Muslim cleric (imam) in Arabic.

When the cleric's words were later translated, his words were interpreted to be highly disrespectful, calling the deceased Americans of Extortion 17 "the companions of the fire" and a number of other questionable comments.

The imam's prayer over the bodies included the following, according to the translator, who had been associated with Congresswoman Michele Bachmann's office:

"In the name of Allah, the merciful forgiver. The companions of the fire (the sinners and infidels who are fodder for hell fire), are not equal with the companions of heaven. The companions of heaven (Muslims) are the winners."

These words, many of the families argued, were highly inappropriate, insulting, and inflammatory because (a) the majority of Americans aboard Extortion 17 were professing Christians and there were no Americans aboard who were Muslim, and (b) the language concerning "companions of fire" and "infidels" appeared to be a direct slap to those who died in the fiery inferno that was Extortion 17. It certainly was not appropriate, and was indeed highly insensitive, that the fallen, non-Muslim Americans, laid out in coffins before the imam, were called "infidels."

Disgusting as that language may be, from a forensics standpoint, the whole hullabaloo over the ramp ceremonies, both at Bagram and then again on August 9, 2011, at Dover Air Force Base in Delaware, where the thirty American caskets and eight Afghan caskets were flown for another ramp ceremony, this time with President Obama present—was a convenient distraction to a bigger point: What happened to the bodies?

Gary Reid spent a portion of his limited time at the congressional hearing defending the imam's comments, but nobody asked the question, "What happened to the bodies?"

Perhaps even more important, no one asked, "Why were the unidentified Afghans flown back to the United States?"

Were they flown back because it had been determined that they were Taliban infiltrators and, if this information got out, that it could be highly damaging to the United States? Not a single member of the congressional panel asked that question on February 27, 2014.

Think of the oddity of bringing foreign soldiers back to the United States to have their bodies disposed of here. It would seem that the Afghans, if they were up to something honorable, would be entitled to a burial with honors in Kabul or an Afghan military cemetery somewhere in Afghanistan.

Think of how odd it would be if, on the beaches at Normandy, the bodies of fallen British and Canadian soldiers had been scooped up by the United States and brought back to the United States for disposal, rather than being left with the military authorities for a dignified treatment and burial in their own countries. Such treatment would have been an arrogant slap in the face to America's British and Canadian allies.

So just why were these Afghans brought back to the USA? And what became of their bodies?

Several family members were flat out told by US military officers that all the bodies had been cremated. One of the family members who received this information was Mr. Charles Strange of Philadelphia, the father of US Navy cryptologist Michael Strange. Mr. Strange has been publicly vocal about this issue and has demanded answers as to why Michael and the others were cremated.

So why is the cremation issue relevant to the forensics puzzle of this case? If the bodies were cremated, DNA evidence was destroyed. If DNA evidence was destroyed, it becomes impossible to identify the unidentified Afghans. Thus, if the unidentified Afghans were Taliban infiltrators or sympathizers, their identities will probably never be known because of the military's decision to cremate. If, in fact, this aircraft was infiltrated, and possibly even sabotaged by Taliban sympathizers who drew weapons while the aircraft was in flight, or possibly communicated with Taliban attackers on the ground, then cremating the bodies might be a way to keep that information from the public. Could this explain why the bodies of the Afghans, strangely, were brought back to the United States?

Going back to the topic of the brief congressional hearing on February 27, 2014, with all those casualty and funeral experts appearing before the subcommittee (four of the five witnesses were military casualty and funeral experts), one would think that there would have been some solid testimony about what happened to the bodies after they were transported back to the United States.

The cremation account, like the black box account, had been reported several times in the public domain, and even Congressman Chaffetz, who was conducting the hearing, was quoted by Bob Cusack in the article in *The Hill* on July 23, 2013, as saying, "The body I saw didn't need to be cremated." Yet, at Chaffetz's own hearing, none of the four mortuary/funeral experts either confirmed or denied the cremation reports. Instead, they opted for absolute silence. Why didn't Chaffetz ask whether the bodies were cremated? Why not ask about the family members who were told by military officials in 2011 that all the bodies from Extortion 17, including

Americans and Afghans, were cremated? Why not ask for a confirmation, a denial, or at least some clarification?

It was as if the military members testifying and the members of the congressional committee were determined not to touch this very important issue, pointing to either gross incompetence or a cover-up.

Is it possible that not all the bodies were cremated? Note that previously in this book, we've qualified the verb "cremate" with the adverb "apparently."

That's because the military has never publicly said that the bodies were cremated, although officers have told some family members that their sons were cremated. To create even more confusion on the issue, one family member of an Extortion 17 crewmember has reported that a local coroner witnessed seeing his son's body in the casket prior to burial. The young man in question was not interred in Arlington. Though most of the SEAL team members are buried in Arlington, some, including most of the National Guardsmen, are buried in their hometowns around the country.

The cremation issue marks another example of inconsistency, contradiction, confusion and stonewalling on the part of the military regarding a subject of crucial importance. The military claims none of the remains are identifiable, even though testimony in the Colt Report, autopsies, and the report from the local coroner clearly contradict that claim.

Then, on top of those contradictions, we have Congressman Chaffetz's remark about the "body not needing to be cremated."

Remember that at the time of this statement, Congressman Chaffetz, as chairman of the National Security subcommittee, had access to confidential, Top Secret information that the general public was not privy to. His comment is very telling.

Remember, too, that cremation is germane to an understanding of this case because it goes to the identity, or lack of identity, of the Afghans who infiltrated the helicopter without legal authorization or authority. Creating the illusion that the bodies were cremated because they were so badly burned and unidentifiable serves as a deterrent against the public demanding the identity of the Afghans.

On this issue, there has been more contradiction and sleight-of-hand from the military. For instance, the official military reports, disseminated by military spokesmen to the public, claimed that the bodies were so badly mangled that there were "no identifiable remains." On August 9, 2011, Pentagon spokesman Marine Col. David Lapan told reporters that there were "no identifiable remains" of the thirty troops.

A *McClatchy* newspaper article written by Nancy A. Youssef and Jonathan S. Landay that same day, August 9, 2011, also reported a Pentagon spokesman as saying "there were no identifiable remains." The *Potomac Local News* reported that Petty Officer Michael Strange was going to be cremated, a procedure not consented to or approved of by his family. Other news outlets reported the same thing in covering the arrival of the bodies at Dover, parroting the Pentagon line that none were identifiable.

This Pentagon-foisted version of events, that "all bodies were so badly mangled that there were no identifiable remains," creates the perfect backdrop for justification of the cremation of bodies. In other words, since "there were no identifiable remains," then we (the military) had no choice but to go ahead and cremate.

Of course, nowhere has the military publicly admitted to cremation. But casualty assistance call officers (CACO) did tell Mr. Strange that his son and the others were cremated.

Mr. Strange later saw a photograph of his son's body, taken at the crash site, and determined that he did not have to be cremated, because his body was still sufficiently intact. Mr. Strange was extremely upset when he saw the photograph, and came to the realization that cremation was in fact unnecessary.

But internal sworn testimony contained within the Colt Report (but not mentioned in the Executive Summary) totally contradicts the military's official "there were no identifiable remains" line.

Remember that the military probably was not anticipating the public release of underlying evidence from the Colt Report, and probably calculated that it could get away with yet another false narrative by publicly claiming that "there were no identifiable remains." Why spread such a false narrative, unless you're embracing justification for cremating bodies?

Consider, for example, the sworn testimony of the J3 operations officer provided at Exhibit 1, page 116 of the Colt Report.

> *So they pulled off there, no signs of survivors. I do want to highlight
> here, and I will show you in the next slide, there was a single, coher-
> ent crash site. It was all together. There were a number of individuals
> outside the wreckage, and those were the individuals, the six friendly
> KIA. Later on, I heard a number that there were actually eight out-
> side—identified as outside the wreckage that were not really burned
> and they were recognizable.*

This is the same officer who also started to testify about the unauthorized Afghans who infiltrated the aircraft, but was cut off midstream
by his boss.

The public claim made by the Pentagon that "there were no identifiable remains" was undercut and undermined by internal sworn testimony
within its own report.

Why would the military disseminate false information about the
bodies' condition? With sworn testimony that at least eight bodies were
"not really burned" and "were recognizable," why would the military publicly claim that there were "no identifiable remains"?

It's important to understand regarding this false claim, as with so
many of the other public contradictions and inaccuracies contained in the
Colt Report, that the data in the report had not been declassified, and
those conveying the false information probably never thought that the
real, underlying data would be quickly declassified and analyzed.

So why disseminate the false reports that *all* the bodies were unidentifiable, contradicting internal evidence that at least eight were recognizable? Here's why: Because if all the bodies were truly mangled and burned
to the point that they could not be identified, then the military could
better justify its decision to cremate.

All these claims about the bodies being unrecognizable would
seem to justify the military's purported cremation of the bodies which,
conveniently, destroyed DNA evidence on the identity of the Afghan
infiltrators.

As the blatant contradictions and inaccuracies mount, it becomes more and more obvious that the military spun a web of lies to hide the truth about what really happened.

CHAPTER 48

British Press Reports: The Taliban Knew

It is worth taking a closer look at the reports in the British press, not only because of their revelation from the Afghan government that Taliban forces were tipped off, but also because they provided yet another source contradicting the official and false Pentagon reports of August 9, 2011, that no bodies were identifiable.

The first of the two British reports came in a *Telegraph* story on August 8, 2011, entitled "US Helicopter Shot Down in Taliban Trap." An unnamed Afghan government official told the *Telegraph* that the Taliban had laid a trap for Extortion 17 to lure the chopper to the area where it was shot down.

The *Telegraph* quoted the Afghan government official, speaking on condition of anonymity, as saying, "Now it's confirmed that the helicopter was shot down, and it was a trap that was set by a Taliban commander." The Afghan official went on to say that "the commander lured US forces to the scene by telling them there was a Taliban meeting taking place there," and that the Karzai government, "thinks this was a retaliation attack for the killing of Osama bin Laden."

Remarkably, the *Telegraph* report gave the name of the Taliban leader the SEALs were targeting, Qari Tahir, which up to that point, had been a guarded secret. The name Qari Tahir did not surface from the American side until later. Here's the exact wording from the *Telegraph* on that point: "Citing intelligence 'gathered from the area,' the official blamed Qari Tahir, a Taliban commander, for masterminding the attack. He alleged that four Pakistani nationals helped Tahir carry out the strike."

The *Telegraph* is a longstanding, credible paper in Britain, having been named National Newspaper of the Year by the British Press in 2010, and also having won journalistic awards for its coverage of the Iraq War in 2004. It is not a gossip-laden tabloid.

But the *Telegraph* wasn't the only British newspaper to run this story. As a follow-up to the *Telegraph*'s report, on August 10, 2011, just four days after the shoot-down, and just one day after the Pentagon claimed that no bodies were recognizable, the UK *Daily Mail*, also a reputable newspaper and one of the oldest in Britain, also quoted unnamed officials of the Afghan government as saying that the Taliban knew in advance the exact flight path of the Chinook.

Consider this stunning section from the UK *Daily Mail* article:

An Afghan official said on Monday that the Taliban lured US forces into an elaborate trap to shoot down their helicopter.

He said that Taliban commander Qari Tahir lured US forces to the scene by tipping them off that a Taliban meeting was taking place.

He also said four Pakistanis helped Tahir carry out the strike.

"Now it's confirmed that the helicopter was shot down and it was a trap that was set by a Taliban commander," said the official, citing intelligence gathered from the area.

"The Taliban knew which route the helicopter would take," he continued.

"That's the only route, so they took position on the either side of the valley on mountains and as the helicopter approached, they attacked it with rockets and other modern weapons. It was brought down by multiple shots."

Another official, who spoke on condition of anonymity to describe the event while the investigation remains ongoing, said that the Rangers, special operations forces who work regularly with the SEALs, secured the crash site afterwards.

38 people—including 30 American Special Forces troops and eight Afghan soldiers—were killed when the blast brought down the helicopter early Saturday.

Of the 30, 22 Navy SEALs from the elite "Team Six" unit that killed Osama bin Laden lost their lives.

On Sunday, the names of the Americans aboard the chopper began to be released.

Aaron Carson Vaughn, from Tennessee, was a 30-year-old Navy SEAL and the first special ops soldier to be identified in the devastating crash that killed 38 on Friday.

This report shows that Navy SEAL Aaron Vaughn's body was *immediately* identifiable, further proving the falsity of subsequent Pentagon reports that "there were no identifiable remains"—[the claim made by Pentagon spokesman Marine Col. David Lapan to reporters]—the narrative they needed to justify cremation—which would have destroyed DNA evidence of the identity of the unidentified Afghans.

Note that neither paper used the Taliban—which we would expect to push a propaganda-laced narrative—as a source. Both attribute their information to the Afghan government. This is significant, because the Afghan government led by President Hamid Karzai, was supposed to be a US ally.

So two major British newspapers reported essentially the same thing, with uncanny detail, specifically naming the terrorist who was the subject of the operation, weeks before the US government confirmed anything about Qari Tahir.

The British press accounts were ignored in the Colt Report, ignored by the National Security Subcommittee, and largely ignored by the American press, as if they had no relevance to a determination of what really happened.

CHAPTER 49

Afghan President Karzai: First to Announce the Shoot-Down

Afghan president Hamid Karzai was the first public official to announce the shoot-down of Extortion 17.

How would Karzai know about the shoot-down of the SEAL team ahead of the US government? Why would he make the announcement rather than the US military? The fact that Karzai was on-the-spot with the announcement, in fact announcing it as soon as the sun rose in Afghanistan, showed that the Afghan government had their fingers on the pulse of this mission and were most likely tipped off either by their Afghan insiders at Base Shank or by the Taliban itself. Karzai's quick announcement gave credence to the UK *Daily Mail* report citing the Afghan government's claims that the Taliban was tipped off. Just how Johnny-on-the spot was the Afghan president in announcing this?

Karzai announced it the very same day. Not only that, but he announced specific details about the shoot-down before the US government had released any details.

An Associated Press story published on August 6, 2011 made two telling references to Karzai.

Here's the first revelation from that article:

Afghan President Hamid Karzai announced the number of people killed in the crash and the presence of special operations troops before any other public figure. He also offered his condolences to the American and Afghan troops killed in the crash.

Why did Karzai announce the shoot-down before the US government announced it? Second, how did Karzai know the specific number of people killed in the crash? Third, how did he know that Special Operations forces were on board? Who told him all this? Was he tipped off like the Taliban? Wouldn't it have been more appropriate for President Obama to have made the first announcement? After all, thirty of the thirty-eight men aboard were Americans, and it was an American helicopter.

Of course no one on the congressional subcommittee asked any of these questions on February 27, 2014.

Karzai clearly had an inside line of communication not only with the Taliban (he had been negotiating with them for months), but also with someone with specific details on the mission, and was eager to announce his knowledge of such, even before President Obama could announce the deaths of the SEALs.

Here's the second revelation from that article:

Night raids have drawn criticism from human rights activists and infuriated Karzai, who says they anger and alienate the Afghan population. But NATO commanders have said the raids are safer for civilians than relatively imprecise airstrikes.

Karzai, who had been negotiating with the Taliban for months and reaching out to them for years, was furious about the presence of US Special Forces. Why? Because US Special Forces, unlike the Russian forces who came in 1970, were highly effective in killing Taliban.

Karzai was furious that the SEALs and Rangers were so effective against the Taliban and wanted them gone. He needed the Taliban to keep alive his political fortunes at the time, and it was hard to achieve that when he was playing host to the government whose Special Forces were killing Taliban.

The increase in US Special Operations was reaching a boiling point, as documented by *New York Times* reporters Thom Shanker, Elizabeth Mumiller, and Rod Norland, in an article published November 15, 2010.

In "Despite Gains, Night Raids Split US and Karzai," the *Times* reported that, "For the United States, a recent tripling in the number of night raids by Special Operations forces to capture or kill Afghan insurgents has begun to put heavy pressure on the Taliban and change the momentum in the war in Afghanistan. For President Hamid Karzai of Afghanistan, the raids cause civilian casualties and are a rising political liability, so much so that he is now loudly insisting that the Americans stop the practice."

The *Times* went on to say that "The difference—and a flare-up over the raids between Mr. Karzai and Gen. David H. Petraeus, the top American commander in Afghanistan—is likely to be a central focus at a NATO summit this week in Lisbon, where the United States and NATO are to present a plan that seeks to end the combat mission in Afghanistan by 2014."

The day before, Sunday, November 14, 2010, Karzai had told *Washington Post* editors in Kabul that it was time to reduce the US military presence in Afghanistan. Reporter Doug Mataconis wrote that Karzai said, "The time has come to reduce military operations. The time has come to reduce the presence of, you know, boots in Afghanistan . . . to reduce the intrusiveness into the daily Afghan life."

The *Post* goes on to report that "Karzai has long been publicly critical of civilian casualties at the hands of US and NATO troops and has repeatedly called for curtailing night raids into Afghan homes."

So over a year before the shoot-down, Karzai was becoming increasingly hostile about US forces, and especially US Special Forces conducting night missions.

Then, to make matters worse, in March 2011, five months before the Extortion 17 shoot-down, US Special Forces killed Karzai's cousin.

CHAPTER 50

NATO Special Operations Forces Kill President Karzai's Cousin

By March 2011, President Hamid Karzai's frustration with US Special Forces operating in his country was festering. He was furious because US Special Forces were killing Taliban, eroding and undermining his attempted negotiations and peace talks.

The American war in Afghanistan, even though there may not have been an end game, was quite different from the Russian war some thirty years before. In ten years in Afghanistan, the Soviets had over fourteen thousand killed and nearly fifty-five thousand wounded. By contrast, in the first years of the American War, from 2001 to 2009, only 569 US military personnel were killed. That number would increase in 2010 and 2011, when President Obama stepped up the war effort, adding 497 killed in 2010. So by the time 2011 rolled around, 1,066 Americans had been killed, versus over fourteen thousand Soviets in nearly the same period of time.

Afghan guerrilla tactics against American Special Operators were not nearly as effective as they had been against the more primitive Soviets, and the Americans were getting the best of the Taliban. And the Taliban didn't like it.

Remember, Karzai was cozying up to the Taliban because he needed their support once the US left. But instead of slowing the tempo of Special Operations missions, US policy was to ratchet up those missions, and Karzai's anger grew.

Then the Special Forces operations became up-close and personal for Karzai. On March 9, 2011, NATO forces mistakenly killed an elderly cousin of President Karzai in a botched night raid in the village of Karz, near the southern city of Kandahar.

According to the UK *Daily Mail,* "Haji Yar Muhammad Khan, 65, a second cousin of the president, was accidentally shot in Mr. Karzai's home village of Karz, near the southern city of Kandahar."

President Karzai's own brother, head of the provincial council, was quoted in the article as saying, "While the operation was going on, Khan walked out of his house and was shot by mistake. He was not the target."

Here's how David Williams of the *Daily Mail* described the effect of Khan's death:

The shooting of such a high-profile figure will fuel the furious row between Mr. Karzai and ISAF, the NATO-led International Security Assistance Force over repeated civilian deaths. The US offered a rare apology this month after nine Afghan boys were gunned down by helicopters as they collected firewood.

When President Karzai was the first to announce the shoot-down of Extortion 17 on August 6, 2011, and when he offered his "condolences" for the lives of the Americans killed, he was offering condolences over a mission that he was furious about to begin with, after Special Forces had accidentally killed his cousin, after he had been complaining for months about the presence of US Special Forces in Afghanistan.

So would it be surprising if the Taliban had been tipped off about this mission? Remember, the unidentified Afghans who boarded Extortion 17 were loyal to President Karzai, who now, after the death of his own flesh and blood, had a special and personal grudge against US Special Forces. And like it or not, martyrdom is a badge of honor for Islamic militants.

Under these circumstances, neither the Colt team nor the National Security subcommittee asked any questions about it? Were they afraid of the answer they might get? Or did they already know the answer and were trying to keep the public from learning the truth?

CHAPTER 51

Karzai and the Taliban Playing Footsie for Years

Years before Extortion 17 was shot down, and long before his cousin had been killed by US Special Forces, Afghan president Hamid Karzai had been playing footsie with the Taliban, thinking of the day when US forces would be gone. Karzai had already been negotiating with the Taliban for at least four years at the time of the shoot-down. President Karzai, as recently as June 2011, two months after his cousin was killed, admitted to personally being in peace talks with the Taliban and even claimed that the United States was negotiating with the Taliban as well. This was reported by Fox News on June 18, 2011. The US government did not confirm or deny Karzai's claim that the United States was negotiating with the Taliban.

Reuters reported on September 11, 2007 that Karzai was urging the Taliban to negotiate peace. On September 29, 2007, NBC reported that "President Hamid Karzai offered Saturday to meet personally with Taliban leader Mullah Omar for peace talks and give the militants a high position in a government ministry as a way to end the rising insurgency in Afghanistan."

On November 17, 2008, the WASHINGTON POST reported that, "Afghan President Hamid Karzai said Sunday that he would guarantee the security of Taliban chief Mohammad Omar if he decides to enter into talks."

On November 3, 2009, the UK *Telegraph* reported that Karzai offered an olive branch to his "Taliban brothers."

On January 29, 2010, the *Los Angeles Times* reported that, "Afghan President Hamid Karzai told world leaders Thursday that he intends to reach out to the top echelons of the Taliban within a few weeks, accelerating a peace initiative that has troubled US and many other Western leaders." According to the *Times*, the Obama Administration was "cool" to the Karzai plan on the Taliban.

On October 6, 2010, the *Washington Post* reported that the Taliban was in "high-level talks"with the Karzai government.

On October 10, 2010, CNN reported that Karzai had "unofficial personal contacts" negotiating with the Taliban on his behalf. The next day, October 11, 2010, the *Christian Science Monitor* reported that Karzai himself was negotiating with the Taliban.

Of course, all these reports, and many others, predated the reports in June of 2011 (two months before the shoot-down) that both the United States and Afghanistan were negotiating with the Taliban.

There is no question that the Afghan government had ties with the Taliban. They were talking with the Taliban and had been doing so for months. Karzai wanted to cozy up with the Taliban and make peace with them because once the United States left, he didn't want the Taliban to be on the other side of him, militarily.

Yet, despite this uncontroverted recent history of talks between the Taliban and the Afghan government, no questions were asked of any Afghans in the Colt investigation, nothing was mentioned about this in the Colt Executive Summary, nothing was said by General Mattis, and no questions were asked about any of this in the congressional investigation.

Reputable British newspapers reported that the Taliban were tipped off. This raises other questions. Was the Taliban in communication with someone inside the helicopter? Could there have been a tracking device on one of the seven unidentified Afghans aboard?

These questions were glossed over and were, in fact, never even addressed in the Colt Report, again, as if the whole subject was the pink elephant in the room. No Afghans were interviewed. There was no follow-up on the UK *Daily Mail* report to either confirm or deny its accuracy.

Why would the Colt Report simply ignore this seemingly important tip? Why would the National Security subcommittee ignore it in questions on February 27, 2014, at a time when Extortion 17 family members were so desperate for answers? How could this question be ignored in the investigation? Is it because the Army doesn't want the real truth exposed? A serious report alleging Taliban infiltration has to be followed up on.

Moreover, despite the fact that Afghans were routinely being ordered on these missions, not one single Afghan was questioned about anything regarding the Extortion 17 mission.

The pink elephant was left to roam.

CHAPTER 52

Another Dirty Secret:
Afghans on Every American Mission

Most Americans have no clue that for every US military mission executed in Afghanistan, because of evolving political agreements and evolving political correctness, the US made the Afghans privy to every mission executed. This means, despite the big-time problem of Green-on-Blue violence and the warnings by former US ambassador Ryan Crocker, the Afghans were brought in and made a part of Top Secret details of each and every mission conducted in Afghanistan. That means the Afghans were tipped off on Top Secret details of the Extortion 17 mission.

Consider the following stunning testimony from the J3 officer of the task force, beginning at page 6 of Exhibit 1 of the Colt Report on the extent of Afghan involvement in US mission planning.

In this testimony, the J3 officer reveals the existence of a group known as the "OCG," for "Operational Coordination Group," made up largely of Afghans:

> *Likewise you see on the left there the OCG. We made some real money with the OCG; they are the Operational Coordination Group and they assist us with the planning, and the vetting, and de-confliction of our operation. Likewise once we are done executing the operation they are able to send the results report, the result of the operations up through their various administrates. They are made up of the ANA, Afghan National Army, the National Director for Security, as well as the National Police Force. They are here on site. They are here on site,*

but we also have them down at the regional level in RC-South and
in September we are going to stand up region site up in RC-North.

The next excerpt revealed that this Afghan "Operational Coordination Group" has visibility on "every operation." Not only that, they knew about every US operation that went on in Afghanistan. Not only that, they were also "briefed" on every operation.

> **IO-DEP:** *So they have visibility on every operation?*
> **TF J3:** *Every operation.*
> **IO-DEP:** *So they knew about the operations.*
> **TF J3:** *Oh yea[h].*
> **IO-DEP:** *And they were briefed on it.*

The US media has not reported about Afghan knowledge of and involvement in these sensitive military operations. In fact, it isn't even clear that the media is aware of it. Most of the American public is wholly unaware of this fact.

Even more shocking was follow-up testimony revealing that these Afghans were simply given authority to cancel or veto any US mission any time they wanted to. From Exhibit 1, pages 6 and 7 of the Colt Report:

> **IO-DEP:** *So they have the ability, do they have approval authority on that, to cancel an operation?*
> **TF J3:** *Technically they do, they don't exercise it, but technically they do have authority.*
> **IO-DEP:** *So they either task or approve the operation.*
> **TF J3:** *Yep. So again another critical enabler as we move more towards Afghanization, as we move towards empowering Afghans, it will be a critical player as well, and we have—that we're figuring those two units as well as the Task Force, those are our primary concerns with transition forward.*

This testimony showed that the Afghans actually approved all missions, and could even veto missions, even though they rarely did that.

Think about the oddity of all this. You have an invading power, the United States, conquering a country, Afghanistan. Then after conquering the country and deposing of the Taliban-supported government, while its forces still occupy the country (Afghanistan), and when the country is still the conquering power, at a time when the country is full of enemy insurgents anxious to kill forces from the conquering power, the conquering power cedes control and information over to the native forces of the conquering power, simply trusting, blindly that there will be no breaches of security from the native forces.

That's what the United States did—foolishly ceded control and access to Top Secret information to the Afghan government. A superpower gave up control and Top Secret operational planning to a government that it propped up and put in power, a country with which it has no longstanding history of trust.

Part of the problem with this strategy of ceding control and providing Top Secret information to the Afghans is the ever-uncertain volatility of radical Islam. With radical Islam being at the heart of the 9/11 attacks that started the Afghan war, and with radical Islam being responsible for countless bloody atrocities from AD 632 mercilessly extending into the twenty-first century, in Europe, Russia, Africa and the United States, it becomes difficult to look under the radical veil and determine who your enemies are and who your friends are.

This is especially true in Afghanistan and neighboring Pakistan, where some of the most violent Islamic atrocities have been reported. The numerous instances of Green-on-Blue violence, whereby Afghans who were supposed to be our friends simply shot Americans in the back, are well documented. Given Ambassador Crocker's frank warnings about widespread Taliban infiltration into the Afghan military, the Green-on-Blue issues should have been on the minds of military planners at all times, with great care and great scrutiny given to the identity and philosophies of any Afghan boarding a US military aircraft undergoing combat operations.

For whatever reason, that never happened with Extortion 17.

Another problem with the US thinking here was that these Afghans, who were given inside information on every US mission, were under the operational command of President Hamid Karzai, who was opposed to US Special Forces operations, who was furious with the United States for continuing these missions, who on many occasions had argued that the United States should get out of Afghanistan, who was cozying up to the Taliban and having peace talks with them, and whose own cousin had been killed by Special Forces in the spring before Extortion 17 was shot down.

As seen in the above testimony, part of the supporting theory behind all of this, at least from the Obama Administration's standpoint, was that eventually control of the country would be turned over to the Karzai government.

That's all well and good. But it seems that the principal and preeminent concern of the Administration should have been the safety of American forces. It seems unnecessary to make unreliable Afghan forces privy to Top Secret American military operations when the Afghan forces had no proven track record of reliability.

Could this explain why, with sweeping powers to investigate, the Colt Report doesn't contain any interviews of any Afghan forces whatsoever? Recall the original directive from General Mattis giving Brigadier General Colt very broad investigative powers, to "conduct your investigation in whatever matter you believe necessary and proper."

Yet, with such broad-sweeping power to investigate and ask anybody anything he wanted about the investigation (unless his question called for a potentially incriminating answer), Colt's sworn interviews did not include one single Afghan, even though (a) the Afghans were in on the mission to begin with; and (b) there were open, unanswered questions about the identity of the seven Afghans who illegally boarded the chopper; and (c) there was a documented history of Green-on-Blue violence whereby Afghan "allies" were killing Americans; and (d) the British press reported an Afghan governmental source saying the Taliban was specifically tipped off on the mission and the specific flight plan of Extortion 17.

Either Colt was incompetent, or he was covering something up and did not want certain information in the record.

Here's a hint: Brigadier General Colt, a decorated Army Special Forces aviator, is not incompetent. Just the opposite is true. All signs point to a cover-up. Remember, this pink elephant never came out of the jungle until the sergeant major's telling comments in the Vaughn home in January of 2013 that "this was a very big deal."

This obvious attempt to hide information about the key security breach in this mission points to the conclusion that the *Telegraph* and *Daily Mail* reports are exactly right—that the Taliban knew the mission, knew the flight plan, and therefore, was waiting near the landing zone with RPGs loaded, ready to fire as the chopper approached to around 100 feet above the ground.

The same conclusion can be drawn about the House National Security Subcommittee's decision to ask no probing questions about the identity of the Afghans who boarded that chopper.

If it leaked out that the Afghans tipped off the Taliban, leading to the deaths of the Extortion 17 crew, it could have proved highly embarrassing to high-ranking US officials, which would have been especially undesirable in the election year of 2012.

But Brigadier General Colt was, by all accounts, an honorable officer with a distinguished record. But still, he was just a one-star general at the time of this investigation. That means he was one rank above a full-bird colonel. That's a very significant honor and achievement in one sense. But in another sense, it's not.

While a brigadier general commands tremendous respect among the troops, and rightly so, the fact is, the guys wearing four stars on their collars, and presidential appointees in the Pentagon are the ones who set policy.

In this case, the case of Extortion 17, the narrative is this: "The shootdown of Extortion 17 is just one of those things that happens in the fog of war. It's no one's fault on the American side, and nothing could have been done to stop it."

That narrative, of course, is an incomplete narrative, and it is a false one. But despite the numerous inaccuracies and shortcomings pointed out in the Executive Summary of the Colt Report, inaccuracies that help paint this false narrative, it is likewise important to remember that the blame for the narrative should not be laid at the feet of Colt.

The decision to paint such a false narrative would have come at a level above Colt. Remember, it was General Mattis, the four-star commander of CENTCOM, who strapped Colt's hands by limiting the investigation with the instructions on Article 31 matters.

Whoever ordered the cover-up—and it may have gone higher in the chain of command than Mattis—was more concerned about protecting someone from a court-martial or guarding against the release of potentially embarrassing information than they were about getting to the bottom of what happened to Extortion 17.

CHAPTER 53

Shocking Discovery: Bullets in the Bodies

Perhaps the most shocking revelation about this whole affair comes in information that has not yet been publicly revealed and was not in the Colt Report. It certainly wasn't touched upon in any of the questions asked on February 27, 2014, by the House National Security Subcommittee.

This author gained access to two autopsies of US Navy SEALs who died aboard Extortion 17. In both of the autopsies, bullets were found and removed from the bodies of the service members, immediately determined to be irrelevant by the pathologist, and then simply thrown away.

How did the bullets get into the bodies of the SEALs?

Why did the pathologist decide to throw the bullets away?

Normally it is up to a prosecutor, not a pathologist, to ultimately determine what's relevant or irrelevant in a crime scene investigation, and pathologists certainly should not throw away bullets found in a victim's body. But, incredibly, that's what happened here. In at least two cases—it is possible more than two bodies contained bullets (the author did not gain access to all the autopsies)—the pathologist unilaterally disposed of the bullets.

The revelations that bullets were found in the bodies appeared on page 4 of both of these autopsies, with these words: "Cook-off rounds recovered at autopsy are not retained by the AFMES because they are of no evidentiary value."

Then, in addition to the revelation about the "cook-off rounds," one of the two autopsies adds these words: "Four grey metal fragments are recovered from the torso and are retained by AFMES."

What is a cook-off round? It is a bullet that has "cooked off," and exploded, usually in a fire. The Armed Forces medical examiner found bullets in the bodies of two SEALs who died aboard Extortion 17. Sounds like a reasonable assumption, right? That the bullets got so hot in the fire that they actually fired off and somehow fired into the torsos of these men? Actually, such an assumption wouldn't be reasonable at all.

Here's the classic example to demonstrate what happens with cook-off rounds that aren't inside the barrel of a gun.

Assume there is a house that catches on fire. Inside the house, inside the master bedroom, say there is a box of .22 caliber bullets in the middle of the fire. Assume that the fire gets hot enough that the gunpowder is ignited inside those bullets. First off, it's not a given that this will happen, as bullets do not always cook off, even in a fire. But even if the rounds do cook off in a box, they are for the most part harmless, unless they are in the barrel of a rifle or a gun. That's because a bullet in a fire, even if it pops, has nowhere to go, unless it's in a gun barrel.

Anyone who understands how a bullet cartridge is put together will understand there is the projectile, that is the bullet itself, which, when fired from a weapon, actually flies through the air at a target, and then there is the casing, which usually falls to the ground, or simply remains in the gun, depending on the type of gun being used.

What we're discussing here is a topic within the field of *internal ballistics*. Internal ballistics is a subfield of ballistics that focuses primarily on the propulsion of the projectile. Internal ballistics studies how far and how powerfully the bullet is propelled through the air, *if at all*, toward the target. The phrase "if at all," is significant, because as will be seen, bullets, even when there is an explosion of the propellant (gunpowder), are not always launched toward a target. This is particularly true of cook-off rounds, because bullets not in a weapon often fizzle and go nowhere.

Usually, a round that ignites inside a box from fire simply separates. The bullet does not go flying off in the air, and usually the casing itself goes farther than the bullet.

The bullet and the casing may separate by a few inches at the most, and that's it.

HATCHER'S NOTEBOOK

Major General Julian Hatcher was the chief of ordnance for the US Army during World War II and later became technical editor for *The American Rifleman*. General Hatcher spent a career studying internal ballistics, and compiled his findings in his seminal work from 1962 entitled *Hatcher's Notebook*.

One of the areas that the general studied and reported on was the subject of cook-off rounds. This study was done in part to address concerns of police and fire departments regarding the safety of working in situations where unchambered ammunition might be threatened by fire.

Here's how General Hatcher addressed the study on page 4 of his book.

> *The second new chapter covers the subject of explosions and powder fires, as well as the behavior of ammunition when it is exploded, accidentally or otherwise, while it is not in a gun. The many inquiries on this subject that I received from Police and Fire Departments, state and municipal authorities, and from readers of the magazine caused me to make a large number of interesting experiments to be able to answer their questions with certainty. The information thus developed is of great value, and is so important that it should be preserved permanently in convenient form for reference.*

General Hatcher specifically examined what happens when an unchambered bullet goes off in a fire. He turned to this very topic at Chapter XXI, page 521 of his book, under the topic of "Explosions and Powder Fires."

General Hatcher covered numerous experiments, under controlled and uncontrolled circumstances, and then, under the topic "Small Arms Ammunition as a Fire or Explosion Hazard," concluded at page 540 that "Enough experiments have been made on this subject so that almost any question that might arise can be answered with definite information based on tests. As for any possible explosion hazard from small arms ammunition, even in large quantities, it can be said with confidence that there is no danger."

Here is an example of one of the tests cited in *Hatcher's Notebook*, at page 533 [author's emphasis]:

A fibreboard case containing 500 12-gauge shotgun shells was placed on a metal rack over a pile of kindling wood and the wood was ignited. After the case was burning, the blazing wood was dragged away. The burning continued until all the shells had burned. At no time did any of the shells explode with violence. The powder charges burned quietly, and barely opened the crimped shells. No propelling of shot charges could be detected. *However, some of the primers did pop off audibly.*

So in this controlled experiment, even with five hundred shotgun shells set on fire and burned, very few actually "cooked off." On the next page, Hatcher was even more to the point demonstrating that (a) cook-off rounds are rare, and (b) even if a round cooks off, it isn't dangerous.

Moreover, in other tests by the same organization, a large number of metallic cartridges and shotgun shells were burned in a fire of oil-soaked wood. The cartridges and shells exploded from time to time, but there was no general explosion or propulsion of shot or bullets with any great force or to any great distance. Throughout the test, the men conducting it remained within 20 feet without injury. The test showed that small arms cartridges, whether they are metallic cartridges or shotgun shells, will not explode simultaneously but rather piece by piece, and that the material of which the cartridges or shells are made will usually not fly more than a few feet.

This point should be emphasized: A cook-off round, which rarely occurs even when there is fire, which is not inside a gun, is not going to penetrate the body of a Navy SEAL. Consider these results, laid out at page 539 of General Hatcher's book [author's emphasis]:

In another exhaustive series of experiments, I took various cartridges for both rifle and pistol, loaded with smokeless powder and with black powder, and placed them downward in a lead melting pot that was arranged to be heated by electricity. On top of the pot I laid a piece of corrugated cardboard, with the cartridge standing on its base so the bullet was pointing directly at the cardboard. Then the heat was turned on until the cartridge exploded. In no case did the bullet pierce the cardboard, or even dent it *deeply*.

Two points should be drawn from General Hatcher's extensive research, points that are now widely accepted in the field of ballistics. First, it is unlikely that ammunition is going to cook off in a fire to begin with. And second, even if the ammunition does cook off, unless that ammunition is in a gun that is pointed directly at the Navy SEAL, it is not going to penetrate through the SEAL's thick Kevlar uniform, let alone penetrate the skin.

Consider the combat uniforms typically worn by Navy SEALs. The SEALs typically wear the AOR1 Navy SEAL combat uniform, made with Kevlar, which is the same material used in bulletproof vests. While a gun pointed at that uniform point-blank would penetrate it, a cook-off round popping off from an ammunition box is *not* going to penetrate it.

Remember also that when Extortion 17 went down, the US military was so unconcerned about the danger posed by cook-off rounds that units approached the helicopter while parts of it were still burning at least twice. Remember that the Pathfinder leader testified that the aircraft was "still smoldering" when they approached it to search for the black box.

General Hatcher wasn't the only ballistics expert to come to this conclusion—that cook-off rounds outside of a weapon, if there is a cook-off at all, are not inherently dangerous.

DR. DI MAIO AND THE HARMLESS COOK-OFF ROUND
One of the nation's most noted forensics pathologists is Dr. Vincent J. M. Di Maio, who some may remember as an expert forensics witness in the George Zimmerman murder trial. Dr. Di Maio, who was a US Army Medical Corps pathologist and served as chief medical examiner for San Antonio, Texas, is a professor of pathology at the University of Texas at San Antonio.

He is among the world's foremost authorities and, indeed, may be *the* foremost authority in the world on the topic of gunshot wounds. His magnum opus, appropriately entitled for the area of expertise for which he is most renowned, is *Gunshot Wounds: Practical Aspects of Firearms, Ballistics, and Forensic Techniques*, published in 1985.

Though Dr. Di Maio's studies on the issue of cook-off rounds may have come more than two decades after General Hatcher's, his observations and conclusions are remarkably similar to the general's.

In Chapter 10 of his book, in a section entitled "Behavior of Ammunition and Gunpowder in Fires," Di Maio comments as follows on pages 284 and 285:

> *Occasionally a story appears in a newspaper describing how fire fighters fought a blaze in a sporting goods store as bullets from exploding ammunition "whizzed by" and cans of gunpowder "exploded" around them. Although this type of story makes fine newspaper copy, it bears no relation to what actually happens in a fire involving ammunition and gunpowder.*
>
> *Smokeless powder is used in all modern cartridges. When it is ignited in a gun, heat, and gas are produced, both of which are confined initially to the chamber. As the pressure of the gas builds up, the chemical processes of combustion are speeded up so that the rate of burning becomes relatively instantaneous, and an "explosion" is produced. This explosion, however, occurs only when smokeless powder is ignited in a confined space such as the chamber of a gun. Outside of a gun, the powder will only burn with a quick hot flame.*

Then, on the next page, after citing some of the experiments conducted by General Hatcher, Di Maio further illustrated his findings on the notion of a cook-off round in a fire.

> *Occasionally one hears that an individual has been "wounded" when a cartridge was accidentally dropped into a fire and detonated. Investigation of such incidents usually reveals that the victim was really injured when they or another individual was playing with a gun.*

When small-arms ammunition is placed in a fire, the cartridge case may burst into a number of fragments and the bullet may then be propelled forward out of the case. In centerfire cartridges, the primer may blowout. None of these missiles, however, is dangerous to life under ordinary circumstances. The bullet in fact is probably the most harmless of all these missiles because with its relatively great mass it will have very little velocity.

All Hatcher and Di Maio's studies point to one conclusion: The bullets found inside the bodies did not come from ammunition just cooking off inside the helicopter, as the autopsies might imply. The bullets came out of the barrel of a gun.

This brings us to another question. What about a cook-off round which explodes inside of a gun?

That's an excellent question, because a round that cooks off inside the barrel of a gun can pose a danger, provided that the gun is aimed at its target.

Think about that. For the bullets inside the bodies of the SEALs to have come from a cook-off inside the gun barrel, someone would have had to aim the gun at the SEALs long enough for the bullet to have gotten hot enough to have cooked off. Or the SEALs would have to have found themselves juxtaposed in front of gun barrels at the moment of cook-off.

This isn't plausible, for two reasons.

First, the SEALs' weapons were found on the ground outside the aircraft, with no indication they were even burned. In Exhibit 65, the Pathfinder leader (PF PLT LDR) and the Pathfinder platoon sergeant (PF PSG), answering questions from the ADSAT officer, testified about where they found weapons.

ASDSAT3: *Any other weapons' components policed up on the battlefield?*

　　PF PLT LDR: *We recovered all three 240H's from the aircrafts. Is that what you are referring to?*

　　ASDSAT3: *No [inaudible]. Keep talking. Anything else? Did you find anything else?*

PF PSG: *Just the personal weapons that the heroes were carrying in the birds. We found those scattered right there on the ground where the main compartment of the bird was at. We collected it up near the crash site thinking that nobody would come in. Once the rain and the flash flood came in, we had to go searching the Wadi looking for the pieces that had floated down with the current.*

Also there simply wasn't enough time from the time the RPG attacked the aircraft until it hit the ground for the weapons to heat up enough to cook off. Going back to the Colt Report, in the Joint Combat Assessment Team Report, we learn, at page 38, that "The entire event (from weapon impact to crash) likely lasted less than five seconds."

So think about that. We have Extortion 17 at an altitude of 100 to 150 feet above ground, struck by an RPG, now dropping violently and chaotically toward the ground, with men and weapons probably flinging about inside during the fall, and we're supposed to assume that the weapons, in less than five seconds during that fall to earth, got hot enough and were then trained on the SEALs and cooked off, and perfectly aimed at the SEALS during that chaotic fall to earth, then fired bullets into the bodies of the SEALs during the less-than-five-second drop of 100 to 150 feet?

That is an impossible scenario to believe.

Moreover, based upon eyewitness testimonial accounts from the AC-130 witnesses and others, there was an immediate explosion contemporaneous with the RPG striking Extortion 17. An explosion erupting in flames would have killed all personnel immediately, strewing bodies and weapons in a chaotic manner and further reducing the likelihood that weapons could have been aimed in such a precise manner at bodies to have "cooked off."

The more likely scenario was a firefight aboard the chopper before the RPG ever struck it.

When the helicopter hit the ground, the weapons, the only possible source of cook-off rounds, were then scattered all over the ground, outside the aircraft, outside the fire, with no evidence that they ever even got hot.

Despite the military pathologist's decision to summarily remove bullets from the bodies of the SEALs at the autopsy, and to call them "cook-off rounds" and throw them away, the bullets found inside the bodies of the Navy SEALs were not cook-off rounds. The math works against that conclusion, the science of ballistics works against that conclusion, the evidence of the weapons being found strewn all over the ground, outside the burning aircraft, with no evidence that the weapons were even heated works against that conclusion, and the law of probability works against that conclusion.

Moreover, it should be pointed out that the military pathologist cannot, by on-the-spot visual inspection, make a determination as to whether a bullet was fired in a "cook-off" situation or fired conventionally by the gun's hammer striking the primer in the center of the base of the casing.

If the rounds were fired conventionally, the primer would have an indentation, made visible when the gun's hammer has struck the hammer. If the round were "cooked off," there would be no indentation in the primer, because heat would have caused the gunpowder to explode, rather than the primers.

The pathologist would need to see the casing and look at the casing and primer to determine if the round had been cooked off or not. All he had, however, were the actual bullets pulled from the SEALs' bodies.

The Joint Combat Assessment Team did not indicate that any casings were recovered. In fact, the report on "Collection Methodology" at page 26 of Exhibit 60 only indicates that "aircraft components" and some "residual" soil were taken from the shoot-down site.

In fact, no ballistics testing was reported at all, with the exception of extensive testing run on the RPG point-of-entry into the helicopter blade. In this regard, the forensics testing and analysis were conducted superbly, and based upon examination of the helicopter blade, the team concluded the angle of strike as being 40 degrees incoming under the wing.

There is absolutely no report of any ballistics testing done on any of the guns or small arms in the aircraft that could have been responsible for firing those bullets into the Navy SEALs. There is absolutely no report of any ballistics testing done on any of the casings or primers or gunpowder from any small arms in possession of either the SEALs or the Afghans on board. None.

No ballistics tests were done to match the bullets found in the bodies of Navy SEALs with the casings from which they were fired. Or, put it this way. If ballistics tests were conducted on the small arms in that aircraft or the discharged ammunition from those small arms, the results of those tests were not reported by the Joint Combat Assessment, nor were those tests reported on or mentioned anywhere in the Colt Report.

So how, then, did these bullets enter the bodies of the Navy SEALs?

And why would the military pathologist simply call these bullets cook-off rounds, declare them to be of no evidentiary value, and throw them away?

Could there have been a struggle for control of the aircraft before it landed?

Could the struggle for control of the aircraft have explained the thirteen to fourteen minute delay in the original landing time of the aircraft?

Could the seven unidentified Afghans, loyal to a president who hated US Special Forces, standing with their Taliban brothers, have pulled their weapons on the SEALs, hoping to keep the aircraft airborne long enough for their terrorist comrades on the ground to take a shot at it?

Could there have been a firefight on board the chopper before it landed?

Is this why the chopper seemed to stall in the air?

Is this why it was delayed and never landed?

Is this why the SEALs have bullets in their bodies?

Could this explain why we don't know the true identities of these Afghans to this day?

Could this explain the military's inconsistent, contradictory, and unbelievable explanation about the black box?

Is this why no Afghans are interviewed in the Colt Report?

Is this why, when the J3 officer started to testify as to how the Afghans got aboard the aircraft, his boss essentially shut him up?

A US Army Ranger who was in the flight control center as Extortion 17 attempted to find its landing zone that night has indicated that near panic broke out among military officers in the room when Extortion 17 actually went into a hover and stopped moving forward in the air.

The sudden stop in the sky could not be explained, according to the Ranger, and some in the room theorized that the chopper was hovering so that the SEALs could rappel down ropes from the chopper to the ground.

If the Ranger who reported this was correct, could the chopper have been delayed and have gone into a strange hover, stopping its forward progress in the sky because of a firefight that was going on inside?

Were the Afghans inside trying to stall and delay the landing so that their Taliban comrades on the ground could move into point-blank position with the RPGs?

Aside from the fact that the bullets are probably not from cook-off rounds, to simply throw away evidence of bullets found in a service member's body, and not preserve those bullets as evidence, borders on criminal negligence. In addition to the fact that the laws of physics make it unlikely that those bullets in the bodies of US service members could have come from cook-off rounds, the pathologist cannot make that determination based upon a visual inspection anyway.

To make that determination, that the bullets were cook-off rounds from a weapon, the bullets would have to be forensically examined, and then matched with the casings from which they were fired to determine whether there was an indentation in the butt of the casing, showing that the rifle's hammer had struck the bullet.

None of that was done. Instead, this crucial and valuable evidence was simply thrown out. Moreover, there is nothing in the Colt Report stating that bullets were found in the bodies of dead US service members. That was discovered by a separate examination of autopsy reports.

Could the Afghans have taken an explosive device on board? The pathologist did recover an unidentified metal fragment within one of the SEALs' bodies. The fragment has still not been identified. How does a small, unidentified metal fragment wind up in a SEAL's body, unless it is propelled there by an explosion? Of course, the fragment could have been hurled into the SEAL's body upon the explosion generated by the RPG strike. So it seems likely to have been propelled into the body by an explosion. The curious element here, however, is that the substance is unidentified. Any substance brought aboard a US helicopter by American forces, or part of that helicopter, should have been identifiable.

The inability to identify the substance suggests that whatever it is, it may have been brought onboard by the mysterious and unidentified Afghans who came onboard in the last-second swap out.

CHAPTER 54

Autopsies Versus "No Identifiable Remains"

There's at least one other point about the autopsies that contradicts the military's odd and false claim that there were "no identifiable remains" among the badly burned bodies of the members of Extortion, a falsehood that is even carried out on the headstone placed in Arlington National Cemetery.

In a cover letter obtained and dated October 20, 2011, from Captain C. T. Mallack, MD, United States Navy Medical Corps, one of the Extortion 17 families was informed of the autopsy with these words.

> As requested, enclosed within this sealed envelope is a complete copy of the Autopsy Report Protocol in the case of your late son, [name redacted for privacy reasons at request of family].
>
> I emphasize that the information contained within this report is graphically described to ensure complete accuracy of the physical details of your son's remains.

Stop and just think about the cover letter.

The military has claimed that the remains of those aboard Extortion 17 were unidentifiable. They've even placed a tombstone at Arlington claiming the remains of the men of Extortion 17 are "unidentified."

Yet, the pathologist was able to identify the bodies well enough to perform autopsies and even send letters and autopsy reports for individual SEALs to their families.

So how do you identify a body well enough to perform an autopsy if the body is "unidentified"?

The autopsy examination report for one of the SEALs provides the following information:

Place of Death: *Afghanistan*
Date of Death: *06 Aug 2011*
Date/Time of Autopsy: *10 Aug 2011/1400-1600 hours*
Place of Autopsy: *Post Mortuary, Dover AFB, DE*
Date of Report: *25 Aug 2011*
Circumstances of Death: *It is reported that the deceased was injured after the CH47 Chinook he was in received enemy fire.*
Authorization for Autopsy: *Armed Forces Medical Examiner, per 10 US Code 1471*
Identification: *Positive identification is established by antemortem and postmortem dental comparison.*
Cause of Death: *Multiple Injuries*
Manner of Death: *Homicide*

From these bullet points alone, several relevant facts emerge. First the date of the autopsy, namely August 10, 2011, was only one day after Pentagon spokesman Marine Col. David Lapan's claim that "Given the nature of the attack, there were 'no identifiable remains' of the thirty troops. It's also only one day after the *McClatchy* newspaper article written by Nancy A. Youssef and Jonathan S. Landay quoting a "Pentagon spokesman" as saying "there were no identifiable remains." It was four days after Army Pathfinders reported that at least eight of the men who had been thrown out of the helicopter were not badly burned and were visually identified on the spot.

Here's the other relevant nugget. Note the means of identification: "Positive identification is established by antemortem and postmortem dental comparison." This same phrase was used in both autopsies obtained by the author.

In other words, positive identification was easily made in this case simply by comparing the SEAL's dental records both before and after death. It is a basic premise of forensic dentistry that a person's teeth will survive fire and, in fact, will survive temperatures of up to 2,000 degrees Fahrenheit.

So the claim of "no identifiable" remains is false on multiple fronts. It allows a false narrative to be spun that "we can't identify those seven Afghans." And, of course, if we can't identify the previously unidentified Afghans, the military doesn't have to publicly deal with the question of whether they were Taliban sympathizers.

So the military perpetrates the false notion of "no identifiable remains," and, hopefully, the question of "who were the Afghans?" doesn't come up and doesn't get asked and doesn't get pressed.

We know already that eight bodies were immediately identifiable at the crash site, per sworn testimony of the Pathfinders, and now there are at least two others identifiable through dental records.

Obviously, the military has a reason to continue the drumbeat of this "no identifiable remains" falsehood. The only logical reason for perpetuating this falsehood: They want to hide the true identities of the Afghans who perpetrated Extortion 17.

CHAPTER 55

All Signs Point to a Cover-Up

Was the downing of Extortion 17 an inside job perpetrated by Taliban infiltrators? The circumstantial evidence is as follows.

The Afghan military is heavily infiltrated with Taliban. Seven unknown Afghans infiltrated the helicopter right before takeoff. The identity of the Afghans remains unknown.

An unexplained loss of communication and a communications delay occurred in the last three minutes before landing. In fact there was an inexplicable delay in landing, and during that delay, the chopper was shot down—three minutes and thirteen seconds after it should have already landed.

One Army Ranger inside flight control center that night reported that the chopper had stalled in the air, in an inexplicable hover at the time of the shoot-down. The flight data recorder is inexplicably missing. Bullets were found in the bodies of at least two Americans, which were summarily discarded by the military doctor on a suspicious determination that they were cook-off rounds, even though there is no evidence that bullets were matched to casings.

Unidentified metal fragments were found in the body of one of the SEALs, raising questions as to how multiple metal fragments wound up in his body, and the source of those fragments.

Although 100–150 feet above the ground when the RPG struck its back rotary blade, the helicopter broke into three parts and fell in a scattered triangular configuration on the ground below. The Colt Report indicated that the attack on the back rotary blade caused a series of stressors resulting in the breakup. But keep in mind that per the report, less than five seconds lapsed from the shoot-down until the crash on the ground. The breakup of the chopper, combined with the unidentified metal found in the SEAL's body, suggests the possibility of an internal explosion. Again, there may be other explanations for this combination of events, but under these questionable circumstances, no one has even asked the question.

Rifles and guns, the only source for possible cook-off rounds that could have penetrated the SEALs' bodies, were found outside on the ground, not in the chopper, and there is no evidence that they were even burned. This leaves open the possibility that Navy SEALs were shot before the chopper went down, perhaps in a struggle to keep the aircraft aloft longer so that it could be spotted and targeted from the ground.

FURTHER UNDERMINING THE COOK-OFF ROUND STORY
Recall from previous testimony that there were at least eight individuals on the ground at the crash site, outside the helicopter, and that their bodies were identifiable. This testimony came from the J3 (operations officer) at Exhibit 1, page 116 of the Colt Report.

The author gained access to information concerning the autopsy of one of the Americans whose body was found outside that helicopter. That American is Navy cryptologist Michael Strange. To be assigned to Seal Team Six, Michael had to be one of the elite cryptologists in the Navy.

Michael's godmother, Cheryl McNamee, spoke these affectionate words about her godson, a tremendous athlete and a tough young man from Philadelphia, four days after his death: "Most guys from Philadelphia, like Michael, love the Eagles, they love Philly cheesesteaks, but he was so much more. He was a thinker, and he loved his job and his family, and his family and all of us are very proud of him."

At the time Ms. McNamee made that statement, to the *Potomac Local News* on August 10, 2011, just four days after the shoot-down, none of Michael's family members had any specific details about Michael's body, other than the military's false claim that none of the bodies were identifiable. The entire family was under the impression that Michael's body was unidentifiable and was to be cremated.

The author has learned that Michael was found on the ground, apparently some distance from the wreckage of the helicopter. Secondly, his body was identifiable. Michael's father and others, including Congressman Chaffetz, have seen photographs of Michael's body lying on the ground outside the helicopter. Remember Chaffetz's comments that "the body I saw didn't need to be cremated."

Also, after seeing the photograph of Michael's body, his father, Charles, was publicly furious because he had been told by Navy officials that Michael had been cremated. This cremation account was also reported in the press, including the *Potomac Local News* as cited above, and Charles Strange brought up this very fact in the press conference on May 9, 2013.

But here is the third important point now known about Michael Strange's body: Cook-off rounds were found in his body at his autopsy and thrown away, apparently tossed away by the Armed Forces pathologist as having "no evidentiary value." But the presence of these so-called cook-off rounds in Michael's body was especially significant because Michael's body was not even inside the helicopter.

The fact that his body was thrown from the helicopter, at the moment of impact, and was away from the wreckage, away from the ammunition that was, according to the implied official narrative, supposedly cooking off and firing into the bodies of these men, makes the cook-off round theory for the bullets in Michael's body an even greater impossibility.

To recap the incontrovertible findings of General Hatcher and Doctor Di Maio, both among America's best and most well-respected ballistics experts, the likelihood of cook-off rounds winding up in the bodies of any of these American servicemen was slim-to-none from the start.

But when we consider the fact that *Michael's body was outside the chopper, away from the ammunition that was stored inside the chopper*, away from the flames, and away from the weapons, the notion that those bullets found inside his body were cook-off rounds is not only incredible, but next to impossible to believe.

There is only one logical conclusion: The bullets inside Michael's body did not come from outside the helicopter. That would be impossible. There were no bullets out there, on the ground, in a fire to cook off. They had to have been fired from inside the helicopter, before Michael's body was thrown out onto the ground.

Moreover, in the less-than-five seconds from the moment the chopper was struck until the moment it hit the ground, there was not enough time to heat any ammunition enough to cook off that ammunition. Thus, logic dictates that those bullets in Michael's body had to be fired *before the rocket-propelled-grenade ever struck the rear blade of Extortion 17.*

This brings us full circle to the pink elephant in the room:

Who were the unidentified Afghans who boarded Extortion 17? And why has the military been deafly silent on the topic of the unidentified Afghans? Why was the J3 (operations officer) basically muzzled when he broached the subject of these Afghan operatives in his sworn testimony during the Colt investigation? Why did Brigadier General Colt not mention them in his Executive Summary to General Mattis? And why did General Mattis not mention them in his final report, dated September 13, 2011?

And why did it take fifteen months after the shoot-down for the significance of this security breach of the seven Afghans to be finally brought to the forefront, when a brave and gutsy sergeant major, sitting in the living room of Billy and Karen Vaughn, right in front of Admiral William McRaven, told the Vaughns that the security breach involving the Afghans on board that helicopter was "a very big deal," and that it "should never have happened"?

These questions scream for answers. And so does this question: Did these Afghans fire the bullets into the bodies of these American servicemen in an internal ambush in the air even before the chopper was shot out of the sky by Taliban operatives on the ground? Does all this explain the odd and seemingly inexplicable behavior of Extortion 17 in the sky on approach to landing?

Remember, the Afghan government was reported as saying that the Taliban knew the flight plan, suggesting someone tipped off the Taliban. We don't know the identity of the seven Afghans who slipped on board, and probably never will know, because it appears that all bodies were cremated, thus destroying valuable DNA evidence. We do know that their president, Hamid Karzai, hated Special Forces, that he wanted Special

Forces out of the country, and that his own cousin was killed by Special Forces just five months before the Extortion 17 mission.

All this evidence is circumstantial and, clearly, there could be other explanations for each of these factors. But the circumstantial evidence of possible infiltration is strong enough that the matter should have been addressed and investigated, something that is not even considered in the Colt Report.

CIRCUMSTANTIAL EVIDENCE OF EITHER GROSS INCOMPETENCE OR COVER-UP

There is also circumstantial evidence of a cover-up. Crucial evidence germane to determining the truth about Extortion 17 disappeared.

At least eleven problem areas immediately stand out: (1) the inexplicable disappearance of the black box with flight data recorder, and failure to address the ELT transmission from the black box; (2) the arbitrary decision to discard bullets found in the bodies of US Navy members; (3) the possible cremation of bodies unnecessarily, and particularly Taliban bodies, which destroyed DNA evidence and made subsequent identification impossible; (4) even without cremation, the false claim that bodies weren't identifiable when they were identifiable; (5) failure of the investigation to focus on or even substantially address the identity of the Afghan infiltrators who entered the helicopter without authority; (6) failure to publicly follow up on reports from the British press that the Afghan government reported that the Taliban knew the flight path of Extortion 17; (7) failure to interview any member of the Afghan military as part of the Colt Report, a seeming oddity now that it has been revealed that the Afghans were part of the planning of every mission and, in fact, retain veto power; (8) the unsubstantiated and mathematically impossible claim that shots were fired from a building 220 meters away—outside the effective range of the RPG; (10) failure to allow pre-assault fire into the landing zone, even when the AC-130 requested permission twice to deliver pre-assault fire; and (11) contradictory, implausible, and inconsistent stories about what happened to the helicopter's black box.

Perhaps it would be possible to explain away one, possibly two of these failures to secure evidence as an errant oversight. But the problem is that the combination of errors, seemingly on a chain linked together, points to one of two inescapable conclusions: either (1) gross negligence in the preservation of evidence or (2) a deliberate cover-up to destroy or hide crucial pieces of evidence.

It does not seem possible that there would be so much incompetence at so many steps along the way. This leads to one inescapable conclusion: There was a cover-up.

The military has ignored the pink elephant in the room (Afghan infiltration and reports of the Taliban being tipped off). They have sold a false narrative that no one was at fault, orchestrating a cover-up to mask the truth of what really happened.

Powerful evidence suggests that this mission was compromised from the moment seven unidentified Afghans slipped aboard the helicopter, until the moment it was shot down. For the families of the crew of Extortion 17, and for every American wearing a uniform who may be subjected to unnecessary danger because of foolish decision-making by the government, someone should be required to answer.

CHAPTER 56

Final Thoughts

They died that night, under the moonless morning, in a valley by a creek surrounded by the rugged, snow-capped Hindu-Cush Mountains a half-world away from their homes, in an obscure Afghan province that most Americans have never heard of.

There were thirty of them. They all gave their lives for their country, the single greatest loss of life in the history of US Special Forces.

Their deaths got some attention at first and, at first, different and conflicting accounts surfaced about what had happened.

Despite the cries of a vocal few, cries barely loud enough to finally achieve a short congressional hearing that gave no meaningful answers to anything, the nation has largely forgotten.

By the time four Americans were murdered one year later in a terrorist attack on the US Consulate in Benghazi, Libya, on September 11, 2012, the tragic cover-up of Extortion 17 was rapidly fading out of the public consciousness. The military's false narrative had seemingly been accepted by the powers that be, and the media grew more anxious to focus on the deaths of four Americans in Libya than the senseless and uncalled for deaths of thirty Americans, mostly US Navy SEALs, in another part of the world, where the Middle East blends into mountainous Central Asia.

Yet, to put all this in perspective, more than seven times as many Americans died in Extortion 17 than at Benghazi. In the words of Major General Paul Vallely (Ret), "Before Benghazi, there was Extortion 17."

But Benghazi is more sound-bite friendly: an ambassador. A secretary of state. A film. The White House. The national security advisor. A refusal for a request to help. A stand-down. Sunday talk shows. Talking points. Plenty of meat for the press to dig its teeth into.

And that's a good thing. The American people deserve to know the truth when their government has foolishly and unnecessarily placed Americans in harm's way, and when life is lost as a result of that foolishness.

But in a glitzy world of sound-bites and ratings and presidential politics, Americans sometimes get lazy and forget to seek the truth on behalf of those average Americans serving their country whose names don't instantly command the attention of a national audience.

With great respect and reverence to the men who died at Benghazi, all who honorably served the United States, the men of Extortion 17 also served their country with honor and sacrifice.

With no disrespect intended for the amazing life lived and service rendered by Ambassador Chris Stevens, was the life of an ambassador somehow more important than that of a twenty-five-year-old enlisted cryptologist serving the Navy SEALs, who was taking up arms and risking himself and his life on behalf of his country?

All life is equally important. The lives of Ambassador Chris Stevens and twenty-one-year-old Specialist Spencer Duncan, of Olathe Kansas, who was killed on Extortion 17, are equally important.

Someone try telling young Braydon Nichols that his daddy's life isn't just as important as any of the men with higher-profile names and titles who were lost, or that Bryan Nichols's life wasn't important enough that the American people should find the collective strength, determination, and doggedness to insist on answers that go beyond the dog-and-pony show of a meaningless congressional investigation.

Someone try telling Charles Strange that his boy Michael's life wasn't important enough to demand answers.

Sadly, the respect and honor they all deserve cannot be adequately expressed in the limited pages of this book, or any forum for that matter.

But their mission and their service should never be forgotten, and their sacrifice should fuel an uncompromising demand for the full truth behind the reason for their deaths.

In the end, the press may lose interest. The pop culture may have been too distracted to have ever known. But God will never forget them.

As General John J. Pershing, the great commander of the American Expeditionary Forces in World War I said: "Time will not dim the glory of their deeds."

Index

About the Author

Don Brown, a former United States Navy JAG officer stationed at the Pentagon and a former Special Assistant United States Attorney, is the author of ten military and legal novels, including the nationally best-selling novels *Treason* and *Malacca Conspiracy*. A graduate of the University of North Carolina at Chapel Hill, the Campbell University School of Law, and holding a certificate of International Law from the US Naval War College, Don served as an administrative law attorney at the Pentagon on the staff of the Navy Judge Advocate General, where he drafted legal memoranda for the Secretary of the Navy and drafted legal opinion papers for the Secretary. Rising to the rank of Lieutenant Commander in the Navy JAG Corps, in addition to having authored the popular Navy Justice Series and Pacific Rim Series, Don has also been published in the prestigious *Navy Law Review*. He lives and practices law in Charlotte, North Carolina.

The author would like to acknowledge his editor, Jack Miller, for his contribution to the text.